Wolf

SPIRIT OF THE WILD

Wolf

SPIRIT OF THE WILD

A Celebration of Wolves in Word and Image

Edited by Diana Landau

Foreword by Douglas H. Chadwick

Sterling Publishing Co., Inc.
New York

A WALKING STICK PRESS BOOK

THE NATURE COMPANY

Frontispiece: One of northern Minnesota's wild wolves, Jim Brandenburg.

The Nature Company exists to provide fine-quality products devoted to the observation, understanding, and appreciation of the natural world.

Wolf: Spirit of the Wild was prepared for publication at Walking Stick Press, San Francisco
    Designed by Linda Herman
    Edited by Diana Landau
    Art research by Lindsay Kefauver
    Miriam Lewis, research associate
    Karen Pike, design associate
    Linda Larsen, typography
    Christine Kristen and Miriam Lewis, production associates
    Laurie Donaldson, editorial assistance
    Verne Lindner, calligraphy
    Reineck & Reineck, cartography

Library of Congress Cataloging-in-Publication Data Available

10 9 8 7 6 5 4 3 2 1

Sources of text and illustrations and acknowledgment of permission to reprint copyrighted material appear on pages 190–191.
First paperback edition published in 2000 by Sterling Publishing Co., Inc.
    387 Park Avenue South, New York, N.Y. 10016
Previously published by The Nature Company, Berkeley, California.
    Copyright © 1993 by The Nature Company; reprinted text copyright by authors or sources named in credits.

Printed in China.

Sterling ISBN 1-4027-2918-9

CONTENTS

Pair of gray wolves (Canis lupus) *cross a river, northern Montana.*
Erwin and Peggy Bauer/ Bruce Coleman, Inc.

For a long time, wolves were seen but not looked at. Grown scarce, they made themselves elusive, and their actions were interpreted more than observed. Recently, though, they have begun to emerge from their night.

PAUL-EMILE VICTOR, *L'Empire des Loups*

In the fairly short time since wolves began to emerge from the shadows of fear and misunderstanding, we have longed to see more and know more of them. There are many reasons why this is so, including pure fascination with the details of how these intelligent, family-oriented animals go about their lives, and regret and sorrow for their historical persecution. But it is more than that. We sense that wolves have a special connection to people, that it's important to have a world in which both wolves and humans can live. We somehow feel that, as we come to regard the wolf in a new light, we ourselves are emerging from a dark age of isolating ourselves as a species from the rest of creation. This book came about because of that passionate interest, because of a need to live wisely with wolves—and with wilderness.

How we see and think about wolves derives in great part from how others have seen and thought about them. This is inevitable; aside from a fleeting, unsatisfying glimpse at a zoo, it's unlikely that most of us will ever see a living, breathing wolf. Even when wolves lived closer to people than they do now, they have always been elusive creatures, more often heard than seen. So we must rely on images received—from those who make careers of observing wildlife, who have ventured into wolf country at times with camera or paintbrush, or who in times past have actually shared the land with wolves.

Our aim is to show how wolves have been seen, and imagined, from the time before stories were written down to the present—in literature, folklore, science, and the arts, and in every part of the world where wolves and humans have cohabited. Despite the fact that they are so rarely observed (or partly because of it?) wolves have inspired an extraordinary array of ideas about their lives,

habits, and spiritual significance. Once we began looking for images of wolves, they seemed to coalesce quickly—as if out of a dark forest in response to an inquiring howl.

So this is a gathering of wolves, as seen by the recorders of classical myths; by Native American storytellers and artists; by the authors of fairy tales, histories, religious tomes, and ethological papers; by nineteenth-century landscape painters and intrepid wildlife photographers; by novelists, poets, reporters, and naturalists—and, not least, by scientists. For until recently all this rich imagery of wolves was long on imagination and very short on fact. Indeed, it is only in the last half century that wolves have been seen in the light of genuine information about their natural history and lifestyle.

We have sought to impose order on this diverse collection of material by assembling related texts and images into thematic sections. We begin with a general look at the "essential wolf": who the creature is, where it lives, where it came from, its chief physical traits. Then we take a closer look at its complex and highly social lifeway, and its relation to the landscapes it inhabits and shares with other creatures. The last section focuses on the troubled yet hopeful history of human-wolf interaction. Within these greater parts, editorial summaries introduce major topics, and sometimes comment on individual excerpts.

As with any big subject, certain sources of information about wolves are seminal: those writers or scientists or photographers who have studied them most deeply, forged the sharpest insights, or captured the most telling moments. This and any contemporary book on wolves owes much to the work of Adolph Murie, the chief pioneer of wolf biology, and L. David Mech, foremost among contemporary field biologists studying wolves and author of several authoritative books about them.

A firmly unscientific but enthralling body of wolf observations is found in Lois Crisler's *Arctic Wild* and *Captive Wild*, accounts of her experiences raising wolves in the Alaska wilderness and at her Colorado home in the 1950s. Crisler combined an immense intuitive sympathy with the animals, breathtaking fearlessness in interpreting their behavior, and a vivid telegraphic writing style, as shown in the excerpts reprinted here.

Farley Mowat's *Never Cry Wolf* is surely the best-known book on wolves yet published; Mowat's graceful and engaging writing has won thousands of readers to their cause. We have included several selections, which should be enjoyed with this caveat: wolf biologists are generally skeptical of the book as science, believing that many episodes are fictionalized. While at times indulging in hyperbole or speculation, Mowat nonetheless has deftly woven in much that is known of wolves.

Undoubtedly the most important work for anyone interested in the relations between wolf and humankind is Barry Lopez's *Of Wolves and Men.* Ranging through ancient myth, Native American cultures, European legend, and American history, as well as synthesizing much current science, it is essential reading for anyone interested in the role animals play in our lives, beliefs, and arts. We have relied on it extensively.

Because of the wide range of texts excerpted—many from folkloric or colloquial sources and dating from many periods—the reader should exercise judgment about what is really true of wolves. Pitfalls include the tendency of writers to exaggerate, anthropomorphize, or voice opinions; as is often noted, wolves have been whatever people have needed them to be. Scientific sources are identified here, and we have endeavored to make editorial summaries as up-to-date and factual as possible. Yet even to scientists, who have studied them as intensively as any carnivore in the world, wolves remain mysterious, contradictory beasts in many ways. Like other intelligent creatures, they exhibit a wide range of individual behavior. "To be rigorous about wolves—" as Barry Lopez wisely notes, "you might as well expect rigor of clouds."

A brief note on wolf classification: There are references in this book to various subspecies of wolves (*Canis lupus lycaon,* or *arctos,* or *mackenzii,* and so on). Biologists have struggled with a history of their predecessors identifying too many different wolf types, especially in North America, but a new proposal to reduce the number of subspecies to just five will probably be accepted soon—making some of these colorful names extinct.

Many people contribute to the creation of a book such as this, and those who most need thanking are recognized in the Acknowledgments. But over and above the formal credit due to holders of copyrights, we wish to extend our appreciation to all those who have written and spoken and sung about wolves so eloquently, or depicted them visually with such imagination and skill, or waited patiently through frozen winters and mosquito-plagued summers to capture a unique image or a newfound pattern of behavior. Of all we have learned in assembling this book, the most striking thing is this : that getting involved with wolves evokes passions as powerful today as those experienced by the first people ever to hear wolves howl.

On Photographing Wolves

Except in a few places where they have never been persecuted, wild wolves tend to melt into the landscape at any sign of human presence—so photographing them is a great challenge. Many of the photos of wolves published here and elsewhere, especially portraits or close views of pack behavior, are of captive wolves in natural enclosures or released temporarily to the wild for photography. Some are of wolves being tracked and studied by biologists; others are opportunistic shots taken from aircraft by researchers or professional photographers. One of the rare places where photographers can often observe and capture wild wolves on film is Denali National Park in Alaska.

Among a few photographers who have accumulated a significant body of work depicting wild wolves, the most notable is Jim Brandenburg. His images of arctic wolves on Canada's Ellesmere Island first appeared in *National Geographic* and in his own book, *White Wolf.* A longtime resident of northern Minnesota, he has also extensively photographed the gray wolves that live in that part of the country.

Good photographs of wolves outside North America are especially hard to come by, and we are grateful to another *National Geographic* photographer, Mattias Klum, for traveling to the Børas Sanctuary in his native Sweden to shoot the wonderful photographs of its resident pack that are published here for the first time.

The Editor

FINDING OUR WAY WITH WOLVES

by Douglas H. Chadwick

It was March when I skied into the western edge of Glacier National-al Park last year. Montana was just on the cusp of spring. The winds gusting off the slopes carried new smells—of rain, swelling buds, and patches of open ground. The snowpack was softening even in the deepest spruce shadows, where varied thrushes sang. Creeks were running high. And, I realized as huge footprints cut across my path, the grizzly bears were out of their dens.

The tracks led to four different deer carcasses. The bear had feasted on each, but I couldn't be sure whether it had killed any of the animals itself. The first looked to have been done in by winter and old age. Another had fallen to a mountain lion. The remains of the third and fourth had been heavily worked over by yet another big predator—the new one, the far-traveler with the scent of magic in its wake. Its pawprints criss-crossed this portion of the hooved animals' late winter range. Absent from the West for most of the past century, such tracks now pattern sever-al other stretches of northwestern Montana as well and loop on into Idaho. With eyes of gold and fur of silver and black, the wolf is coming back. A lot more music is going to echo through these hills, and a lot of crea-tures are going to have to be better than ever at what they do to survive.

Portions of the northern Rockies have stayed pretty wild over the years. But now the ecosystem is closer than ever to its true natural state, with silvertipped bears, black bears, cougars, lynx, wolverines, coyotes, and, finally, wolves all roaming out there, competing for moose, elk, deer, beavers, snowshoe hares, grouse, and leftovers; challenging, fighting, exploring, learning;

honing every sense and skill they possess; knitting whole landscapes back together with their trails; reinforcing old, lovely rhythms with each beat of their untamed hearts.

These days, when you spot eagles and ravens circling in the dis-tance you find yourself wondering if wolves are watching the same sight, for they home in on the birds to locate kills made by other predators, just as African lions follow the flight of vultures. Before long, a cougar with fresh blood on its muzzle may be leaping for safety into the branches of a tree, or some great grizzled bear will be whirling with a roar to defend its meat against the pack. You don't need to hustle halfway around the world to Africa to experi-ence the excitement of a community full of grand beasts. One is being reshaped right here.

Gray wolf, Nova Scotia, Canada. Peter McLeod/First Light.

The wolf's face is familiar to us through our companion dogs, and we share a kindred intelligence.
Steven C. Kaufman/Peter Arnold, Inc.

Canis lupus, the grey wolf, is the canine family's largest member. Before modern traps, firearms, and poisons, this was the most widespread large wild species on the planet's surface. More than any other predator, wolves resembled us, both in their success and in the reasons for it. They hunt in cooperative, stable family units using an elaborate array of body language and vocal signals. Their capacities include loyalty, altruism, keen sensitivity to emotions, and a degree of forethought that permits wolfish levels of planning and strategy.

Scientists faced with portentous behavior in nonhumans tend to scramble for cover behind jargon like "metacommunication," yet the rest of us speak easily of qualities we share with dogs. Is there someone who hasn't seen a dog display guilt, for example? Or a dog shimmying with anticipation as it trots over with a stick to play keep-away? What about the one that has the stick right in front of it but keeps looking all around pretending that it can't find the thing, until the instant before you try to grab it? Well? Dogs are essentially domestic varieties of wolf. That is, *Canis familiaris* arose directly from *Canis lupus,* and the two species remain close enough genetically that they can freely interbreed. What we did was take wolves and turn them into cherished members of millions of human families.

Another way in which we recognize wolves' similarities to us is through folklore and the arts. For millennia, the creatures have appeared as ancestors, gods, spirit guides, or demons, shifting shapes with shamans and ordinary folk alike. It is particularly because of their kindred intelligence that wolves make such powerful stand-ins for our kind. Werehumans. In the collection you are about to enjoy, authors from Aesop to Willa Cather illustrate the wolf's enduring niche in the curious habitat of the human imagination.

Barry Lopez, another contributor, pushed the subject further in his seminal work, *Of Wolves and Men.* He pointed out how each culture makes of these beasts what it needs, imbuing them with human qualities to be admired or else loathed and then righteously purged—destroyed. Western societies have put a rather bizarre amount of effort into vilifying wolves. Yet that in itself was an admission of the extent to which we felt the beasts competing with us at both a psychic and physical level. Wolves cast doubt on our claims to be wholly separate from, and superior to, nature, and people hated them for it. Some still do.

But times have changed; the planet has changed, more comprehensively than anyone from a previous generation could have envisioned. Suddenly we find that what we need is not more proof that humanity can conquer other beings but reassurance that some of the splendor and variety of life on this planet will endure. The pinnacle of creation, where we ensconced ourselves,

Arctic wolf bares its teeth in a status display with a pup from the pack; in general, adults wolves are very tolerant of pups. Ellesmere Island, Canada. Jim Brandenburg.

turns out to be a lonely and precarious perch. Many have begun to seek a greater sense of communion instead. You may step onto that path in the writings of naturalist-philosophers such as Aldo Leopold and Edward Hoagland, who suggest parallels between accepting wolves and learning some much-needed humility.

Perhaps the hardest thing is simply to see wolves for what they are, apart from our needs and fears. Even among wildlife managers, data never intruded very far among opinions until just a half century ago, when biologist Adolph Murie published *The Wolves of Mount McKinley*. His studies showed for the first time what now amounts to standard knowledge: Over the long run, wolves do no harm to populations of hooved animals. Weather cycles and range conditions set the crucial limits on numbers; predators cull the less fit individuals, ultimately strengthening their prey. The pages that follow include Murie's insights along with those of Dave Mech and other field researchers who have added immeasurably to our portrait of the species.

Solid facts are still just coming in. But as they do, they continue to open up our understanding of how native wildlife communities operate and how to conserve their vital balance. We don't really know yet why wolves sing, but then we would be hard put to explain exactly why humans do, either. At one level, the reasons are surely alike: to reinforce bonds between members of a group; to express sheer excitement, joy, or sorrow. The farther we follow the wolf's tracks, the closer they lead toward a vision of wholeness in the living world, the more clearly we can see our connections to that realm, and the better our chance of finding wholeness within ourselves. This is why I feel that if there were any one way to grasp the deeper meaning of nature, it would be to practice understanding wolves. You will find that this volume makes a fine place to start.

A mountain with a wolf on it stands a little taller.

EDWARD HOAGLAND, *Red Wolves and Black Bears*

Despite all efforts to banish them, wolves still roam free in the remoter parts of the northern hemisphere, all over the world, as they have for more than a million years. Now mainly confined to the wilderness margins—places where people tend not to go because they are too cold, too barren, too far from any road—wolves once were

The Essential Wolf

the premier predator in every temperate landscape north of the equator, from the steppes of Eurasia to the Sierra Madre to the Siberian tundra. More widespread than any other large carnivore that has ever lived, the wolf has good claim to the title of most successful predator on earth—man excepted. Just what sort of creature is the mammal that Linneaus in 1758 named *Canis lupus*, and that we variously call the gray wolf, timber wolf, tundra wolf, or lobo? How did it evolve over a few hundred million years from a raccoon-sized, all-purpose mammalian ancestor into the big, powerful, highly intelligent and socially subtle wolf of modern times? Who are its close relations in the canine clan, including other types of wolves, coyotes, foxes, and the like—and how are wolves linked to our beloved domestic dogs? Finally, what are the chief physical gifts that lend the wolf its adaptability to so many earthly habitats, its awesome efficiency as a hunter, its uncanny communication skills, and the graceful and expressive beauty that entrances people who have lived closely with wolves, and seduces many who declare themselves its enemy? Though much about wolves remains mysterious, here are a few partial answers . . . .

MEETING WOLF

The wolf is the original dog and most resembles such races of dog as the Eskimo sled dog, husky, malamute, or German shepherd. Still, the wolf differs from them in build by being narrower, leaner, and more streamlined. And in the north of its range throughout the world, the wolf usually grows larger, and has bushy, fuzzier fur and larger feet.

Most wolves are a mottled gray, with tawny legs and flanks. However, in the far north wolves are a creamy white, sometimes with a light gray mane. In parts of Canada, Alaska, and the northern forty-eight states, some are pure black. Farther south, almost all wolves are tawny gray. In the Superior National Forest of Minnesota, however, I once saw a pack with three gray wolves, one black, and one white.

Scientists have long recognized two main types, or species, of wolves, the gray wolf *(Canis lupus)* and the red wolf *(Canis rufus).* Gray wolves originally lived throughout the northern hemisphere above about 20 degrees north latitude, which runs approximately through Mexico City and southern India. The only exception was the southeastern United States, where the red wolf lived. However, whether the red wolf is really distinct from the gray wolf, or whether it is really a large coyote, or a hybrid between wolves and coyotes, are still subjects of debate among biologists.

In North America, gray wolves have several common names depending on just where they live. For example, in the eastern forested areas of North America they are known as "timber wolves," in the High Arctic as "arctic wolves," on the tundra, as "tundra wolves," and in the southwestern United States and Mexico as "lobos," the Spanish name for wolf. To add to the confusion of names all designating the gray wolf is one other name that refers not to the gray, but to the wolf's

PRECEDING SPREAD: *Gray wolf,* Canis lupus. *Stephen J. Krasemann/ Peter Arnold, Inc.* THIS PAGE: *"Wolf" (1986), by Joan Brown.* FACING PAGE: *Members of the Sawtooth Pack in an Idaho winter. The gray wolf's narrow-chested build helps it move easily through deep snow. Jim Dutcher.*

4

SONG OF A CHEYENNE SCOUT
▼▼▼▼▼▼

Wolf I am,   everything
In darkness   will be good
In light   because Maheo
whenever I search   protects us.
wherever I run   *Ea ea ea ho.*
wherever I stand

KARL H. SCHLESIER, *The Wolves of Heaven*

5

Gray wolf pup, Montana. This dark pup may have siblings of different shades. Carl R. SamsII/Peter Arnold, Inc.

smaller cousin, the coyote, which is called the "brush wolf" in many areas.

Like most other animals, gray wolves vary slightly across regions. Differences appear in size, color, and in minor skull measurements. Scientists interested in these minor geographic variations recognize different wolf races or subspecies.

However, because wolves vary in these characteristics even within one region, scientists disagree on how many races of wolves there are. In North America, for example, twenty-four subspecies were originally recognized. But individual wolves are very wide travelers, and often they cut across the arbitrary lines that the old-time scientists drew around the ranges of subspecies. . . . In reality, one race of wolf is pretty much the same as any other. The behavior and natural history are similar among the various races and between North American and Eurasian wolves. In fact, any real differences seem to be more related to the precise living conditions such as food type, climate, and geographic area. . . .

Wolves do differ from coyotes, although the two can interbreed. Coyotes generally are a quarter to a half the size of wolves, and they have more sharply pointed noses, as well as proportionately larger, outward-pointing ears and smaller feet. Coyotes generally live on

smaller prey such as rabbits and hares, and inhabit smaller territories, reach higher densities, breed earlier, and live in smaller groups than wolves. . . .

Wolves vary in size in different areas of the world. The smallest live in the southern part of the wolf's range, especially in the Middle East; there they may weigh only thirty pounds. The largest wolves inhabit midlatitude Canada, Alaska, and the Soviet Union, where they occasionally reach 175 pounds. One report that has some documentation involves a wolf from the Yukon area that supposedly weighed an unconfirmed 227 pounds! Males are usually about 20 percent larger than females.

Whatever their adult size, wolves can achieve it within their first one to two years of life. In fact, many of them reach almost adult weight by their first autumn. . . . Presumably a wolf pup's fast growth is related to the need for pups to travel with the adults by fall. Since the wolf is a northern species, it must contend with snow for much of the year. If the pups were not adult size by snowfall, they would struggle hard to keep up with their parents during the pack's travels. In some areas of northern Canada and Alaska, where the wolf's main prey is caribou, the pups must follow their migrating food supply as far as three hundred miles to its winter range.

Wolves possess keen senses and excellent learning ability—both to be expected from a hunter. Under some conditions, wolves can hear as far as six miles away in the forest and ten miles away on the open tundra. I've watched them seem to smell a moose a mile and a quarter away, and they appear to see at least as well as humans.

L. DAVID MECH, *The Way of the Wolf*

L. David Mech is recognized as the world's leading wolf biologist, as closely associated with wolves as is, for example, George Schaller with lions or Jane Goodall with primates. His studies of wolves and moose on Isle Royale in Lake Superior are considered a classic work on predator-prey relationships, and he is the author of several books including his comprehensive The Wolf. *A wildlife research biologist with the U.S. Fish and Wildlife Service, he is vice chair of the International Wolf Center and consults with conservation groups around the world.*

Long legs, narrow chest, slender muzzle, and alert expressive ears are among the wolf's distinguishing features. Michael Francis/The Wildlife Collection.

PICTURE A WOLF

Hardly anyone realizes what wolves look like. I know of only two artists, Olaus Murie and Bill Berry, who draw real wolves; the rest draw myth wolves, stocky and brutal-muzzled.

Real wolves are slender, invincibly aristocratic-looking. They have disarmingly sweet faces!

They are slender all over and as sinuous and graceful as cats. Bodies are long, and carried high on long legs. Paws and legs are unlike those of dogs. Legs are twined "nervously" with veins and sinews. (By nervous I mean innervated, alive and sensitive all over.) Paws are nervous too—not mere clumps like most dog paws, but long-fingered and spreading. Trigger's forepaw made a track as long and almost as spreading as that of my own long hand.

Beside a wolf, the most graceful dog looks wooden. Wolves seem to have a fineness and delicacy of articulation lost to dogs through centuries of breeding. In motion they ripple, they flow. Even in walking, the spine has a slight side-wise ripple.

And how wolves leap! Lifting leaps—straight up, all bushy and flowing, to the tip of the tail. Straight down. That is their way of participating in gaiety. They leap upward as if pulled at the shoulders by a skyhook. Or they leap perpendicular, standing straight up in the air; that is the "observation leap." They leap sidewise. They leap backward. They twirl into a doughnut in midair and wind up the incredible act with a flourish—chest to ground, paws spread, and an inimitable, flashing wolf-toss of the head. Heads too are slender, long.

LOIS CRISLER, *Arctic Wild*

In 1953, Lois Crisler and her husband went to Alaska on assignment for Walt Disney to film arctic wildlife. For over a year they lived in tent camps in the Brooks Range, where they adopted and raised two orphaned wolves—Lady and Trigger. Both wolves died before the Crislers left Alaska, but they returned home with five pups for whom they built a network of enclosures at a remote Colorado cabin. Crisler's observations of these animals in her books Arctic Wild *and* Captive Wild *are among the most precisely detailed and deeply felt writing that exists about wolves.*

WHENCE CAME THE WOLF?

▼▼▼▼▼▼

It's ironic, as David Mech points out, that wolves and their chief prey—the large hoofed herbivores—probably evolved from a common ancestor: a rodentlike, insect-eating creature far removed from both the carnivores and the splendid hoofed mammals that followed. Quite a bit later, say a hundred million years ago, a group of primitive meat-eaters called creodonts appeared, from which descended all the major families of carnivores—canids, cats, bears, weasels, and raccoons and their kin.

The next major step toward wolfness is pegged at around 55 million years ago, namely the first mammal with specialized meat-shearing teeth, called carnassials. One of them, a beast called *Miacis*, is considered the key ancestor of both wolves and bears. Around 20 million years ago, the dog and cat families became more or less distinct, the first moving out onto open country and growing longer limbs for speed, and the latter staying behind to pursue a tree-based hunting style, developing retractable claws to facilitate it. Another

intermediate animal, *Tomarctus*, was still more genuinely doglike.

It was in the Pleistocene, around 1 million years ago, that the true proto-wolf, or *Canis*, emerged. "We can imagine it," says Barry Lopez, "pulling down camels hundreds of thousands of years ago in what is now Oklahoma." *Canis* had a bigger brain and a longer jaw than earlier models, and from it sprang our hero *Canis lupus* as well as a short-lived cousin, the dire wolf. Even larger than today's wolves, this must have been a fearsome beast, but (scholars suppose) it was neither as fast as the gray wolf or as socially organized, thus it fell off the evolutionary ladder. *Canis lupus,* however, thrived and continued to pioneer in new environments and new kinds of prey, probably including a few early hominids. Mankind's fear of wolves may indeed have such atavistic roots, but in truth humans have never provided more than an incidental meal in the wolf's pursuit of its favored ungulate prey. Rather, the wolf has done man the inestimable service of being parent to our first and most cherished of domestic animals, the dog.

ABOVE: Artist's reconstruction of Miacis, *by John McLoughlin.* LEFT: *This fragment of Mimbres pottery from New Mexico dates from 1050-1250 A.D. and depicts a wolflike beast devouring part of another animal.*

THE WOLF HELPS MAN TO BECOME

While science strives through empirical evidence to trace the descent of animals and their links to humans, the creation myths of native cultures often show animals playing an important role in helping mankind to evolve. The Tewa people of New Mexico tell a story in which wolves test the human hero in a kind of initiation rite, endowing him with their power and with knowledge of life and death:

In the primordial time before this world, people, animals, and supernaturals lived beneath [a great salt] lake in a place called Sipofene. This world was dark, and time and death were unknown. Two of the supernaturals, Blue Corn Woman (the summer mother of the people) and White Corn Woman (the winter mother), asked one of the men to go forth and discover a way through which everyone might be able to leave the lake.

Three times the man pondered this request, and on each occasion he refused. Finally after a fourth demand he agreed, going first to the north. He found only mist and haze, saying the world was unripe *(ochu)* or green. On successive tries he went to the west, then to the south and east. The two mothers instructed him to go to the above. Here he came to an open place and here he saw gathered all the *tsiwi,* or predators.

The wolves, mountain lions, coyotes, foxes, vultures, and crows were there waiting for him. He was afraid. On seeing him, the predators rushed him, knocked him down, and fiercely scratched him. Then they told him to get up, that they were his friends. His wounds disappeared and they bestowed on him a bow, arrows, and quiver. They dressed him in buckskin and painted his face black and they tied feathers of carrion-eating birds in his hair.

"You have been accepted," the wolves and other predators told him. "These things we have given you are what you shall use from now on. You are ready to go."

JAMES C. BURBANK, Vanishing Lobo

James Burbank is an Albuquerque journalist specializing in environmental reporting. His Vanishing Lobo: The Mexican Wolf and the Southwest *is a wide-ranging report on the fate of this near-extinct wolf subspecies, and how wolves fit into the web of the Southwest's Native, Spanish, and Anglo cultures.*

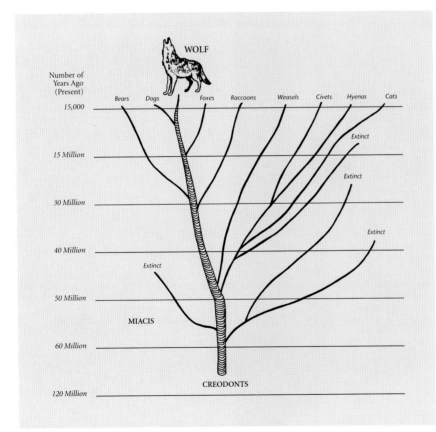

<small>ABOVE: *Hopi Wolf kachina standing on a kiva, by Tino Youvella, 1970s. Jerry Jacka photo.* LEFT: *The wolf's evolutionary tree, showing how the various carnivore families branched off from a common ancestral group. Adapted from* The Wolf, *by L. David Mech.*</small>

WOLF

Number of Years Ago (Present)

Bears Dogs Foxes Raccoons Weasels Civets Hyenas Cats

15,000

Extinct

15 Million

Extinct

30 Million

Extinct

40 Million

Extinct

Extinct

50 Million

MIACIS

60 Million

CREODONTS

120 Million

THE ADAPTABLE SURVIVOR

This sketch of how the wolf evolved in Alaska is taken from James Greiner's The Red Snow, *a fictional narrative that follows a wolf pack living in the Tanana River valley through the course of a year as they struggle for their livelihood on the rugged flatlands below the Alaska Range. A wilderness guide and bush pilot who lives in Fairbanks, Greiner writes about wolves with the authority of one who knows them well.*

One hundred and forty centuries ago seems to be a handy place to begin the story of the gray wolf, providing one does not forget the fact that he was here for [at least a] million years before that in a form virtually identical to the one in which he appears today. The wolf has always been a predator, and before the appearance of grasslands in Alaska he had successfully competed with other hunters such as the jackel-like dole, the short-faced bear, the lion, and even the awesome saber-toothed tiger.

Since his role as a hunter remained virtually unchanged through the ages, the wolf became a highly flexible survivor. With the coming of the grasslands, other species which relied specifically upon forest prey began to disappear, seemingly unable to adapt to hunting the grazing animals which replaced the forest dwellers. That the wolf was successful in this venture is obvious, for today, in spite of man's intrusion and sometimes misplaced concern, he exists in numbers which may very well surpass those of fourteen thousand years ago.

He quickly learned how to hunt hairy mammoth calves, primitive bison, camels, sheep, wild ponies and donkeys, and other grass-eating ungulate prey species. Though there were others that competed with him for survival on the treeless land, none was more impressive than the gray wolf's close relative, the dire wolf. Though the latter possessed a massive lower jaw, he competed with the gray wolf only after the kill had been made, a kill which he seldom helped consummate, for the dire wolf was a carrion eater by choice.

The land continued to change. Vast plains began to

Gray wolf in winter snow, Alaska. Tom and Pat Leeson.

disappear and with continuation of the cycle came the inexorable disappearance of those animals that depended upon grass for survival. Then as the plentitude of grazing prey species shriveled, the dire wolf came upon hard times, and he too vanished from the scene. The gray wolf remained, however, and today is the undisputed king among the large Arctic predators, as much at home on the barren treeless tundra as he is among the spruces and down timber of the interior. . . .

It is known that man was here and had already established himself eleven thousand years ago, and it seems probable that he was here before that time. It is also logical to assume that, from his westerly landfall, he moved inland and that he met the gray wolf. Why man came here and how he survived are questions which have long fascinated modern generations. One fact stands clear—the ancients were hunters of supreme ability. They possessed a refined technology which provided functional weapons and crudely tailored garments made from the skins of animals they killed. Most astounding is the fact that they accomplished all of this in a land where, in its northern reaches, bitter winters lasted virtually all year, as they still do. Like the gray wolf, early man in Alaska was an adaptive competitor, and because of this, he too has survived to the present time.

As the forebears of the modern Alaskan native peoples moved eastward into the interior, they discovered a land in transition. Though not true nomads, they moved with opportunistic purpose on a seasonal basis. Such movement occurred within shifting territories, and was triggered by changing game populations. Also like the wolf, early man quickly learned that to follow was to survive. . . . Because of familiarity, the Alaskan native sees the gray wolf through different eyes than does his white counterpart. As a result, even among the impressionable Eskimos and Indians of the big land, the wolf has never become the creature of legend that Caucasians have demanded. The native learned during the passage of thousands of years to share the land with the wolf, and to compete but never dominate. It is, perhaps, the final irony that the wolf has lived here for at least [a] million years, the native for more than fourteen thousand, and white man for a mere seventy-five, yet it is the latter who seems bent upon the task of domination.

JAMES GREINER, *The Red Snow*

"U?Mata Ya," by Kwakiutl artist Frances Dick, 1990. Kawadelakala, one of the two wolves represented in this print, has torn his younger brother Kwalili into small pieces. The fur blows upward to the sky as he chants, "Wherever your pieces fall, these will become nations among themselves." For the artist, this legend signifies that from every loss or violent act in nature comes a gift of new creation.

"Amaguk is like Nunamiut. He doesn't hunt when the weather is bad. He likes to play. He works hard to get food for his family. His hair starts to get white when he is old."

BARRY LOPEZ, *Of Wolves and Men*, quoting an old Alaskan Eskimo man on the parallels between wolves and his people.

WOLVES AND THEIR KIN

▼▼▼▼▼▼

The genus *Canis,* to which wolves belong, contains just nine species but is represented on all the world's continents—in part because one species, *Canis familiaris* (the domestic dog) goes wherever humans go. Besides wolves and dogs, the other members of *Canis* are the coyote, several kinds of jackals, and the Australian dingo. Other doglike carnivores closely related to wolves include foxes (found nearly all over the world), African wild dogs, and maned wolves—not true wolves at all, but a long-limbed South American predator more closely akin to foxes.

Among true wolves, two species are recognized. *Canis lupus* refers to the gray, or timber, wolf as well as the arctic, or tundra, wolf, and all other creatures called lobos, buffalo-wolves, and so on. All variations on *Canis lupus* are either subspecies or races, including the Mexican wolf *(Canis lupus baileyi).* And all the wolves still found in Europe and Asia are likewise subspecies of *Canis lupus.*

Because wolves are so widespread, great potential exists for variety in size, weight, color, and other traits. At one time, scientists tended to announce new subspecies at the least opportunity (up to twenty-four were identified in North America alone). Animal classifiers have traditionally formed camps of "splitters" (those who distinguish many subspecies) and "lumpers" (those who recognize fewer); more lately, the lumpers have gained sway where wolves are concerned.

The other generally recognized species is the red wolf, *Canis rufus.* This fascinating critter has long been the subject of genetic controversy: is it indeed a separate species or just another geographic race? Native to the Southeast but virtually extinct in the wild, a few have been reintroduced to a limited refuge in North Carolina. The red wolf's fate is recounted in the following excerpt by Edward Hoagland.

Part of the problem in making hard-and-fast distinctions among wolves and their kin is that all the members of *Canis* may interbreed (normally different species do not). The coyote, for example, which has proven far more adaptable than wolves to living near people, has crossed with wolves at times. Besides coyotes, the other animal most often mistaken for a wolf is the dog—again, because they freely crossbreed, either by human intent or accident.

And when, on the still cold nights, he pointed his nose at a star and howled long and wolflike, it was his ancestors, dead and dust, pointing nose at star and howling down through the centuries and through him.

JACK LONDON, *Call of the Wild*

Coyote (Canis latrans) *hunting on a frosty fall morning. Coyotes tend to hunt singly or in pairs rather than in packs, pursuing smaller prey than wolves do. Tom and Pat Leeson.* OPPOSITE: *Various wolf types and coyote, original art by Cynthie Fisher, 1993.*

VARIATIONS ON A THEME

GRAY WOLF
Black phase. Black wolves are commonest in Alaska, Canada, and northern regions generally.

GRAY WOLF
Canis lupus. Largest individuals are from northern subspecies such as *occidentalis* or *pambasileus.*

MEXICAN WOLF
Canis lupus baileyi. Strongly contrasting face markings distinguish this handsome, medium-sized wolf.

ASIAN WOLF
Canis lupus. These are the smallest wolves; several sub-species, including *arabs*, *pallipes*, and *campestris.*

COYOTE
Canis latrans. Confusingly known as the "brush wolf," coyotes are smaller and have different lifestyles than wolves.

RED WOLF
Canis rufus. The second wolf species, midway between the gray wolf and coyote in size, with gray to reddish pelage.

LAMENT THE RED WOLF

▼▼▼▼▼

Essayist Edward Hoagland, whom a Washington Post *reviewer called "the Thoreau of our time," has written eloquently and incisively about animals, wild country, and conservation issues; his books include* Walking the Dead Diamond River. *In researching* Red Wolves and Black Bears, *he spent time with the scientists who track wolves in Minnesota and the trappers who pursued them in east Texas. Both contributed to his insights.*

Red wolves are short-coated and long-eared, with stilty, spindly legs for coursing through the southern marshes or under tall forests. They have the neck ruff, almond eyes and wide nose pad of other wolves, but not the massive head and chest, and so their angular ears and legs seem to stick out plaintively. Anatomically their brains are primitive, almost foxlike among the canids, and they have im-

pressed naturalists as being rather rudimentary animals, fragile in their social linkups, not very clever, unenterprising and almost easy to trap. Besides the pacing gait that they share with larger wolves and a flat dash, they bound along like modest rocking horses, standing up on their hind legs to peer over a patch of all weeds. They are an unemphatic, intermediate sort of animal, behaviorally like wolves, ecologically more like coyotes. They howl like wolves, not like coyotes, and snarl when threatened instead of silently gaping the mouth, as coyotes do. They scout in little packs, unlike coyotes, which have stripped away a good deal of the pack instinct for better secrecy in crowded country and better efficiency at gleaning small game. A grown male weighs about sixty pounds, midway between a coyote's thirty or forty and a gray wolf's average of eighty pounds; but skinny as he is, the red wolf can live on a coyote's diet of cotton rats and marsh rabbits. . . . Five square miles supplies his food, and ten to forty is enough to stretch his legs and psyche with other members of the pack, about half what a pack of Minnesota timber wolves requires. . . .

Red wolves are so far gone by now—none has been photographed in the wild since 1934—that the main effort to protect them involves not only shielding them from human intervention but from encroachment and dilution by coyotes. This situation is unusual. The rarest breeds of ferret, parrot, and so on, even

The red wolf, Canis rufus, *is the second of only two recognized species of wolves. Tom and Pat Leeson.*

manatees and prairie chickens, depleted in numbers though they are, seldom require protection from other animals, and it is this peculiar rattle-headedness—that these last wolves will so amenably let a coyote mount them—which has called into question their right to be regarded as a species. . . .

Nearer the East Coast, there were no other predators to replace the wolves when they had been killed off, but west of the Mississippi, coyotes from the plains slid in as soon as the shattered packs stopped defending an area. Coyotes could withstand the poisoning and trapping campaigns better, and the hard logging that the settlers did among the old-growth trees actually benefitted them by breaking down the forest canopy. According to the evidence of skulls in the National Museum, the red wolves of Missouri, northern Arkansas and eastern Oklahoma met their end in good order as a species, not mating with the coyotes as they were superseded. . . . But around the turn of the century [in Texas], the demoralized red wolves for some reason began to accept coyotes as their sexual partners, and in the delirium of catastrophe created with them a "Hybrid Swarm." Bigger, "redder" than coyotes, with such a piquancy of wolf blood already, these hybrids absorbed the wolves of Texas's Hill Country and Big Thicket all the more readily. They bred with true wolves and true coyotes and wild-running domestic dogs (even a few escaped pet dingos)—anything they met and couldn't kill—becoming ever more adaptable, a shoal of skilled survivors in a kind of canine Injun-territory situation.

EDWARD HOAGLAND,

Red Wolves and Black Bears

LEFT: *Anubis, the only canine god in the Egyptian pantheon, has been variously identified as a wolf or dog, but most likely represents a jackal. XIX Dynasty.* ABOVE: *The maned wolf, Chrysocyon brachyurus, is not a true wolf. Sometimes called the "stilt fox" of the pampas, this South American canine is very rare in the wild. Erwin and Peggy Bauer/Bruce Coleman, Inc.*

THE RED WOLF

Over the heart of the west,
    the Taos desert,
Circles an eagle,
And it's dark between me and him.

The sun, as he waits a moment,
    huge and liquid
Standing without feet on the rim of
    the far-off mesa
Says: *Look for a last long time then!*
    Look! Look well! I am going.
So he pauses and is beholden, and
    straightway is gone.

And the Indian, in a white sheet
Wrapped to the eyes, the sheet bound
    close on his brows,
Stands saying: *See, I'm invisible!*
Behold how you can't behold me!
The invisible in its shroud!

Now that the sun has gone, and the
    aspen leaves
And the cotton-wood leaves are fallen,
    as good as fallen,
And the ponies are in corral,
And it's night.

Why, more has gone than all these;
And something has come.
A red wolf stands on the shadow's
    dark red rim.

Day has gone to dust on the
    sage-grey desert
Like a white Christus fallen to dust
    from a cross;
To dust, to ash, on the twilit floor
    of the desert.

And a black crucifix like a dead tree
    spreading wings;
Maybe a black eagle with its wings out
Left lonely in the night
In a sort of worship.

And coming down upon us, out of the
    dark concave
Of the eagle's wings,
And the coffin-like slit where the
    Indian's eyes are,
And the absence of cotton-wood leaves,
    or of aspen,
Even the absence of dark-crossed
    donkeys:
Come tall old demons, smiling
The Indian smile,
Saying: *How do you do, you pale-face?*

I am very well, old demon.
How are you?

Call me Harry if you will,
Call me Old Harry, says he.
Or the abbreviation of Nicolas,
Nick, Old Nick, maybe.

Well, you're a dark old demon,
And I'm a pale-face like a homeless dog
That has followed the sun from the
    dawn through the east,
Trotting east and east and east till the
    sun himself went home,
And left me homeless here in the dark
    at your door.
How do you think we'll get on,
Old demon, you and I?

You and I, you pale-face,
Pale-face you and I
Don't get on.

Mightn't we try?

Where's your God, you white one?
Where's your white God?

He fell to dust as the twilight fell,
Was fume as I trod
The last step out of the east.

Then you're a lost white dog of a pale-face,
And the day's now dead....

Touch me carefully, old father,
My beard is red.

Thin red wolf of a pale-face,
Thin red wolf, go home.

I have no home, old father,
That's why I come.

We take no hungry stray from the
    pale-face....

Father, you are not asked.
I am come. I am here. The red-
    dawn-wolf
Sniffs round your place.
Lifts up his voice and howls to the
    walls of the pueblo,
Announcing he's here.

The dogs of the dark pueblo
Have long fangs...

Has the red wolf trotted east and east
    and east
From the far, far other end of the day
To fear a few fangs?

Across the pueblo river
That dark old demon and I
Thus say a few words to each other

And wolf, he calls me, and red.
I call him no names.
He says, however, he is Star-Road.
I say, he can go back the same gait.

As for me...
Since I trotted at the tail of the sun as
    far as ever the creature went west,
And lost him here,
I'm going to sit down on my tail
    right here
And wait for him to come back with a
    new story.
I'm the red wolf, says the dark
    old father.
All right, the red-dawn-wolf I am.

D. H. LAWRENCE

Wolf at sunrise. D. Robert Franz/
The Wildlife Collection.

WHERE WOLVES LIVE

▼▼▼▼▼▼

Wolves were once the most widely distributed land predator the world has ever seen. Since they first evolved—probably more or less simultaneously in several places around the globe—wolves have followed their prey into just about every kind of habitat in the northern hemisphere: arctic tundra and taiga, high plains or steppes, lowland savannahs, and every type of forest. Just about the only places they don't thrive in are true desert lands and rainforests.

In North America, wolves once lived as far south as Mexico City (they may survive in small numbers in Mexico today) and north to the Greenland coast and the Canadian arctic. They are fairly numerous in the less settled parts of Canada and Alaska, but relatively few live in the lower forty-eight: in northern Minnesota, Michigan, Wisconsin, Montana, and possibly Idaho and Washington. There are occasional reports of wolves as far south as the Yellowstone area, and serious efforts are being made to reintroduce them to that ecosystem.

Wolves have vanished from most of western Europe, except for a few pockets of wildness in northern Scandinavia, the Alps, the Pyrenees, and the Italian Appenines. In eastern Europe, wolf numbers apparently increased during the 1950s and '60s in response to strict controls on hunting by Communist regimes; it seems reasonable that they are still more common there, but their true numbers are a mystery. Likewise in the former Soviet Union, where only rudimentary conservation efforts exist and wolves are routinely shot from military aircraft in Siberia.

For the rest of Asia, wolves once roamed from the Arabian peninsula to the islands of Japan, including the Indian subcontinent. In fact, the only part of Asia where no evidence of wolves has been found is Indochina. Today they linger mainly in the remoter provinces of China, Iran, and Afghanistan. There are some in India and the Near East; again, reliable figures are hard to come by. (See Appendix A, page 176, for current worldwide population estimates.)

The theme of the wolf devouring the world is common in northern European mythology. This Celtic vessel, dated around 50 A.D., shows the wolf, representing destruction, in close association with the horned god Cernunnos and his stag, signifying rebirth.

OPPOSITE: *Gray wolf in the Børas Sanctuary, northern Sweden. Perhaps only a dozen free-roaming wolves survive in that country. Mattias Klum.*

On the ragged edge of the World
I'll roam.
And the home of the Wolf
Will be my home.

ROBERT SERVICE

Arctic or tundra wolf, *Canis lupus arctos,* Northwest Territories. Wolves are most numerous today in the far north, and range through northern Canada and Alaska. J. D. Taylor/ Bruce Coleman, Inc.

Gray wolf, *C. lupus lycaon,* north-central U.S. *Lycaon,* the subspecies native to the Great Lakes area, is most numerous in Minnesota, where wolves are fully protected. Scot Stewart.

PACIFIC OCEAN

Red wolf, *Canis rufus,* southeastern U.S. The only wolf species other than *C. lupus,* the red wolf is rare in the wild but was reintroduced in North Carolina in 1988. Tom and Pat Leeson/ DRK Photo.

NORTH AMERICA

NORTH ATLANTIC OCEAN

SOUTH AMERICA

LEGEND

▓	Present Wolf Distribution	▓	Past Wolf Distribution
▓	Tundra	▓	Prairie
▓	Forest	▓	Steppe
▓	Mountain Vegetation	▓	Desert

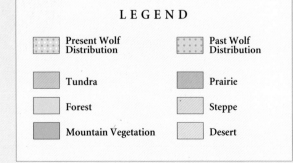

Mexican wolf, *C. lupus baileyi.* Probably fewer than a dozen survive in the wild in Mexico. Protected status is unenforced. Scot Stewart.

THE WORLD OF WOLVES

This map shows how extensively wolves were distributed around the world at the height of their past range, and the reduced area where they still live today. In some of their present range—for example, India, China, central Europe, and parts of southern Canada and Siberia—wolves are not widely distributed but exist only as isolated remnant populations. Also shown are the varied habitats where wolves can thrive, though they were never numerous in desert regions.

Gray wolf, *C. lupus lupus,* northern Europe. Only scattered individuals or pairs survive in the wild in Scandinavia. Wolves are more numerous in eastern Europe but are still hunted there. Mattias Klum.

Chinese wolf, *C. lupus chanco,* northern China. She-wolf and young in captivity; population numbers for wild wolves are unknown. Kenneth W. Fink/ Bruce Coleman, Inc.

Persian wolf, *C. lupus campestris.* A viable wolf population inhabits Iran, but elsewhere in the Middle East their numbers are low or unknown. Jeff Rotman/Peter Arnold, Inc.

Indian wolf, *C. lupus pallipes.* Asian wolves are smaller and more slender of build. Between 1,000 and 2,000 wolves still inhabit the remoter parts of the subcontinent, but they are endangered. Anup Shah/Animals Animals.

ARCTIC OCEAN

ASIA

EUROPE

AFRICA

INDIAN OCEAN

PACIFIC OCEAN

AUSTRALIA

SOUTH ATLANTIC OCEAN

WOLF AND DOG: THE ANCIENT BOND

▼▼▼▼▼▼

Everyone knows that wolves howl and dogs bark. Yet even the wisest cannot tell what moves these animals to call or explain why wolves howl and dogs bark when they do.

After CHANG TZU

"A very long time ago," notes animal authority Roger Caras, "man assumed responsibility for the genetic alteration of a species of wolf because it pleased him to do so. Later on he was to find he couldn't get along without that companion carnivore...."

If the relationship between humans and wolves is in many ways a puzzle, the dog is the key. Our dogs are intermediaries between us and nature, or as John McLoughlin says, "windows on the disappearing wild." Directly descended from wolves and among their closest relations, dogs provide even the casual observer with firsthand evidence of wolfish behavior, and have greatly aided wolf biologists in their investigations. The ways dogs display status-linked behavior among themselves and with their human masters, their territorial marking rituals, their wide range of vocal and facial expressions—all these are part of the wolf's legacy.

Dogs were first domesticated around fourteen thousand years ago, and since they are man's creature, their bond with wolves has been full of contradictions. There are old attractions, as described in *The Call of the Wild* and other stories, but also old antipathies, based on the dog's first and most important job: guarding its master's flocks from marauding predators. Dogs and wolves will interbreed under the right circumstances, and wolf blood was traditionally used to strengthen the sled dog strain. Wolf-dog hybrids, or demiwolves, have been bred for many purposes, justifiable and dubious. Specialized dogs have been bred over the centuries for the express task of hunting wolves, and hungry wolves will readily kill an available dog, like any other prey. In all its permutations, the link between wolves, dogs, and people has produced some of the most fascinating accounts in animal literature.

Jed, a one-quarter wolf/three-quarters malamute hybrid trained by Clint Rowe, played the title role in the 1991 Disney film White Fang, *based on the Jack London classic. Jed's broader chest and blockier muzzle reveal his predominatly dog heritage, but his intent gaze is very wolfish. Photo © The Walt Disney Company.*

HOW IT MAY HAVE STARTED

To pinpoint the actual beginning of the man-dog relationship requires a good bit of conjecture, as do most things that happened between one hundred and two hundred centuries ago. In most parts of the world the dog was probably the first domestic animal man extracted from the living forms around him. There seems to be little argument on that point. Most likely it happened somewhere in the Middle East or southwestern Asia. The date suggested for the event is often fourteen thousand years B.P. (before the present). . . .

The first issue, however, is how and why it happened. Man the carnivore—more properly the omnivore, because he was surely hunting, gathering, and eating everything in sight, including his neighbor in some instances—appears to have suddenly reached out and taken a fellow carnivore and therefore competitor into the cave and made him a partner. All this with no history or tradition of domestication. It almost seems as if there had to have been some kind of revelation.

There have been any number of romanticized views of how it came to pass. One day Mrs. Flintstone supposedly said something to the effect that the kids would love a puppy and Fred should bring one home from work. Unlikely. Slightly more plausible, but still probably less than likely, is the idea that some small species of wolf not unlike one still to be found from India to Israel and probably once even more widely distributed than that *(Canis lupus pallipes)* began hanging around human dwellings to get the offal tossed aside by the hunting families and clans. Eventually, the theory goes, it became a habit for man and wolf to stay near each other, and it stuck and went on from there. Possible, but again I think unlikely.

What does seem likely is that man had a hard time making ends meet and brought home everything he could chew and swallow. There was a constant plaint back at the nest: more food, more food! A raid on a wolf den when the adults were away or had been neutralized with a shower of rocks would have periodically yielded a batch of tender puppies. Dogs are still eaten in Asia, so I have no problem with this speculation so far. Even cavemen would have discovered that meat goes high if it is dead and cannot be kept

Rock painting of archer and dog, c. 6000 B.C., Tassili N'Ajjer Plateau, North Africa. Photo by Douglas Mazonowicz.

cold. Meat on the hoof stays fresh. It is my guess that pre-dog man began keeping puppies from kidnapped wolf litters around for food as needed. It is not difficult to imagine that sooner or later some kid would ask some father to spare a puppy. It was probably done as a temporary measure, but a habit came into being with which we are still enchanted. That little scene in the cave, however, is still a long way from purebred dogs genetically engineered to fulfill a job like sheepherding or game tracking or guard duty. There was still a way to go. A wolf puppy cannot grow up to be a dog no matter how much you love it.

And what does the record show? For a long time it was assumed that there were two ancestors to the dog, the wolf and the jackal. That has pretty much gone by the way, although wolves, jackals, and domestic dogs can all interbreed. There is a lot of liberal democracy in the canine genetic package. But the wolf generally gets full credit today for giving us our dogs.

ROGER CARAS, *A Celebration of Dogs*

Roger Caras is the dean of American popular writers about animals. Author of The Custer Wolf, Dangerous to Man, In Celebration of Dogs, *and many other volumes, he is especially well known as an authority on the far-flung dog tribe. He currently serves as president of the ASPCA.*

"Canoe of Fate," by Roy De Forest, 1974.

THE WOLF AND
THE INDIAN DOG

As Barry Lopez observes, wolves and dogs occupied very different places in the perception of Native Americans. The wolf was an honored fellow being, sometimes connected with sacred rituals, whereas dogs were simply kept for their usefulness: in hunting game, pulling loads, or guarding camps. Many Indians had a vivid sense of the dog's unique and sometimes confused position somewhere between the wolf and human tribes, as this Crow story shows:

Crow woman was digging roots when a wolf came by. The woman's dog ran up to the wolf and said, "Hey, what are you doing here? Go away. You only come around because you want what I have."

"What have you got?" asked the wolf. "Your owner beats you all the time. Kids kick you out of the way. Try to steal a piece of meat and they hit you over the head with a club."

"At least I can steal the meat!" answered the dog. "You haven't got anything to steal."

"Hah! I eat whenever I want. No one bothers me."

"What do you eat? You slink around while the men butcher the buffalo and get what's left over. You're afraid to get close. You sit there pulling dirt balls out of your tail."

"Look who's talking, with camp garbage smeared all over your face."

"Hrumph. Whenever I come into camp, my owner throws me something good to eat."

"When your owner goes out at night you follow along to eat the droppings, that's how much you get to eat."

"Listen, whenever they're cooking in camp, you smell the grease, you come around and howl, and I feel sorry for you. I pity you. . . ."

"When do they let you have a good time?" asked the wolf.

"I sleep warm, you sleep out in the rain, they scratch my ears—"

Just then the woman shouldered a bundle of roots, whacked the dog on the back with a stick, and started back to camp. The dog followed along behind her, calling over his shoulder at the wolf, "You're just full of envy for a good life, that's all that's wrong with you."

Wolf went off the other way, not wanting any part of that life.

R. H. LOWIE, *Myths and Traditions of the Crow*, adapted by Barry Lopez

WOLF DOGS

The wolf dog—offspring of dog and wolf—is said to be liable to be more dangerous than either parent. That is easy to understand. Dogs have fierce hearts but are human-oriented; their fierceness shows toward animals, even their own kind. Wolves have gentle hearts but are not human-oriented. A human means no more to them than does a fox, but they are tolerant of other species, even of prey species when not hungry. If the combination occurred of a dog's fierce heart and a wolf's indifference toward man, the animal could be ruthless.

But the opposite combination is possible too: a wolf's solicitude and intensity, plus a dog's human orientation. Then you get an animal that has greatness.

LOIS CRISLER, *Arctic Wild*

BUCK HEARS THE CALL

One night he sprang from sleep with a start, eager-eyed, nostrils quivering and scenting, his mane bristling in recurrent waves. From the forest came the call (or one note of it, for the call was many noted), distant and definite as never before—a long-drawn howl, like, yet unlike, any noise made by husky dog. And he knew it, in the old familiar way, as a sound heard before. He sprang through the sleeping camp and in swift silence dashed through the woods. As he drew closer to the cry he went more slowly, with caution in every movement, till he came to an open place among the trees, and looking out, saw erect on haunches, with nose pointed to the sky, a long, lean timber wolf.

He had made no noise yet it ceased from its howling and tried to sense his presence. Buck stalked into the open, half crouching, body gathered compactly together, tail straight and stiff, feet falling with unwonted care. Every movement advertised commingled threatening and overture of friendliness. It was the menacing truce that marks the meeting of wild beasts that prey. But the wolf fled at sight of him. He followed, with wild leapings, in a frenzy to overtake. He ran him into a blind channel, in the bed of the creek, where a timber jam barred the way. The wolf whirled about, pivoting on his hind legs after the fashion of Joe and of all cornered husky dogs, snarling and bristling, clipping his teeth together in a continuous and rapid succession of snaps.

Buck did not attack, but circled about him and hedged him in with friendly advances. The wolf was suspicious and afraid; for Buck made three of him in weight, while his head barely reached Buck's shoulder. Watching his chance, he darted away, and the chase was resumed. Time and again he was cornered, and the thing repeated, though he was in poor condition, or Buck could not so easily have overtaken him. He would run till Buck's head was even with the flank, when he would whirl around at bay, only to dash away again at the first opportunity.

But in the end Buck's pertinacity was rewarded; for the wolf, finding that no harm was intended, finally sniffed noses with him. Then they became friendly, and played about in the nervous, half-coy way with which fierce beasts belie their fierceness. After some time of this the wolf started off at an easy lope in a manner that plainly showed he was going somewhere. He made it clear to Buck that he was to come, and they ran side by side through the somber twilight, straight up the creek bed, into the gorge from which it issued, and across the bleak divide where it took its rise.

On the opposite slope of the watershed they came down into a level country where were great stretches of forest and many streams, and through these great stretches they ran steadily, hour after hour, the sun rising higher and the day growing warmer. Buck was wildly glad. He knew he was at last answering the call, running by the side of his wood brother toward the place from where the call surely came. Old memories were coming upon him fast, and he was stirring to them as of old he stirred to the realities of which they were the shadows. He had done this thing before, somewhere in that other and dimly remembered world, and he was doing it again, now, running free in the open, the unpacked earth underfoot, the wide sky overhead.

JACK LONDON, *Call of the Wild*

Gray wolf vocalizing, Montana. Alan and Sandy Carey.

THE EMBODIED WOLF

▼▼▼▼▼

The physical wolf is superbly constructed and adapted for its role in life—that of a coursing hunter pursuing large and small prey over many kinds of terrain: open plains, dense forest, deep snow, steep slopes, and into the water if need be. Red wolves have even been known to leap onto the lower limbs of trees.

Evolution has shaped the wolf with a rangy, muscular body set high on long, powerful legs. All the canids are adapted for running, and wolves especially so. They can average around 25 miles per hour for several miles, and 35 to 40 mph for short bursts—not as fast as a healthy deer or caribou, but their hunting success relies on

a combination of speed, stamina, and tactics. The wolf's narrow chest and outward-splayed forelegs enable its hind legs to move in the same track as the front, an advantage in covering ground efficiently and in moving through deep snow. The feet are notably large and well-padded, the better to spread weight over snow or crust, and to grip securely on irregular shapes like rocks and logs.

Far-ranging travelers built for endurance as well as speed, wolves carry relatively little flesh for their size. People typically exaggerate their size and weight; full-grown gray wolves average around 80 pounds (the range is about 45 pounds for small Asian wolves up to a record 175 pounds for an Alaskan wolf).

The strength of wolves is also the stuff of legends. Trappers tell of wolves dragging heavy objects such as tree trunks for miles, or exerting enough force to straighten a quarter-inch-thick iron "drag hook" commonly attached to traps. Immense power is concentrated in the wolf's jaws, which can attain a crushing pressure of nearly 1,500 pounds per square inch (compared with around 750 for a large dog). The jaws themselves are massive, bearing 42 teeth specialized for stabbing, shearing, and crunching bones. Not surprisingly, wolf digestion is also well adapted to deal with meat fresh off the hoof.

The wolf's coat is both its crowning glory and a buffer against harsh surroundings. As with most mammals, it comprises a layer of soft underfur beneath longer, coarser guard hairs; this outer layer is what gives each wolf its distinctive color pattern. Wolves generally take all summer to shed their old coats and grow a new one, which reaches maximum lushness in winter. Wolves vary in color more than any other furred beast, ranging from pure white to solid black with all shades of cream, gray, fawn, and brown in between.

In the realm of the senses, wolves are most richly endowed with smell and hearing, probably surpassing most dogs in these powers. They are relatively nearsighted and cannot discern the full color spectrum, but their vision is excellent at detecting movement. Their learning capacity is great, as survival dictates, and their reactions and responsiveness are incredibly sharp and finely tuned.

LEFT: *Engraving of wolf anatomy from an eighteenth-century German volume.*
OPPOSITE: *Leaping wolf, Yukon Territory. Jack Couffer/Bruce Coleman, Inc.*

The wolf's strong, long-toed feet make it an agile climber, and they favor high rock outcrops as lookouts. Mattias Klum.

The wolf is kept fed by its feet.
Russian proverb

WOLF TAILS

A wolf's most undoglike feature is his tail. He runs with his tail, thinks with it, marks mood with it, even controls with it. "They run with their tails as much as with their spines," observed Cris. The tail floats. The one position it never assumes is up and curled like a sled dog's tail. . . .

The higher the wolf's spirits, the higher his tail. You glance at his tail to learn his mood. A typical tail position for a cheerful wolf is out an inch, then down. You can talk a gloomy wolf's tail into that position. Wolves are wonderfully responsive to a truly cheerful voice.

Since wolves have complete "differential relaxation," they don't wag their tails quite as dogs do. They wag them on about the same occasions but take the trouble to start only the base of the tail. The rest of the tail follows through, drifting languidly in a Delsarte gesture, the stump starting east while the tip drifts west. When the tail is not in use the wolf withdraws every ounce of residual tension; the tail hangs like a great tassel, subject only to wind and gravity.

On the other hand, wolves use their tails strongly and controllingly, like fifth arms. A wolf will flap his tail strongly over the back of another wolf running alongside.

LOIS CRISLER, *Arctic Wild*

Wolves have marvelous legs. The first thing one notices about wolves is how high they are set on their skinny legs, and the instant, blurred gait these can switch into, bicycling away, carrying them as much as 40 miles in a day. With brindled coats in smoky shades, brushy tails, light-filled eyes intense sharp faces which are more focused than an intelligent dog's but also less various, they are electric on first sighting, bending that bushy head around to look back as they run. . . . scientists watching pet wolves in the woods speak of their flowing joy, of such delight in running that they melt into the woods like sunlight, like running water.

EDWARD HOAGLAND,
Red Wolves and Black Bears

Down on my hearth-rug of
  desert, sage of the mesa,
An ash-grey pelt
Of wolf all hairy and level,
  a wolf's wild pelt.

D. H. LAWRENCE,
from *"Autumn At Taos"*

Wolf fur has been favored for parka ruffs by Eskimos, trappers, and the U.S. Army, for good reason. Its thick winter underfur allows a wolf to curl up and sleep comfortably in weather as cold as 40 degrees below zero. The long guard hairs shed moisure and protect the underfur. Tom and Pat Leeson/DRK Photo.

MAKING TRACKS

The going was rough and rocky at first, and I took a great deal longer to cover the intervening ground than the wolf had done, but eventually I scaled the low crest where I had last seen him (or her). Ahead of me I found a vast expanse of boggy muskeg which promised well for tracks; and indeed I found a set of footprints almost immediately, leading off across a patch of chocolate-colored bog.

I should have felt overjoyed, yet somehow I did not. The truth is that my first sight of the wolf's paw-prints was a revelation for which I was quite unprepared. It is one thing to read in a textbook that the footprints of an arctic wolf measure six inches in diameter;

but it is quite another thing to see them laid out before you in all their bald immensity. It has a dampening effect on one's enthusiasm. The mammoth prints before me, combined as they were with a forty-inch stride, suggested that the beast I was proposing to pursue was built on approximately the scale of a grizzly bear.

I studied those prints for quite a long time. . . .

FARLEY MOWAT, *Never Cry Wolf*

Gray wolf, Alaska. M. A. Chappell/Animals Animals.

EYE CONTACT

Although we perceive the outer, physical world with our eyes, we can also touch and sense something of the inner world through eye contact. This avenue into the inner being of another is not a mystical illusion but a very real key to communion. Emotions, fleeting reactions, and even intentions are reflected in the subtle changes in the size of the pupils and in the movements of the muscles that control the eyes.

As in man, so in the wolf: a direct stare is a threat; looking down and away is a submissive or friendly signal; and a wide "innocent" gaze, an infantile open face, is associated with playful intentions. Changes in pupil size in both man and wolf correlate with changes in emotion—pleasure, pain, fear, and anger.

The wolf's eyes glow in the dark; there is a light-reflecting layer called the *tapetum lucidum* that may facilitate night vision. A carnivore's eyes are also usually extremely sensitive to movements, while color perception and visual acuity may be inferior to man's. The use—conscious or unconscious—of the eyes in social contexts, however, is virtually identical in man and wolf. . . .

Rarely will one make direct eye contact with a wolf, wild or captive, unless the intention is to threaten (and possibly attack), or to engage in play. More usually, the wolf elusively avoids eye contact, but in a Mona Lisa way. You always know that the wolf is following you with its eyes whenever you are in its vicinity. . . . The more submissive, dependent, or fearful wolf or human being makes more eye contact than does one who is more self-assured and of high status.

Both wolf and man have eyes set in the front of the face, a mark of the hunter who searches and penetrates his visual field for prey.

MICHAEL W. FOX, *The Soul of the Wolf*

Michael W. Fox is Vice President of the Humane Society of the United States, a renowned animal behaviorist, and the author of many books on our relationship to animals. He has raised and kept wolves, who became his "mirror and teacher."

We stared at one another in silence. I do not know what went on in his massive skull, but my head was full of the most disturbing thoughts. I was peering straight into the amber gaze of a fully grown arctic wolf, who probably weighed more than I did, and who was certainly a lot better versed in close-combat techniques than I would ever be.

For some seconds neither of us moved but continued to stare hypnotically into one another's eyes. The wolf was the first to break the spell. With a spring which would have done justice to a Russian dancer, he leaped about a yard straight into the air and came down running. . . . Within seconds he had vanished from my sight.

FARLEY MOWAT, Never Cry Wolf

BEFORE BIOLOGY

Published in 1607, this source was among the first to attempt any detailed natural history of wolves—almost wholly based on myth.

The brains of a wolf do decrease and increase with the moon. The neck of a wolf is short which argueth a treacherous nature. If the heart of a wolf be kept dry, it rendereth a most pleasant or sweet-smelling savor. . . .

There are divers kinds of wolves in the world. . . . The first which is swift hath a greater head than other wolves, and likewise greater legs fitted to run, white spots on the belly, round members, and his colour betwixt red and yellow, he is very bold, howleth fearfully, having firy-flaming eyes, and continually wagging his head. The second kind hath a greater and larger body than this, being swifter than all other . . . his sides and tail are of a silver color. . . . The third kind inhabiteth sharp and inaccessible places, being worthily for beauty preferred before the others, because of his Golden resplendent hairs. . . . He is exceedingly strong, especially being able to bite asunder not only stones, but Brasse and Iron: He feareth the Dog star and heat of summer. . . .

EDWARD TOPSELL, A Historie of Foure-footed Beastes

TOOLS OF THE TRADE

A mammal's most important food-processing tools . . . are the teeth. The early insectivores possessed, in both upper and lower jaws on either side of the head, three incisor teeth for cutting; one long, sharp, stabbing "canine" tooth—so called, of course, because of its great importance to our friends the Canidae; four shearing premolar teeth; and three grinding molar teeth. . . .

This is the standard arrangement, from which all tooth specializations for different ways of higher mammalian life may be derived. We human beings, for example, are tool-using omnivores (we'll eat almost anything but prepare it before eating with tools held in our hands); while our tools take the place of stabbing canine teeth and shearing premolars, we still retain good incisors—but only two on a side—and good grinding molars for such coarse vegetable food as we take. But we have lost two of the shearing premolars and our canines, while still there, are no longer any good for stabbing. . . .

In carnivorous land mammals, the incisors are still essential nippers for cutting flesh. Behind them, the aptly named canine teeth tend in such animals to be long and daggerlike, as they are used to seize and stab comparatively large prey. Carnivorous mammal are efficient eaters; except in times of unusual plenty, they are not content simply to eat the sirloin of their prey and abandon the rest. No, they eat it all, and to cope with the inevitable gristle, tough hide, and other "low cost meats" with which they are forced to deal, mammalian carnivores need some sort of carnassial (flesh-shearing), or "knife" teeth.

JOHN C. MCLOUGHLIN, The Canine Clan

In The Canine Clan, *zoologist and scientific illustrator John McLoughlin traces the evolution of dogs, wolves, and other canids, and compares and contrasts the characteristics of all modern-day canines.*

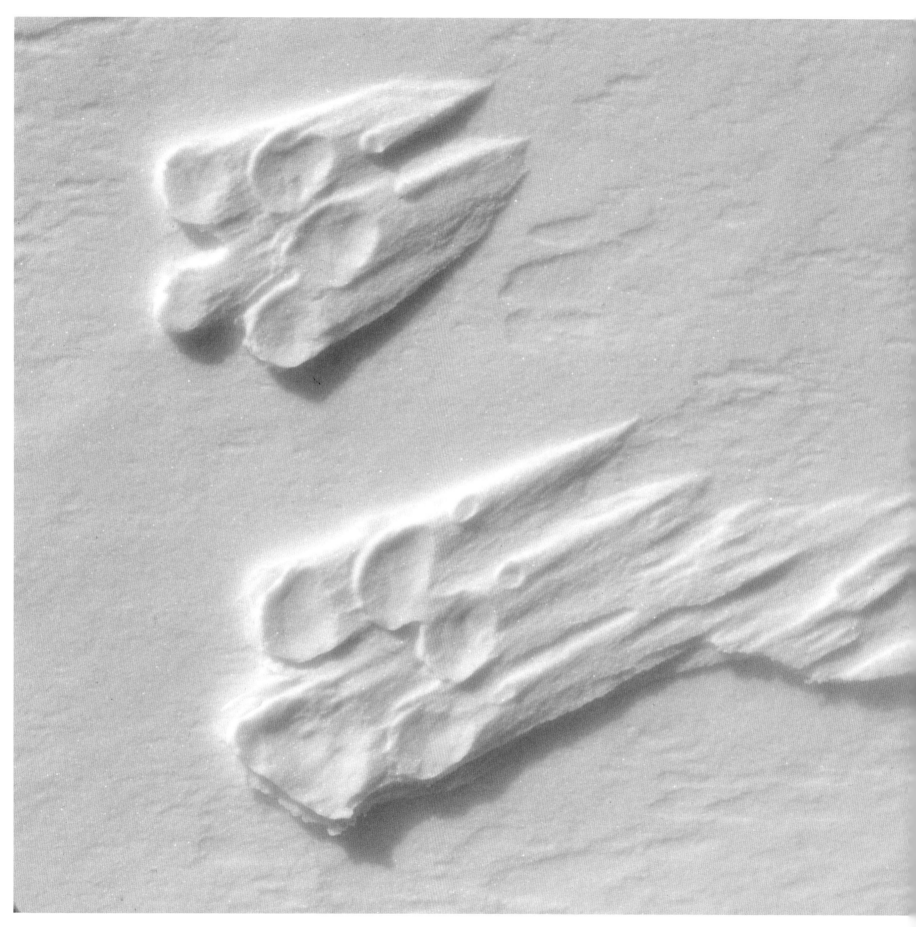

MOON WHEN WOLVES RUN TOGETHER
▼▼▼▼▼▼

Long ago, an old wolf
came to that time
when his life on earth
could last no longer.
"My people," he said,
"you can follow in my footsteps
when the time comes for you
to join me in the skyland."
Then he left the earth,
climbing higher and higher,
and each place he stepped
the sky filled with stars.

Shunk man-i-tu tan-ka,
we call the wolves,
the powerful spirits
who look like dogs.
When they climb the hills
to lift their heads and sing
toward that road of stars,
their songs grow stronger
as they join their voices.

So, in this moon, we climb the hills
lift our eyes toward the Wolf Trail
and remember that our lives
and songs are stronger
when we are together.

JOSEPH BRUCHAC
AND JONATHAN LONDON,
Thirteen Moons on Turtle's Back

Drifted tracks of an arctic wolf, Ellesmere Island, Canada. Jim Brandenburg.

Survival rules,
but after that comes conviviality!

RICHARD GROSSMAN, from *The Animals*

Wild wolves live about ten years, if they're lucky, and for most of
that time they are either learning how to live from older wolves, or
passing those lessons on. Their livelihood hangs on an intimate
knowledge of their surroundings—what's good to eat and what
should be left alone, where to den and where the caribou
will be tomorrow, where they can   freely range and

The Lifeway of Wolves

where they   risk   trespassing on another's turf.
Not to   mention the skill and strategy required to
kill animals   considerably larger and faster than themselves.
    Some of this knowledge is inborn but much must be
learned, by example or experience. Because of how wolves evolved
and the special demands of their lifeway, they have become the
most highly social of all carnivores. They live in packs linked by
close blood ties, in which each wolf's role is understood and
serves the common good. They communicate with voice, face,
and body in ritualized ways that enhance hunting success and min-
imize combat between well-armed foes. Mates form close bonds,
and all pitch in to nurture and train the young, a two-year commitment. Wolves usually tolerate and feed the old and less fit
among them, and keep peace with neighboring packs by respecting
territorial boundaries.   Since people have come to know
wolves better, we have found much to admire in their efficient organization and their dedication to family and tribe. We've also
observed—perhaps with a touch of envy—the wolf's lifelong gift
for joyful play.

*I*magine a wolf moving through the northern woods. The movement, over a trail he has traversed many times before, is distinctive, unlike that of a cougar or a bear, yet he appears, if you are watching, sometimes catlike or bearlike. It is purposeful, deliberate movement. Occasionally the rhythm is broken by the wolf's pause to inspect a scent mark, or a move off the trail to paw among stones where a year before he had cached meat.

The movement down the trail would seem relentless if it did not appear so effortless. The wolf's body, from neck to hips, appears to float over the long, almost spindly legs and the flicker of wrists, a bicycling drift through the trees, reminiscent of the movement of water or of shadows.

The wolf is three years old. A male. He is of the subspecies *occidentalis*, and the trees he is moving among are spruce and subalpine fir on the eastern slope of the Rockies in northern Canada. . . .

It is early September, an easy time of year, and he has not seen the other wolves in his pack for three or four days. He has heard no howls, but he knows the others are about, in ones and twos like himself. It is not a time of year for much howling. It is an easy time. The weather is pleasant. Moose are fat. Suddenly the wolf stops in mid-stride. A moment, then his feet slowly come alongside each other. He is staring into the grass. His ears are rammed forward, stiff. His back arches and he rears up and pounces like a cat. A deer mouse is pinned between his forepaws. Eaten. The wolf drifts on. He approaches a trail crossing, an undistinguished crossroads. His movement is now slower and he sniffs the air as though aware of a possibility for scents. He sniffs a scent post, a scrawny blueberry bush in use for years, and goes on.

The wolf weighs ninety-four pounds and stands thirty inches at the shoulder. His feet are enormous, leaving prints in the mud along a creek (where he pauses to hunt crayfish but not with much interest) more than five inches long by just over four wide. He has two fractured ribs, broken by a moose a year before. They are healed now, but a sharp eye would notice the irregularity. The skin on his right hip is scarred, from a fight with another wolf in a neighboring pack when he was a yearling. He has not had anything

but a few mice and a piece of arctic char in three days, but he is not hungry. He is traveling. The char was a day old, left on rocks along the river by bears.

The wolf is tied by subtle threads to the woods he moves through. His fur carries seeds that will fall off, effectively dispersed, along the trail some miles from where they first caught in his fur. And miles distant is a raven perched on the ribs of a caribou the wolf helped kill ten days ago, pecking like a chicken at the de-caying scraps of meat. A smart snow-shoe hare that elud-ed the wolf and left him exhausted when he was a pup has been dead a year now, food for an owl. The den in which he was born one April evening was home to porcupines last winter. . . .

The underfur next to his skin has begun to thicken with the coming of fall. In the months to follow it will become so dense be-tween his shoulders it will be almost impossible to work a finger down to his skin. In seven months he will weigh less: eighty-nine pounds. He will have tried unsuccessfully to mate with another wolf in the pack. He will have helped kill four moose and thirteen caribou. He will have fallen through ice into a creek at twenty-two below zero but not frozen. He will have fought with other wolves.

He moves along now at the edge of a clearing. The wind com-ing down-valley surrounds him with a river of odors, as if he were a migrating salmon. He can smell ptarmigan and deer droppings. He can smell willow and spruce and the fading sweetness of fire-weed. Above, he sees a hawk circling, and farther south, lower on the horizon, a flock of sharp-tailed sparrows going east. He senses through his pads with each step the dryness of the moss beneath his feet, and the ridges of old tracks, some his own. He hears the sound his feet make. He hears the occasional movement of deer mice and voles. Summer food.

Toward dusk he is standing by a creek, lapping the cool water, when a wolf howls—a long wail that quickly reaches pitch and then tapers, with several harmonics, long moments to a tremolo. He recognizes his sister. He waits a few moments, then, throwing his head back and closing his eyes, he howls. The howl is shorter and it changes pitch twice in the beginning, very quickly. There is no answer.

The female is a mile away and she trots off obliquely through the trees. The other wolf stands listening, laps water again, then he too departs, moving quickly, quietly through the trees, away from the trail he had been on. In a few minutes the two wolves meet. They approach each other briskly, almost formally, tails erect and moving somewhat as deer move. When they come together they make high squeaking noises and encircle each other, rubbing and pushing, poking their noses into each other's neck fur, backing away to stretch, chasing each other for a few steps, then standing quietly together, one putting a head over the other's back. And then they are gone, down a vague trail, the female first. After a few hun-dred yards they begin, simultaneously, to wag their tails.

In the days to follow, they will meet another wolf from the pack, a second female, younger by a year, and the three of them will kill a caribou. They will travel together ten or twenty miles a day, through the country where they live, eating and sleeping, birthing, playing with sticks, chasing ravens, growing old, barking at bears, scent-marking trails, killing moose, and staring at the way water in a creek breaks around their legs and flows on.

BARRY LOPEZ, *Of Wolves and Men*

Of Wolves and Men, published in 1978, is Barry Holstun Lopez's groundbreaking investigation of wolf-human relations. The author's researches spanned the mythology and history of many lands; he worked with biologists in the field and lived with the Nunamiut Eskimo in Alaska, close to wolves. Like other keen ob-servers of wolves, he used what we know of them to imagine in detail this passage of a wolf through a day in its life—tracking it with the mind's eye.

THE SOCIAL WOLF

▼▼▼▼▼▼

Nearly everything wolves do, they do together. Genetically programmed for cooperative living, a wolf begins learning the law of mutual dependence from the moment its mother licks it dry at birth, and group-consciousness dominates every feature of its life from then on: sibling play, the choice of hunting and denning grounds, breeding, feeding, and relations with "outside" wolves and packs.

For pack life to work, wolves had to develop a wide range of ways to express their emotions, perceptions, and intentions, and they passed on much of that gift for communicating to their descendents, our dogs. The affection and loyalty of wolves toward their fellows—and the ability to convey them clearly—are the qualities we most value in our companion animals.

Packs can vary in size from a pair up to a recorded maximum of thirty-six (old reports of packs containing "hundreds of wolves" are almost surely apocryphal). So many factors influence pack size that an "average" is hard to come by, though around seven wolves seems common. Determining factors include how many wolves are needed to bring down large prey, how many can feed at a single kill, and social stresses that develop when packs reach a certain size.

Most often, wolves in a pack are related by blood, because the bonds that hold packs together are strongest between parents and their pups, and among siblings from the same litter. Mated pairs may be related, or may form an attachment during the breeding season; this is one way an outside wolf may come into the pack. "Lone wolves" may be young animals who compete too hard for breeding and feeding rights, socially ostracized members of any age, wolves orphaned by some catastrophe, or old wolves who have lost long-time mates—but in any case, solitude is hardly ever a voluntary state. Wolves are "always seeking to enroll themselves."

Packs typically consist of a breeding pair—usually the "alpha" male and female—a middle layer of subdominant wolves, whose relative positions may shift around; the pups of the season (who have their own pecking order); and sometimes one or more very low-ranking wolves at the bottom. It was once thought that only the alpha male and female would breed and bear young, but subdominant males do sometimes mate with the alpha female.

Much has been made of the "hierarchical" structure of wolf packs, but as Barry Lopez says, notions about rigid rankings, harsh discipline, and alpha male leadership owe more to human than to wolf culture. Wolf social organization is more dynamic, responsive to individual personalities and circumstances. Roles may change, over time and depending on the business at hand.

PORTRAIT OF A PACK

The wolf was a drifting blot of gray as she ascended the ravine, her winter-long claws rasping faintly as she slipped on the ice-sheathed rocks. Not trotting as wolves usually do, she seemed to move in a leisurely manner, but her panting and sagging belly betrayed the illusion. Pregnant with what would likely be her last litter of pups, she stopped frequently to sniff the invisible trail she followed among the rocks and broken tapestries of blue ice. . . .

There were six adult wolves in the St. George Creek pack, including the little gray bitch. A huge black male, her conjugal mate since her first period of annual heat, was as much an exception to standard size as was the small female. During times of seasonal prime, he weighed almost 130 pounds and stood three feet high at his roached shoulder. There was little doubt that his physical size and age were factors which established him as leader of the pack, yet his position of dominance was not absolute. Though he bore undisputed authority over most of the others, his mate, the small gray bitch, was also an influential member of the St. George Creek pack. Though she respected and followed him, her reaction to his dominance within the group was less rigid, and was probably a normal result of both her sex and the fact that he was her full brother.

Two buff-tan males, both two-year-old sons of the black leader and the gray bitch, formed the hunting nucleus of the pack in company with their sire. With the passage of their second winter of life and recent sexual maturity, they had attained true adulthood.

The remaining members of the St. George Creek pack were adult females. Each bore the white coloration of their common father, and were the only members of the pack that did not claim the bloodlines of the black leader. Whelped during a heavy rainstorm which flooded the den occupied by their mother before she had licked them dry, they were the only survivors in a letter of seven pups. Then, during their second winter, both of their parents fell victim to an experienced trapper. . . . They had traveled alone during the balance of a severe winter, and during the following spring joined with the small group led by the black.

OPPOSITE: Howling is usually a group event. Peter McLeod/First Light. ABOVE: Grey wolves during breeding season, light-colored male and black phase female, Michigan. Carl R. Sams II/Peter Arnold, Inc.

The merger was a rarity, for seldom do wolves join the packs of other leaders, or more properly, are they allowed to join by the strange pack. . . . Both were, as a result of the absence of parents during their second year, more inexperienced where hunting was concerned than they would have been after a more normal adolescence. As resident members of the pack, they occupied the lower end of the social order headed by the huge black but more rigidly enforced by his mate, the gray bitch.

JAMES GREINER, *The Red Snow*

41

WOLF
▼▼▼▼▼▼

The basis for friendship is
community of interest. Wolves
mate for life.

Yet they call our families "packs"
like decks of cards.
A communard who knows

how to have a good time with others,
I object to this moniker
of shuffling beast. It's true

that the only way to eat
is ultimately to rip something apart,
but you can't swallow

with your eyes, and besides,
we wolves have big hearts:
We are gentle, bright,

and penultimately kind.
Survival rules,
but after that comes conviviality!

A wolf attack on a moose
is no worse
than the conventions

of nations,
or the strategies
of most political parties.

RICHARD GROSSMAN, *The Animals*

SOCIAL STRUCTURE OF A WOLF PACK

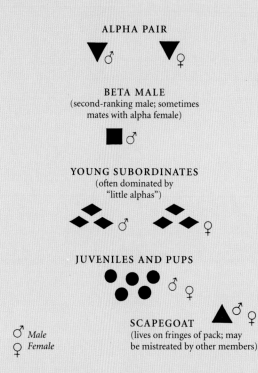

ALPHA PAIR
▼♂   ▼♀

BETA MALE
(second-ranking male; sometimes
mates with alpha female)
■♂

YOUNG SUBORDINATES
(often dominated by
"little alphas")
◆◆♂   ◆◆♀
◆   ◆

JUVENILES AND PUPS
●●●♂ ♀
●●

♂ Male
♀ Female

SCAPEGOAT   ▲♂ ♀
(lives on fringes of pack; may
be mistreated by other members)

Observers have noticed the similarities between the intricate life of a wolf pack and the most primitive grouping of man, the family-sized band. Often there is a "peripheral wolf," for instance, which is tolerated but picked on, and as though the collective psyche of the pack required a scapegoat, if the peripheral wolf disappears another pack member may slip down the social ladder and assume the role, or a stray that otherwise might have been driven off will be adopted. The strays, or "lone wolves," . . . are always seeking to enroll themselves.

EDWARD HOAGLAND,
Red Wolves and Black Bears

Muzzle licking and a lowered head and tail are usually part of the greeting ritual offered by a subordinate to a more dominant wolf. Tom and Pat Leeson.

The act of seeking and receiving acceptance is an oft-repeated ritual that helps hold packs together. Flattened, outward-pointing ears are an element of the "wolf smile," conveying affection in the clearest terms. Mattias Klum.

STATUS SHOW

Canadian wildlife writer R. D. Lawrence got well acquainted with a pack of captive wolves in Minnesota while researching In Praise of Wolves. *Most of the detailed observations that have been made of wolf social behavior have occurred with captive animals that are not tamed but kept in large enclosures containing many elements found in their wild habitat. Shawano was the alpha male of this pack.*

Shawano, standing erect and courtly as a monarch, accepted the homage of his subjects, allowing his muzzle to be nibbled but advertising his status by holding his tail high, his head up, his ears erect, his mouth partly open. His lips were wrinkled by a benevo-lent grin. This in contrast to the other wolves, who were careful to keep their tails low and who flattened their ears and whined as they sought their leader's approval and reassurance. The exchange was typical of wolves everywhere, an interaction often mistaken by human observers for a manifestation of dictatorial tyranny on one side and fawning subjugation on the other. What soon followed would have served to confirm that impression, for Shawano suddenly stopped grinning and peeled back his lips in a seemingly ferocious snarl as he concentrated his attention on Toivo, who, in his enthusiasm, had become overly bold, allowing his tail to rise as he pressed too tightly against his leader.

R. D. LAWRENCE, *In Praise of Wolves*

The strongest impression remaining with me after watching the wolves on numerous occasions was their friendliness. The adults were friendly toward each other and amiable toward the pups, at least as late as October. This innate good feeling has been strongly marked in the three captive wolves which I have known.

ADOLPH MURIE,
A Naturalist in Alaska

ABOVE: *Wolves are very oriented toward each other's mouths. Gently grasping the muzzle of another wolf can be a gesture of dominance, but is also used by subordinates greeting a leader or by any adult wolf mildly chastising an unruly pup. Charlie Palek/Animals Animals.* OPPOSITE: *Dominance challenges sometimes occur around food but are usually settled with no more than a flash of teeth and a firm shouldering.*

TABLE MANNERS

As the subordinate members approached them, I observed something I don't think anyone has ever seen before, at least in wild wolves around a kill: The subordinates performed an astounding submissive ritual that seemed to have strong elements of homage-paying, begging, or placating.

When the subordinates came to within about six feet of Alpha Male, who was standing over the half-eaten carcass, each seemed to be drawn to the leader like a magnet. The subordinate would lower itself, point its nose toward Alpha Male, pull its ears in and its lips back, and continue forward reluctantly, almost as though it had lost control and was being pulled. The closer it got, the lower and more submissive it became. Alpha Male stopped feeding and began to pay attention, more out of duty, it seemed, than because he really wanted to.

The first subordinate, a male, was now within inches of Alpha Male in a very tense half-crouch, head pointed up and wavering. Then the subordinate lifted a front foot and tried to paw Alpha Male around the head.

Alpha Male, lord wolf king of the surrounding one thousand square miles, snapped half-heartedly, and his subject fell to the ground. It was hard to believe. The subordinates acted like tiny pups, yet each was at least three years old and probably more, and they had all just helped kill the musk ox like equals. Now here they were, each a fawning mass of insecurity in the face of their leader.

I still don't really understand it. Why were they so drawn to the alpha? Were they anxious to feed but reluctant to buck the head honcho? Was there some other reason to approach and demonstrate their submissiveness? They often go through a similar, although lower-intensity, ritual on awakening and grouping up for the hunt. However, in this case they seemed much more highly motivated.

L. DAVID MECH, *The Arctic Wolf*

THE JUBILATION OF WOLVES

▼▼▼▼▼

The wolf's howl has epitomized wildness since time immemorial. No other aspect of wolf behavior has so seized the human imagination—with terror or dread in times past, and with a spirit-lifting thrill for most listeners today.

It was pioneering biologist Durward L. Allen who described howling as "the jubilation of wolves." Often it does express joy or sheer excitement, as when members of a pack reconvene after time apart, or prepare to set out on a hunt. But howling seems to have other purposes, such as gathering a scattered pack, announcing the whereabouts of a kill, serenading or pining for a mate, and lamenting an absent member of the tribe. Wolves also howl to advertise their presence to neighboring packs, reaffirming territorial rights.

One member of the pack usually begins a group howl, and others join in one at a time, each taking a different pitch. ("Wolves avoid unison singing"; notes Lois Crisler, "they like chords.") Even young pups join in. Though howling often follows a pattern, starting with long, low howls and proceeding to shorter, higher ones, each animal has a distinctive voice, so they can recognize each other over distance.

Wolves vocalize in ways other than howling. These sounds—short or prolonged whimpers, barks, growls, and squeaks—are used to greet, solicit, warn, or challenge other wolves nearby. They are less often heard by humans because they are not used for long-range communication.

Biologists have found that wolves will respond to humans imitating their howls (and, to a lesser extent, to tape-recorded wolf howls). This has been an important research tool, and also a way for visitors in wolf country to make contact with the elusive creatures. The International Wolf Center in Minnesota sponsors "howl nights," naturalist-led field trips on which people can express some of their own wildness and hope for an answering howl from over the hills.

BELOW: "Howl," lithograph by Luis Jimenez, 1977. OPPOSITE: Wolves often howl at day's end, when they set out for the hunt. Alan and Sandy Carey.

Farley Mowat, like many other observers, found himself deeply moved by the wolf chorus, part of the early evening ritual that took place before the pack set out to hunt:

This was one of the high points of their day, and it was certainly the high point of mine. The first few times the three wolves sang, the old ingrained fear set my back hairs tingling, and I cannot claim to have really enjoyed the chorus. However, with the passage of sufficient time I not only came to enjoy it, but to anticipate it with acute pleasure. And yet I find it almost impossible to describe, for the only terms at my disposal are those relating to human music and these are inadequate if not actually misleading. The best I can do is to say that this full-throated and great-hearted chorus moved me as I have very occasionally been moved by the bowel-shaking throb and thunder of a superb organ played by a man who had transcended his mere manhood.

FARLEY MOWAT, *Never Cry Wolf*

SANTEE SIOUX SONG

▼▼▼▼▼

At daybreak I roam
ready to tear up the world
I roam

At daybreak I roam
shivers coming up my spine
I roam

At daybreak I roam
awake to who is following
I roam

At daybreak I roam
eyes in the back of my head
I roam

*Sung by Weasel Bear, comparing himself to a wolf
to warn young men of the dangers they faced*

WOLF SONG

Music recorded for a wordless Blackfeet wolf song.

GIVING VOICE

We were awakened about midnight by the wolves' howling. It was a new howl, one we had never heard before, and very probably the most beautiful animal sound in the world, the "call howl" of wolves.

The two voices changed incessantly, rising and falling, always chording, never in unison. The chord changed in minor thirds and fifths. Sometimes there was a long note from one while the voice of the other interwove around it. The notes were hornlike and pure. The wolves would break off suddenly and there would be listening silence. We were sure they heard the voices of other wolves at the margin of sound.

We lay listening, only the thin wall between, and I almost feared. Not real fear; I would have gone out to them without hesitation. But uncanny fear because of the wildness of the sounds. "It's wild and beautiful and eerie," whispered Cris.

There are many howls—the happy social howl, the mourning howl, the wild deep hunting howl, the call howl. All are beautiful. The wolf's voice is pure except when the wolf is crushed by despair. The only set pattern is that of the mourning howl. The others vary but the meaning is clear. Mountain men in the old West gathered valuable clues about movements of Indians and wild animals from the changeful voices of the wolves. Few humans now have ever heard the howl of a wolf and at that only the captive howl, like the howling of the slave dogs of the North.

LOIS CRISLER, *Arctic Wild*

Ye blessed Creatures, I have heard the call
Ye to each other make; I see
The heavens laugh with you in your jubilee;
My heart is at your festival,
My head hath its coronal
The fullness of your bliss, I feel—I feel it all.

WILLIAM WORDSWORTH,
"Ode on the Intimations of Immortality"

Timber wolf howling. Lynn and Donna Rogers.

BODY LANGUAGE

▾▾▾▾▾

Since survival is a group effort, wolves need to communicate clearly in every aspect of life. Messages are conveyed vocally, through scent, and most important, through a visual vocabulary of body movements and facial expressions. How a wolf uses body language is determined by his place in the pack structure and by the situation: Is he warning others of an outside danger, asserting or acknowledging dominance, asking to be fed, or instigating a game of tag?

Charles Darwin was among the first to observe how a dog's body posture reflects its aggressive or friendly intentions. These basic patterns—aggression signaled by an enlarged body, forward-pointed ears, raised hackles and tail, and stiff-legged walk; submission or peacemaking by reversing those actions—were directly inherited from wolves, and are the basis for studying wolf social behavior.

Displays of dominance and submission take place frequently in packs, reaffirming the social balance and reminding each wolf of its place. In "passive" submission, a lower-ranking wolf simply rolls on its back and offers its belly to the wolf asserting dominance, or it may "actively" submit by approaching in a semi-crouch (sometimes with a lifted forepaw) and then rolling. Spontaneous "mobbing" of the alpha wolf, where others crowd near with tails wagging and nuzzle or lick the leader's face, often precedes a hunting expedition.

How a wolf tilts its ears and moves its tail, narrows or rounds its eyes, wrinkles its muzzle to show teeth or relaxes its lips in a grin—all these signs, emphasized by its face fur markings, speak volumes to other wolves. People often misread wolf body language, interpreting dominant behavior as ferocity, submission as a sad loss of dignity. But animals cannot afford to equivocate; these actions keep the peace, keep the pack fed, and reassure each other of the most important fact of their lives—that they belong.

Gray wolf female and pup. Pups lick the muzzles of adult wolves at any opportunity, a gesture that stimulates feeding by disgorging. The mother's splayed ears signal affection. Laura Riley/Bruce Coleman, Inc.

THE WOLF SMILE

Then came a revelation—our first real nugget of wolf knowledge. Lady whirled and ran back toward Cris and as she came she demonstrated what is surely one of the prettiest, most endearing gestures in the world, the wolf "smile." We had not known it existed.

She smiled with her whole body. She humped her back like an inverted smile. She sleeked her ears into her fur and tossed her big forepaws gaily to either side as well as back and forth, as if they were on universal joints. Nearing Cris, she produced the most bewitching part of the smile: she tilted her head aside and lifted her opposite forepaw high, as if entreating friendliness. She looked up at Cris with an expression of pure joy, such as we had never seen on her keen little black face before. . . .

For the first time we realized the beauty of a wolf's eyes. The whole wolf face is considered by Dr. Rudolph Schenkel to be one of the most expressive of animal faces, and much of the expression resides in the quick-changing eyes. . . . The black pupils, enlarging readily with emotion, may be radiant or lighted by the fierce spark of anxiety or anger.

The rest of the wolf's face changes with feeling too. Eyelids knot or smooth, ears point alertly or snug flat in friendliness. Also . . . there are changes in the slight but very complex musculature of the muzzle.

The smile goes on naturally into the "full wolf greeting." When the wolf tilts head aside, bowing his neck, he may proceed to lay his neck clear down on the ground and unroll his eel-supple spine to follow—a dancer's maneuver no dog could perform. A wolf can perform it without falling over only because he takes a remarkably wide base with hind paws. And he does it all in one fluent gesture, accompanied by the dazzling sweetness of the eyes.

LOIS CRISLER, *Arctic Wild*

LEFT: *Wolves often solicit play with a graceful bowing gesture. In the next instant, this animal may leap up and lead one of its pack members in a mock chase. Jim Dutcher.* ABOVE: *Wolf body studies, by Ernest Thompson Seton.*

TALKING LIKE A WOLF

Julie of the Wolves is a remarkable novel for young readers about an Eskimo girl who runs away from an arranged marriage and loses her way on the Alaskan tundra, where she meets and is accepted by a wolf pack. Author and naturalist Jean Craighead George tells the tale with great warmth and realism.

Miyax stared hard at the regal black wolf, hoping to catch his eye. She must somehow tell him that she was starving and ask him for food. This could be done, she knew, for her father, an Eskimo hunter, had done so. One year he camped near a wolf den while on a hunt. When a month passed and her father had seen no game, he told the leader of the wolves that he was hungry and needed food. The next night the wolf called him from far away and her father went to him and found a freshly killed caribou. Unfortunately, Miyax's father never explained to her how he had told the wolf of his needs. . . .

She had been watching the wolves for two days, trying to discern which of their sounds and movement expressed goodwill and friendship. Most animals had such signals. The little Arctic ground squirrels flicked their tails sideways to notify others of their kind that they were friendly. Miyax had lured many a squirrel to her hand. If she could discover such a gesture for the wolves she would be able to make friends with them and share their food, like a bird or a fox.

She had chosen [the black wolf] because he was much larger than the others, and because he walked like her father, Kapugen, with his head high and chest out. The black wolf also possessed wisdom, she had observed. The pack looked to him when the wind carried strange scents or the birds cried nervously. If he was alarmed, they were alarmed. If he was calm, they were calm.

"*Amaroq, ilaya,* wolf, my friend," she finally called. "Look at me. Look at me."

She spoke half in Eskimo and half in English, as if the instincts of her father and the science of the *gussaks,* the white-faced, might evoke some magical combination that would help her get her message through to the wolf. . . ."I never dreamed I could get lost, Amaroq," she went on, talking out loud to ease her fear.

It had been a frightening moment when two days ago she realized that the tundra was an ocean of grass on which she was circling around and around. Now, as that fear overcame her again, she closed her eyes. When she opened them her heart skipped excitedly. Amaroq was looking at her!

"*Ee-lie,*" she called and scrambled to her feet. The wolf arched his neck and narrowed his eyes. He pressed his ears forward. She waved. He drew back his lips and showed his teeth. Frightened by what seemed a snarl, she lay down again. When she was flat on her stomach, Amaroq flattened his ears and wagged his tail once. Then he tossed his head and looked away. . . .

She thought about Amaroq. Why had he bared his teeth at her? because she was young and he knew she couldn't hurt him? No, she said to herself, because he was speaking to her! He had told her to lie down. She had even understood and obeyed him. He had talked to her not with his voice, but with his ears eyes, and lips; and he had even commended her with a wag of his tail.

She scrambled up the frost heave and stretched out on her stomach. "Amaroq," she called softly, "I understand what you said. Can you understand me? I'm hungry—very, very hungry. Please bring me some meat."

[Miyax ponders how to make herself understood; then one of the puppies claims her attention.] The black puppy was looking at her and wagging his tail. Hopefully, Miyax held out a pleading hand to him. His tail wagged harder. The mother rushed to him and stood above him sternly. When he licked her cheek apologetically, she pulled back her lips from her fine white teeth. They flashed and she

52

[Miyax notices that the pups have other ways of expressing love for the leader, approaching on their bellies, eyes raised in adoration and tails wagging. Then the pack departs on a hunt, leaving a submissive wolf to babysit the pups, who continue to entertain Miyax. She practices giving them commands in body language, with some success.]

Sliding back to her camp, she heard the grass swish and looked up to see Amaroq and his hunters sweep around the frost heave and stop about five feet away. She could smell the sweet scent of their fur.

The hairs on her neck rose and her eyes widened. Amaroq's ears went forward aggressively and she remembered that wide eyes meant fear to him. It was not good to show him that she was afraid. Animals attacked the fearful. She tried to narrow them, but remembered that was not right either. Narrowed eyes were mean. In desperation she recalled that [the pup] Kapu had moved forward when challenged. She pranced right up to Amaroq. Her heart beat furiously as she grunt-whined the sound of the puppy begging adoringly for attention. Then she got down on her belly and gazed at him with fondness.

The great wolf backed up and avoided her eyes. She had said something wrong! Perhaps even offended him. Some slight gesture that meant nothing to her had apparently meant something to the wolf. His ears shot forward angrily and it seemed all was lost. She wanted to get up and run, but she gathered her courage and pranced closer to him. Swiftly she patted him under the chin.

The signal went off. It sped through his body and triggered emotions of love. Amaroq's ears flattened and his tail wagged in friendship. He could not react any other way to the chin pat, for the roots of this signal lay deep in wolf history. It was inherited from generations and generations of leaders before him. As his eyes softened, the sweet odor of ambrosia arose from the gland on the top of his tail and she was drenched lightly in wolf scent. Miyax was one of the pack.

JEAN CRAIGHEAD GEORGE, *Julie of the Wolves*

smiled and forgave her cub. *[Miyax decides to call the beautiful female wolf Silver, and watches the reprimanded cub and his sister wrestle over an old bone.]*

"I understand that," she said to the pups. "That's tug-o-war. Now how to do you say 'I'm hungry'?"

Amaroq was pacing restlessly along the crest of the frost heave as if something were about to happen. His eyes shot to Silver, then to the gray wolf Miyax had named Nails. These glances seemed to be a summons, for Silver and Nails glided to him, spanked the ground with their forepaws, and bit him gently under the chin. He wagged his tail furiously and took Silver's slender nose in his mouth. She crouched before him, licked his cheek and lovingly bit his lower jaw. Amaroq's tail flashed high as her mouthing charged him with vitality. . . .

She had seen the wolves mouth Amaroq's jaw twice before and so she concluded that it was a ceremony, a sort of "Hail to the Chief." . . . It was plain to see that he was their great spirit, a royal leader who held his group together with wisdom and love. She needed only to be accepted by him to be accepted by all. She even knew how to achieve this—bite him under the chin. But how was she going to do that?

THE SECRETS OF SCENT

▼▼▼▼▼▼

We can hear wolves howl and watch them interact physically, but the significance of scent in the wolf's lifeway is harder for humans to interpret. We know that wolves rely heavily on scent to locate and track their prey (and probably to get clues about its condition), as well as to interpret the ever-shifting gestalt of their environment: winds, weather, the presence of other animals or humans; sorting out the harmful from the benign.

Scent also plays a key role in wolf social life. Like dogs, wolves explore each other's anal regions on meeting, and also sniff around the head and neck. Scent signals come from the other wolf's urine, feces, and various glands; dominant wolves may be "invading the social sphere" of a lower-ranking wolf by anal sniffing. Scent-marking is another way to show status within the pack; and as with most mammals, females ready for mating emit an unmistakable olfactory call.

Scent-marking is especially important in communicating with other wolves outside the pack. Wolves—usually the alpha animal—mark their territorial boundaries methodically and periodically; neighboring wolves judge the relative hazard of trespassing by the freshness of those marks.

Then there is the mystery of why wolves roll in their decaying kills and other pungent substances. Some speculate that this "self-scenting" helps draw other pack members to a kill or camouflages

their own scent to aid sneaking up on prey. Hardest to prove is the possibility that wolves simply *like* powerful stinks. And it doesn't seem to matter what kind. Lois Crisler writes of receiving a gift of perfume in her Arctic camp; when she and her husband put some on, their hand-raised wolves went into ecstacies.

BELOW LEFT: *This wolf may be scenting a prey animal that scratched itself on the tree. Leonard Lee Rue/Bruce Coleman Inc.* ABOVE: *Pack members often become excited on locating a new scent. Layne Kennedy.*

The mighty sense of smell in canids may be illustrated by the fact, experimentally shown, that a dog can detect the scent of a human fingerprint some six weeks after the trace was laid. It is this acuteness of smell that permits one wild canid to detect, for example, the odor of fear in the urine of another which has long since passed by, and thus to be on the lookout for trouble in advance. Canids are aided in their sense of smell by a pair of small openings, Jacobsen's organs, in the front of the roof of the mouth. Using these, a canid "tastes" the air as he smells it, curling his lips to do so in a motion referred to by the German word *Flehmen*. In *Flehmen*, the animal raises his nose, wrinkles his snout, and ceases breathing while he bares his fore-teeth and samples the air with his Jacobsen's organs. *Flehmen* may be observed in any dog testing a urinary scentpost, and produces a sort of silly smile characteristic of this sort of canine newspaper-reading.

JOHN C. MCLOUGHLIN, *The Canine Clan*

Timber wolves sniff around a new landscape. Stouffer Productions/Animals Animals.

THE INVISIBLE WALL

A graduate student in psychology in the 1970s, young Roger Peters had the chance to work with L. David Mech on a wolf study in northern Minnesota. Peters' agenda was to show that wolves, like humans, use cognitive maps to navigate their territories—maps whose landmarks are different kinds of scent marks, scats, and other physical signs, as well as the wolves' spatial and temporal memories. On one occasion, he observed from the air an erratic set of wolf tracks on a snowy lake. Landing for a closer look, he concluded that this pack tried to move onto the lakeshore, but were repeatedly turned back by recent signs of a rival pack's presence: "A clear depiction of what psychologists call approach-avoidance behavior had been inscribed into the snow, a paradigm of territorial behavior." Peters imagines the scene thus:

It had been more than a week since they had killed.

There were no deer in any of the old places, and the moose they had found had stood watching and waiting. After an hour of silent staring the wolves had moved on. That moose was not yet ready to die.

Their leader took them north, past an old kill, where they had gnawed dry and brittle bones. Now they were at the edge of the land they knew. Fresh snow had fallen during the night. It lay knee-deep on the lake ahead. Nevertheless, the big brown male would not relinquish the lead. Even breaking trail for the others, he drew farther and farther ahead. He was heading straight for the foreign shore.

Suddenly he stopped. He sniffed the breeze coming from the nearby trees, then dropped a scat, dry and white from the bones he had chewed. As he moved on, each of the others paused to sniff his scat, then trotted to catch up. The shore was only a few leaps away when the leader's ears went back. He clamped his tail down over his rectum and veered away from the dark forest. The others turned, too, cutting the corner he had made, running to fall in behind him as he skulked along the shore, never taking his eyes from the shadows among the trees.

Again he approached the shore, close enough to smell sweet spruce boughs, but again he froze. He urinated in his tracks like a pup. Time and again he tried to go ashore, but each time the shadows turned him away. Finally, when the pack reached the end of the lake, he plunged into a swampy valley that would take them back to the moose.

ROGER PETERS, *Dance of the Wolves*

TERRITORIAL ACTS

▼▼▼▼▼

Anyone whose dog has marked a fencepost or sounded a warning bark at the door is familiar with the phenomenon of territoriality, common to all canids and many other mammals. An animal's territory is defined as the area that it will defend against others of the same species. While the concept of territoriality is still not well understood, observers have seen ample evidence of wolves' turf consciousness.

Territoriality among wolves operates at the pack level: all members of a given pack share the same territory, but usually show intolerance for other packs or individuals that trespass. A pack's territory apparently encompasses most of the area in which they hunt and travel. Both David Mech and Adolph Murie report cases of packs encountering single wolves or pairs from other packs, and punishing them harshly or chasing them for long distances. Mech believes that in at least one case, if the pursuing wolves had caught the intruder, they would likely have killed it.

Wolves have two chief ways of declaring their territories: howling and scent-marking. Researchers have heard wolves respond to the howls of nearby packs; with their keen hearing, wolves can hear their neighbors over a span of fifty square miles. Animal ethologist Fred Harrington has studied the different ways packs react to such vocal challenges. If they howl back, they usually stand their ground; failing to respond often signals a retreat. (Factors include the relative size of each pack, and the presence of a fresh kill or young pups at a particular site.) Scent-marking boundaries and trails probably serves a double purpose, helping wolves orient themselves within their territory, like a map, as well as warning outsiders away.

The current prevailing theory is that wolf territories are not just spatial—each pack operating within strict geographic limits—but *spatial-temporal,* so that packs may move in and out of each other's turf to some extent, depending on how recently the "no trespassing" signs (howls and scent marks) were posted.

Aerial, wolf pack follows a freshly broken trail through its territory, Minnesota. David Hiser/Photographers Aspen.

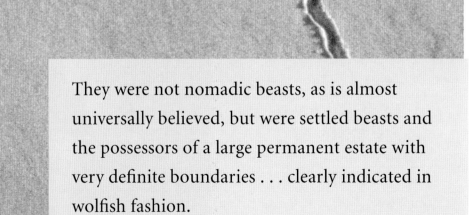

They were not nomadic beasts, as is almost universally believed, but were settled beasts and the possessors of a large permanent estate with very definite boundaries . . . clearly indicated in wolfish fashion.

FARLEY MOWAT, *Never Cry Wolf*

STAKING A CLAIM

The territory owned by my wolf family comprised more than a hundred square miles, bounded on one side by a river but otherwise not delimited by geographical features. Nevertheless there were boundaries, clearly indicated in wolfish fashion.

Anyone who has observed a dog doing his neighborhood rounds and leaving his personal mark on each convenient post will have already guessed how the wolves marked out their property. Once a week, more or less, the clan made the rounds of the family lands and freshened up the boundary markers—a sort of lupine beating of the bounds. This careful attention to property rights was perhaps made necessary by the presence of two other wolf families whose lands abutted on ours, although I never discovered any evidence of bickering or disagreements between the owners of the various adjoining estates. I suspect, therefore, that it was more of a ritual activity.

In any event, once I had become aware of the strong feeling of property rights which existed amongst the wolves, I decided to use this knowledge to make them at least recognize my existence. One evening after they had gone off for their regular nightly hunt, I staked out a property claim of my own embracing perhaps three acres, with the tent at the middle, and including a hundred-yard-long section of the wolves' path.

Staking the land turned out to be rather more difficult than I had anticipated. In order to ensure that my claim would not be overlooked, I felt obligated to make a property mark on stones, clumps of moss, and patches of vegetation at intervals of not more than fifteen feet around the circumference of my claim. This took most of the night and required frequent returns to my tent to consume copious quantities of tea; but before dawn brought the hunters home the task was done, and I retired, somewhat exhausted, to observe results.

Wolves explore new territory during the making of Never Cry Wolf. *Photo © The Walt Disney Company.*

It could be argued that wolves are never more wolflike than when they're exploring, trying to claim, or reclaim, new territory, rather than holding on and defending old borders. It could be argued that our perverse resistance to wolves helps them *remain* wolves, that they need that great arm's distance to remain always outside other communities. . . .

RICK BASS, *The Ninemile Wolves*

58

I had not long to wait. At 0814 hours, according to my wolf log, the leading male of the clan appeared over the ridge, padding homeward with his usual air of preoccupation. As usual he did not deign to glance at the tent; but when he reached the point where my property line intersected the trail, he stopped as abruptly as if he had run into an invisible wall. He was only fifty yards from me and with my binoculars I could see his expression very clearly.

His attitude of fatigue vanished and was replaced by a look of bewilderment. Cautiously he extended his nose and sniffed one of my marked bushes. He did not seem to know what to make of it or what to do about it. After a minute of complete indecision he backed away for a few yards and sat down. And then, finally, he looked directly at the tent and at me. It was a long, thoughtful, considering sort of look.

Having achieved my object—that of forcing at least one of the wolves to take cognizance of my existence—I now began to wonder if, in my ignorance, I had transgressed some unknown wolf law of major importance and would have to pay for my temerity. I found myself regretting the absence of a weapon as the look I was getting became longer, yet more thoughtful, and still more intent. I began to grow decidedly fidgety, for I dislike staring matches, and in this particular case I was up against a master, whose yellow glare seemed to become more baleful as I attempted to stare him down.

The situation was becoming intolerable. In an effort to break the impasse I loudly cleared my throat and turned my back to the wolf (for a tenth of a second) to indicate as clearly as possible that I found his continued scrutiny impolite, if not actually offensive.

He appeared to take the hint. Getting to his feet, he had another sniff at my marker, and then he seemed to make up his mind. Briskly, and with an air of decision, he turned his attention away from me and began a systematic tour of the area I had staked out as my own. As he came to each boundary marker he sniffed it once or twice, then carefully placed his mark on the outside of each clump of grass or stone. As I watched I saw where I, in my ignorance, had erred. He made his mark with such economy that he was able to complete the entire circuit without having to reload once, or to change the simile slightly, he did it all on one tank of fuel.

The task completed—and it had taken him no longer than fifteen minutes—he rejoined the path at the point where it left my property and trotted off towards his home—leaving me with a good deal to occupy my thoughts.

FARLEY MOWAT, *Never Cry Wolf*

Farley Mowat's Never Cry Wolf *is probably the best-known book about wolves, a witty and engaging account of the author's experiences as a young biologist sent out to the Barren Lands of arctic Canada with all the wrong equipment and the vaguest of missions. Mowat's observations were enhanced by his conversations with Eskimo hunters and his unique (if sometimes unscientific) research methods.*

LEFT: *Marking a scentpost. Dennis W. Schmidt/Valan Photos.* BELOW: *What a wolf's "cognitive map" might look like. From* Wolf and Man: Evolution in Parallel.

KEY
- Home pack
- Strange pack
- Good marking or scent
- Bad marking or scent
- Cover
- People
- Water
- Kill or cache

BORDER GAMES

The most interesting correspondence between wolf and Indian . . . may be that involving the perception of territory.

When Indians left their own country and entered that of another tribe—a group of young Assiniboin warriors, for example, sneaking off on foot into the country of the Gros Ventre to steal horses—they moved like wolves: in small packs; at night and during the crepuscular hours; taking advantage of ground contours to observe but remain hidden; moving in and out of the foreign territory quickly. Often on foot and in unfamiliar surroundings, they had to remain invisible to the inhabitants. Elusiveness, therefore, was a quality Indians cultivated and admired. It served them as well as it served the wolf who, after a hard winter, tres-

passes into neighboring packs' territories to look for food, to make a kill, and to go home before anyone knows he's been there.

The definition and defense of home range was as important to the Indian as it seems to be to the wolf. The defense was mostly of food resources in general and of the physical area adjacent to the village in particular; under certain circumstances trespassers were killed. If a party of Flathead warriors was surprised in northern Idaho by a party of resident Kutenai, the Flatheads might be attacked and killed to a man. If it was bitter cold and storming, they might signal each other that it was too cold to fight (wolves probably wouldn't). If the Flathead party was reduced to one man who fought bravely and was thought, therefore, to have strong medicine, he might be let go. Fatal encounters and nonfatal encounters between trespassing and resident wolves bear a striking similarity. In Minnesota, for example, in 1975, a small pack of wolves moving through the territory of a much larger pack was suddenly surprised by the larger pack. One animal in the small pack was killed, two ran off, and the fourth, a female, held ten or eleven wolves to a standoff in a river before they all withdrew and left her.

Some tribes were stricter about boundaries and more bellicose about trespassing incidents than others, as are some wolf packs. The boundaries of most Indian territories, like those of wolves, were fluid; they changed with the movements of the game herds, the size of the tribe, the evolution of tribal divisions, and the time of year. For both wolf and Indian, where the principal game animal was nonmigratory,

"Buffalo hunt under the wolf-skin mask," by George Catlin, 1832-33.

as deer and moose are, territorial boundaries were more important than they were in areas where principal game species were migratory, like caribou. There are instances where neighboring wolf packs have fought each other and then joined territories, just as some tribes established alliances—the five nations of the Iroquois, for example. . . .

The Indian practice of passing family hunting territories on to succeeding generations throws even more light on this interesting correspondence of territorial spacing, hunting rights, and trespassing. Family hunting territories were important, again, where food could be found in the same place all the time. The salmon-eating tribes on the northwest coast and the Algonkian deer eaters in northeastern woodlands both had appropriate family and clan hunting territories that were passed on from one generation to the next. Among the Tlingit, a northwest coast tribe, each family had its own place on the river where it fished and an area where it gathered berries. No one else would fish or berry there unless invited to do so. In the eastern woodlands, especially in northeastern Minnesota, resident wolves seem to have a strong sense of territory as defined by the major food source (white-tailed deer), at least as strong as the family hunting territories that existed in the same country when the Chippewa lived there.

Which leads to another thought, more abstract, about trespassing. It was often assumed that Plains Indians went out intending to kill their rivals. This was not true. They went out to deliberately face rivals in a very dangerous game. The danger itself, the threat of death, was the thrill, not killing; and to engage in it repeatedly was recognized as a way to prove strength of character. Analogously, it might be valuable to consider the encounters of rival wolves as a similar kind of deadly recreation. Just as intriguing is the idea that some game animals assent to a chase-without-death with wolves. Caribou and yearling wolves, for example, are often seen in harmless chases getting a taste of death. Building spirit. Training. Wolf *and* caribou.

BARRY LOPEZ, *Of Wolves and Men*

Timber wolf in summer, Alaska. Johnny Johnson/Valan Photos.

FLIGHT BEFORE FIGHT

▼▼▼▼▼▼

Like families, wolf packs can be well-adjusted or dysfunctional. In a socially stable pack, where each wolf is assured of its status, frequent displays of dominance and submission suffice to keep real fights from breaking out—obviously undesirable among animals armed with lethal weapons. But if a pack is under stress—from overpopulation, rapid introduction of new members, unusually strong challenges by maturing wolves, or conditions of captivity—then ritualized aggression can escalate into serious or mortal combat. Sometimes, too, a very low-ranking "scapegoat" is physically abused to the point of real damage, or driven from the pack. This might be a former alpha wolf fallen from grace, a noncontributor, or possibly a sick animal.

Fights involving serious injury or death are very rare within packs, however. If an attack is imminent, the target wolf will usually flee first. More often, combat occurs when a pack encounters one or more strange wolves, especially in its own territory. Several observers have witnessed chases or battles between wolves of different packs, or when a lone wolf tried to join a pack. However, recent studies indicate that lone wolves successfully join packs more often than was once thought.

People have often mistaken the actions that signal when a wolf truly means to fight, and when it is simply making a show threat. Renowned behaviorist Konrad Lorenz contributed to the confusion when he described a standoff between aggressive wolves: "Notice carefully the position of the two opponents; the older wolf has his muzzle close, very close against the neck of the other, and the latter holds away his head, offering unprotected to his enemy . . . the most vulnerable part of his whole body!" In fact, the less dominant wolf more likely will be snapping at its opponent's neck, while the superior party offers his, thus defusing the other's readiness to fight.

The so-called "biting inhibition" in wolves, which keeps them from harming each other in play fights or dominance shows, is apparently not inborn but learned—as evidenced by the yelp-inducing bites that pups give each other and the humans who sometimes rear them.

Dominance displays may escalate into more serious encounters if a subordinate wolf does not back down from its challenge; this happens most often during breeding season. Tom and Pat Leeson.

NO VISITORS

"The modern study of American wildlife may be said to have begun with Adolph Murie," wrote Edward Hoagland. *As a young government biologist in 1939, Murie was dispatched to Mt. McKinley National Park to study the effects of wolf predation on Dall sheep. Murie was what Hoagland called a "bedroll scientist," following his subjects on foot or with dogsled, camping wherever the day ended. His resulting book,* The Wolves of Mt. McKinley, *remained the only reliable work on wolf biology for some thirty years.*

Shortly after noon the four wolves at the den joined the mantled male and they all bunched up, wagging tails and expressing much friendliness. Then I noticed a sixth wolf, a small gray animal, about fifty yards from the others. No doubt it was the presence of this wolf that had kept the mantled male so alert during the preceding two hours.

All the wolves trotted to the stranger and practically surrounded it, and for a few minutes I thought there was just the suggestion of tail wagging by some of them. But something tipped the scales the other way, for the wolves began to bite at the stranger. It rolled over on its back, begging quarter. The attack continued, however, and it scrambled to its feet and with difficulty emerged from the snapping wolves. Twice it was knocked over as it ran down the slope with the five wolves in hot pursuit. They chased after it about two hundred yards to the river bar, and the mantled male crossed the bar after it. The two ran out of my sight under the ridge. . . .

Four of the wolves returned to the den, but the mantled male stopped halfway up the slope and lay down facing the bar. Presently he walked slowly forward as though stalking a marmot. Then he commenced to gallop down the slope again toward the stranger, which had returned part way up the slope. Back on the bar the stranger slowed up, waiting in a fawning attitude for the mantled male. The latter snapped at the stranger, which rolled over on its back, again begging quarter. But the stranger received no quarter, so again, it had to run away. The male returned up the hill, tail held stiffly out behind, slightly raised. When he neared the den the four wolves ran out to meet him, and there was again much tail wagging and evidence of friendly feeling.

ADOLPH MURIE, *A Naturalist in Alaska*

DEGREES OF AGGRESSION

The first and mildest form of aggression in wolves is *passive;* it is physically advertised by the way in which an animal carries itself, its positive movements and calm manner denoting self-assurance. The second stage is *passive-active,* displayed when an individual continues to demonstrate self-assurance, but at the same time signals elevated arousal by exaggerating its behavior and movements: in this case, a wolf keeps its ears stiffly erect and forward-pointing; its hackles rise, its tail is carried high, its eyes stare fixedly, and it is likely to emit low, rumbling growls, all of these signals being directed at the object of its arousal, the intent being to intimidate and thus to preclude fighting. Stage three is *defensive,* and is most often observed in subordinate animals who feel themselves threatened. Such individuals exhibit the usual signs of submission, but at the same time, by growling, baring their teeth, and raising their hackles, they give warning that they will fight if pressed, behavior that also serves to prevent actual combat because a dominant wolf, accepting the submissive signs and noting the defensive signals, does not wish to precipitate a fight during which it may itself suffer injury, even if it emerges the victor. The fourth stage of aggression is *offensive* and will result in action if an opponent or a prey animal does not escape.

R. D. LAWRENCE,
In Praise of Wolves

Erik Zimen's model of aggression combined with fear. From bottom left to right: increasing tendency to attack. Bottom left to top: increasing fear, which inhibits attacking.

ON THE HUNT

▼▼▼▼▼

"Wolves are hunting whenever they are traveling," observes David Mech—another way of saying that wolves tend to stay put when they have a fresh kill, but as soon as hunger calls, they are on the move again through their large territories. They are opportunistic, feeding on whatever comes their way and is catchable; they favor large hoofed prey like deer and moose but can subsist on mice in lean times. Wolves hunt in a smaller radius from their pups' den in summer and range farther in winter, when prey is spread out and frozen waterways expand travel routes.

Wolves find their prey by direct scenting (if it is quite near), by chance encounter, or by tracking. This accomplished, they go into a stalk, followed by the actual encounter with the animal—which may stand its ground or run. Flight triggers a "rush response" in the wolves, setting off a chase that may last up to a few miles, rarely longer. Wolves prefer to kill on the run, quartering up behind prey and aiming for the vital organs just ahead of its dangerous hind legs. (Contrary to legend, wolves rarely disable prey by "hamstringing," which puts them at risk of injury from a kick.) Large prey that stand still to defend themselves, like moose or musk oxen, pose a more formidable challenge, and a pack often gives up if it cannot induce the creature to run.

All the big wild herbivores have a slight speed advantage, so wolves try to select the less able individuals—the young, old, sick, or injured—often by staging one or more "test" rushes. Strategy plays some part in hunting success, but probably less than people imagine. Wolves do "head off" or turn running prey toward pack members who have left the main chase, traverse high ridges to charge from above, and hunt from ambush—but often a kill is simply a matter of chasing the right animal or lucking onto a terrain obstacle that slows it down.

Netsuke wolf with skull, Edo Period, 18th century, Japan.

Wolves are geared to a "feast or famine" existence, and when they do kill, can consume huge amounts at a feeding—often the only way to save it from scavengers. They may return to a large kill for weeks if a new one isn't made, and also cache food in the earth or snow. Food is freely shared among the pack when abundant, though at other times dominant members do pull rank; this helps keep the strongest wolves healthy for the good of the pack.

STALKING BY RANK

Less than a hundred yards separated the beaver from the wolves, and the gray bitch flattened her ears as the cool musky scent finally ran into her dilating nostrils. The pair was closer to the pond's edge than were their buff-colored sons, but due to a shift and lull in the breeze, all four of the wolves were now guided by the ribbon of scent that flowed and ebbed above the top of the wet grass. Though they moved toward the same goal, each was pulled by his or her own nose, and only when one of them initiated the final rush would the chase become a visual exercise. Finally, and as if on signal, the stalking wolves flattened themselves in the nodding sedges, the only movement their slowly wagging tails. . . .

Though the gray bitch was the first to locate the beaver's sign on the pond's surface, she accepted directional clues from her mate during the stalk, thereby relinquishing leadership to the big black. Though the position he occupied in the pack hierarchy demanded it, it was not an act of aggressive competition as much as an exercise in automatic cooperation, the employment of which was unquestioned. Were it not so, the concept of the pack would have been a useless one. In this hierarchy, the old bitch was second only to her mate, and were he to be lost, the priority of such leadership would probably become hers alone, as a result of habit patterns sustained and honed during the passage of twenty million years.

They will eat like wolves and
fight like devils.

WILLIAM SHAKESPEARE, *Henry V*

*LEFT: Wolves sometimes travel in streambeds
to avoid soft snow; these, in Minnesota, are
on a stalk. Lynn and Donna Rogers. BELOW:
Young beaver feeding in a pond. Tom and
Pat Leeson.*

It was a result of this same system that had caused the white resident bitches to remain above the stalking wolves. No only were they the lowest members in the social order of the pack and strongly subservient to the old gray bitch, they were simply inexperienced hunters. The two factors made them spectators to the events occurring below them and near the pond.

No movement met the leader's eyes as he slowly raised his broad head above the whispering grass. The wind had gained velocity as a passing squall turned the undersides of the new leaves to silver; and crouched low, he had swung with it instinctively. The gray bitch had followed at his hip, and the new course which they followed had led them downwind from the scent source, giving it new strength and more positive direction. . . . [She] heard the soft sounds of the beaver's teeth, and still belly-crawling, she once more froze. Her black mate glanced back over his shoulder, and followed suit. The short pathway to the object of their intense search had now become clearly marked and impossible to lose.

Instants later, tail down and running low to the ground, the pack leader's blurred rush carried him past the beaver. To compensate for his mistake, he leaped high, somersaulting over himself and turning in midair. The gray bitch had been more fortunate, and her teeth locked in the powerful mass of muscle tissue at the base of the beaver's skull. Her own final fifteen-foot bound tumbled both herself and her prey into a rain-saturated clump of red-barked willow. . . .

The stilt-legged shorebird screamed again as it lifted haltingly into the wind, and the sound broke the silence that had attended the stalk and kill.

JAMES GREINER, *The Red Snow*

THE WOLF AND
THE CHIPEWYAN

The Chipewyan are a Native people of central Canada. The following report is taken from Wolf and Man: Evolution in Parallel, *a collection of studies in comparative wolf-human ethology.*

The wolf and the Chipewyan, though occupants of different econiches, are competitors for the caribou. For both species, the  caribou is the primary food source, yet neither species has been able to or has attempted to displace the other in past millennia. Even with the putative advantage of European weapons and technology the Chipewyan have made no headway in displacing the wolf. . . .

Both wolf and Chipewyan kill caribou at almost all opportunities by whatever means possible, but the thousands of actual kills fall into a few patterns. The Chipewyan utilize three basic patterns, involving (a) watching and ambushing, (b) walking, and (c) using pounds and drives. By watching and ambushing I mean all variations of hunts that involve choosing a location from which to watch for caribou, moving to the caribou or to a point on their projected path once they are seen, and attacking. This strategy is the one most commonly used and is particularly favored during periods of high caribou density.

The second strategy, walking, is the simplest and most basic approach to hunting. It simply involves covering as much ground as possible in the hope of contacting caribou, at which point the appropriate tactics are applied. . . . The third strategy, using pounds and drives, is now obsolete except for the occasional spearing of caribou while they are swimming. This basic strategy always involves the concentrating of caribou in a small area, usually *(continued)*

ABOVE: *Wolf mask, Kuskokwim River Eskimos, Alaska, c. 1935. Painted wood with separately carved teeth and ears.* RIGHT: *Wolf and caribou appraise each other on a mountain meadow, Denali National Park, Alaska. Leo Keeler/Animals Animals.*

ACOMA HUNT SONG
▼▼▼▼▼▼

On the eastern edge

Wolf the hunter has come out.

With glittering paint

With white head feather tip waving.

He has gone

Bravely I will go

To get spruce,

Acquiring blessings.

JAMES C. BURBANK, *Vanishing Lobo*

Pack members at a well-stripped deer carcass. Peter McLeod.

through a created canalization of a known migration route, where the caribou may be killed in large numbers. . . .

The Chipewyan preference for the watch and ambush and pounds and drives in contrast to the wolf's preference for watch and ambush and walking derive from the Chipewyan practice of working from a central location at which the nonhunting part of the hunting unit is located, and from the greater mobility of the wolf. . . . Clearly, the greater capacity of the wolf to approach and close with the caribou compensates for the range of killing power of the rifle, bow, and spear. Though both species are locked into a struggle for utilization of the caribou it is not a direct struggle. . . . Both species must be viewed together as predators that bring pressure upon the caribou in a way that tends to keep a more uniform predation pressure upon the caribou than either species could manage alone.

HENRY S. SHARP, *Wolf and Man: Evolution in Parallel*

A point of great significance . . . is the keen sensitivity to the wolf to the condition of its prey. In judging what he can handle and what should prudently be left alone, this carnivore brings to his daily work sophisticated skills completely beyond our human ken. These are made possible by inborn capacities effectively tuned and developed in the young animal through an apprenticeship that only the capable survive.

DURWARD L. ALLEN, *Wolves of Minong*

CACHING FOOD

Wolves, in common with most flesh eaters, often cache excess food for future use. Once I noted a sheep horn which had been carried some distance and buried in the snow; another time the head of a ram was hidden in the snow; again, two pieces of sheep meat were cached, only to be consumed shortly by foxes. But the food is not always cached. When there is an abundant supply, the bother of caching the food is often omitted. I have found calf caribou on the calving grounds left untouched where killed. The wolves were seemingly aware that there was not much point in caching them, since food was readily available on all sides.

I observed a good example of provident caching on July 19, 1941, after a wolf had killed a caribou calf on the bars of the East Fork River. . . . The wolf was hungry, for she ate voraciously for more than half an hour. Three times during the meal she walked to the stream for a drink. After feeding she got my scent, circled above me, barking and howling, then retreated toward the den, still not having seen me. I waited for almost an hour before I saw her coming down the river bar along the opposite shore. She trotted directly to the carcass and, after feeding on a few morsels, she chewed until a foreleg and shoulder had been severed. With this piece in her jaws she waded the stream and trotted about three hundred yards up the bar. Here she stopped and, still holding the leg in her mouth, pawed a shallow hole in the gravel and placed the leg in it. Then, with a long sweeping motion of her head she used her nose to push gravel over the leg. The job was quickly completed and she trotted back to the carcass, chewed off the head and, this time, buried it about three hundred yards away without crossing the stream. On the third trip she carried another leg and cached it on the side of the river from which I was watching.

ADOLPH MURIE, *A Naturalist in Alaska*

There is a wolf in me . . . fangs pointed for tearing gashes . . . a red tongue for raw meat . . . and the hot lapping of blood—I keep this wolf because the wilderness gave it to me and the wilderness will not let it go.

CARL SANDBURG, *"Wilderness"*

LEFT: Wolf carries a deer haunch to a cache. James D. Markou/Valan Photos. BELOW: Pack members hastily depart from a kill as the alpha male approaches. Peter McLeod.

THE TIES THAT BIND

▼▼▼▼▼▼

The close ties among all members of a wolf pack are reflected and focused in the special bonds forged by mating and parenthood. Sexual activity is also intimately linked to the social structure of the pack. Mates are sometimes a mother and her offspring, or siblings from the same or different litters.

It's commonly thought that wolves mate for life, and this is sometimes true. Wolves do show a strong preference for one mate, and their mutual affection endures well past the breeding season. They remain partial to each other's company throughout the year, and year after year. However, a female may have to accept a new mate if her long-time partner dies or is displaced from the leadership position; surviving males do likewise.

The other truism about wolf sex is that only the alpha male and female can breed in a given season. Again, it generally works this way, though occasionally an alpha male will inexplicably lose interest in his female counterpart, clearing the way for a lower-ranking male to mate with her.

The courting season can stretch over many weeks during late winter and early spring, during which conflicts over mating rights can be sharp and frequent—the alpha female enforcing her position as the only one to breed, and the male fending off challenges from others of his sex. Once the issue is settled, the pair focuses on each other, indulging in teasing play, trading dominance moves, grooming each other, or just lying together. The sex act itself takes about a half hour, during which the pair becomes locked in a "copulatory tie" and cannot separate, a phenomenon unique to the dog family and thought to reinforce the emotional bonds between mates.

Pups are born a relatively short sixty-three days after conception, an occasion of great social excitement for the whole pack. Both the father and other wolves will bring gifts of food to the denned she-wolf, or disgorge food for her (as they do later for the pups). The pride and delight that both dam and sire take in their young has been noted often; that wolves are devoted parents is beyond dispute.

Gray wolves, mated pair. Lynn and Donna Rogers.

MATING DANCE

Alatna was enchanted with the stately dog. Like Trigger and Lady, she looked up to size, maturity, "presence." Baranof disregarded her. He applied himself to examining and re-marking every scent spot in both pens. Alatna crouched wooing beside him. . . .

Significantly in playing with him she always lowered her height, either by bowing her chest or by tilting her head below and aside from his. Once she lay clear down on her belly. As she started to rise, she made a stirringly lovely gesture. In the flash of a second she reared her head to one side and curved and reared it to the other, all in one sinuous movement, so gay, so graceful and vital—and always with that accompanying eye expression, black and electric and gay—that a dancer would have longed to rival it. Alatna was in estrus, her second with a mate. . . .

"Sex means more to wolves," I thought, "at least to this female wolf, than it does to dogs. It is not transitory but is a kind of continuing happiness—to have a mate near—and a cause of concern if the mate is absent."

LOIS CRISLER, *Captive Wild*

LOVING LIKE WOLVES

Some ethologists and anthropologists believe that sex, for man, is an essential part of the nonreproductive social and emotional bonding system. It is interesting and illuminating to see other species, such as the wolf and coyote, that stay together throughout the year independent of sex. Such an order of seasonal celibacy for all but two months of the year does not impair social bonds as it might in man, who has instead evolved a very different sexuality. Wolves can enjoy mutual love and affiliation without year-round conflicts over and desire for sex. Perhaps if the reproductive consequences had been separated from the physical, emotional, and social needs and benefits of sex in our own evolution, it is unlikely that the biosphere today would be threatened by overpopulation of human beings. Wolves can stay together and love in their own way without sex, and do no harm to the earth.

MICHAEL W. FOX, *The Soul of the Wolf*

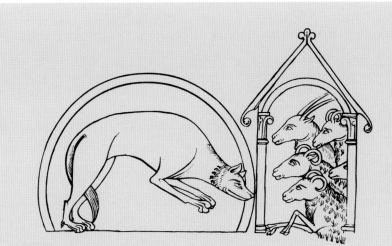

LUPINE LECHERY

In times past, wolves have been associated with ravenous lust; the wolf's predatory instinct toward sheep easily became a symbol for sexual predation. T. H. White's translation of a 12th-century Latin bestiary tells us, "Wolves are known for their rapacity, and for this reason we call prostitutes wolves, because they devastate the possessions of their lovers."

Werewolf legends feature both blood lust and sexual lust, as does the most famous of fairy tales, Little Red Riding Hood. Wearing a red cap that proclaims her sexual maturity, a young girl is lured off the moral path by the seducer wolf. And the sex link endures in colloquial use:

A wolf	A sexually predatory man
Wolf whistle	His call
"Elle a vu le loup"	"She has seen the wolf." she has lost her virginity

Medieval bestiaries were full of such images. Solinus reported that "on the backside of the wolf there is a small patch of aphrodisiac hair." Others said of wolf hair that "If the eyebrows are annointed with the same, mixed with rose-water, the annointed one will be adored by the beholder." Or that "backward men and women can be brought to lust by the tie of a wolf's pizzle (dried in an oven)."

There are classical references to sexual wolfishness too: *lupa* in Latin means both a prostitute and a female wolf; the Lupercal temples were brothels. And the Greek word for wolf sometimes meant a homosexual lover, as in Plato's couplet:

The eager lover to the boy aspires,
Just as the wolf the tender lamb desires.

THE WOLF WAY OF BIRTH

Midnight passed, and half-darkness had settled over the meadow, leaving the sky a pale lemon dome which shaded to green where it met the southwestern horizon. During the dark hours, the gray bitch made several trips to the surface, and doing so seemed to still the waves of trembling that had begun earlier. Then her stays on the surface became increasingly shorter, and though consumed by a powerful urge to quench her thirst, she did not go to the creek. She had already felt the first of the mild cramps beneath her rib cage that signaled the approaching birth of the pups she had carried for sixty-six days, three days longer than normal term. . . .

Another hour passed slowly, during which her cramps became rhythmic spasms, and the first pup was born quickly, pushed by muscle contractions so powerful that no adult wolf could have survived them. The air in the den was heavy with the brassy scent of placental fluid as the gray bitch licked the tiny, roan pup dry. She had carried this litter longer than any that had preceded it, and the lateness of the birth was probably the result of her advancing age. . . .

Moments after the birth of the first pup, the old bitch nipped the convoluted bluish cord attached to its naked belly, a process made efficient by its very simplicity. The short, blunt-edged incisor teeth between the canines crushed the cut edges of the cord as it was severed, thus closing it, stanching the insignificant flow of blood, and thereby promoting healing.

Though she continued to lick the squirming pup, the gray bitch seemed almost disinterested in it, and two more hours passed before she once more felt the building spasms, forerunners of the second pup's birth. Then, panting rapidly in the darkness, she circled nervously, somehow avoiding the first pup with her long-clawed feet. Females of lesser experience often stepped upon their young even as the process of whelping continued, or lay upon them accidentally, yet if practice made the process of reproducing easier and more efficient, better results did not stem from conscious thought on the part of female wolves. The phenom-

ABOVE: *A mother and her newborn litter. Jim Brandenburg.* OPPOSITE: *Courtship play before mating often includes dominance gestures (by both male and female) such as placing a leg over the mate's back. Scot Stewart.*

enon of birth, though basic to all wild species, is a uniquely instinctive process, and the inherited reactions to it sharpen as each breeding and whelping season is experienced.

One of the gray bitch's buff-colored sons barked sharply outside, and the sound reached the bitch's ears as she rested during midmorning. Her labored breathing had ceased sometime after the birth of her fourth pup, and she dozed with an almost desperate need for time during which to regenerate the energy she had burned during the long night. . . . In the darkness she found each pup with her nose, methodically rolling them onto their backs to facilitate licking their bellies, while cleaning her own vulva, which still seeped the residual fluids of birth. . . .

Stretching her neck until she lay flat on her side, the bitch made her udders available to the pups, udders swollen with the milk produced under the complex influence of the rapidly changing hormonal balance in her own bloodstream and the catalyzing effect of the afterbirth she had eaten. Then, testing the slight movement of air in the den tunnel with a nose a hundred times more powerful than man's, she sighed raggedly and once more closed her eyes.

JAMES GREINER, *The Red Snow*

GROWING UP WOLF

▼▼▼▼▼

The yearly rhythms of a pack revolve around the birth and rearing of each season's litter of pups. They are born as winter is loosening its grip on the land—late April and early May is most common—and take all summer and fall to grow into young wolves equipped for the next winter's wanderings. During the easy-going summer, the pack limits its travels and devotes much attention to its newest members.

Weighing about a pound, fuzzy, round-headed, pug-nosed, and stump-tailed, the pups (an average of six per litter) start life with their eyes closed, aware of little but their mother's voice, scent, warmth, and tongue, and their siblings' bodies, these stimuli forming lifetime bonds. In about a week their eyes open and after another week they may venture out of the den; for their first two weeks no adult wolf besides the mother is allowed inside.

At around a month old, the pups start to range farther out into their world, and at two months or so begin the transition from mother's milk to meat—getting their first servings straight from the mouths of adult wolves. About then, too, the den is abandoned and the pack moves to a "rendezvous"—an outdoor home base where the pups romp and stalk their first insects and mice, until they are old enough to travel with the pack. By fourteen weeks, their tails have filled out, legs and muzzles have lengthened, and they have become "fair copies of adult wolves."

A three-month old pup cautiously descends from his high lookout. Rod Allin/Bruce Coleman, Inc.

All the adults fuss over, play with, and feed the pups by the efficient method of regurgitation. Wolves make much of puppies and put up with their pestering graciously. They will also easily adopt young from outside the pack, as did Lois Crisler's semi-tame wolves. Once the mother rejoins the hunting sorties, a low-ranking subordinate is often tagged as babysitter.

While it's hard to imagine the hilariously inept pups transformed into tough, capable wolves, their bumbling play in fact hones skills they will depend on all their lives— "chasing, fighting, and chewing," as one writer says in a nutshell. And by the time they are a few months old, littermates have sorted into a social pattern that mimics the adult hierarchy.

A SEASON TO GROW IN

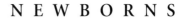

About a week after their eyes open they begin to make the first exploratory trips to the den entrance to try out their new gift of sight on a strange new world. And it is a new world they see in every sense of the word. When their parents mated in February, the earth lay buried under an apparently lifeless blanket of snow; lake and river were scarcely to be told from forest, and the main concern of every living thing was to keep itself alive. Often at night the temperature went far below zero, moisture in the trees exploded like rifle shots throughout the forest, and the lake ice rumbled and groaned like a restless giant turning in his bed. But every day the sun climbed a little higher, the wind blew more often from the south, and now the transition is complete. A landscape that seemed so lifeless and colorless three months ago is rich with the pastel shades of spring. Grass is green on exposed hillsides, insects are on the wing, the air is filled by day with the songs and calls of birds, and at night with the voices of a million frogs come to mat and lay eggs in the abundant water left from the melted snow. Ravens and gray jays have already brought off young from nests built while the snow was still deep; every day more infant animals, from mice to moose, add to the expanding demand for more and more food. But if there are many to be fed there are also many to be eaten, and only the luckiest and strongest will survive to insure the balance of a healthy population for another year. Even among the young wolves, with comparatively little to fear from enemies, only the most alert and physically perfect will complete the two years of apprenticeship necessary before they are to begin raising families of their own.

RUSSELL J. RUTTER AND DOUGLAS H. PIMLOTT,
The World of the Wolf

NEWBORNS

Newly born wolf puppies look more like tiny bears than like members of the dog family. They are blind, their hearing is poor, their ears are flattened forward, and their noses are squashed, as though someone had pressed them down with a forceful thumb. The legs are short and underdeveloped and the beautiful, plumelike tail sported by the adult bears no resemblance to the short, skinny appendage of the wolfling. These babies come into the world wearing dark brown or slate-blue coats of fine, woolly hair. . . . [Thus the wolves we knew] emerged into the world: wriggly, mewling little bundles that weighed about one pound, each of which was to experience immediately the pleasantly warm stimulation of their mother's tongue and then, perhaps abruptly, the small, sharp pain that stabbed them briefly when the maternal incisor teeth nipped through the umbilical cord to liberate the newborns from their embryonic ties. . . .

R. D. LAWRENCE, *In Praise of Wolves*

ABOVE: Two-week old pup near the den entrance. Scot Stewart. BELOW: Littermates in a lily-strewn meadow. Scot Stewart. OVERLEAF: Pups explore the edge of a snowfield, Ellesmere Island, Canada. Jim Brandenburg.

LOVING THE LEADER

That evening after the day's sleep, as the shadow of the mountain to the north grayed the mesa, Trigger arose, stretched luxuriously across the den mouth and uttered the "puppy call." Out from the den boiled the pups. Lady lay quiet outside the pen, watching what now ensued, the cajolery of wolf pups toward the adult wolf.

It is one of the gayest, prettiest sights in the world. The pups themselves are the softest and gentlest of creatures, blue-eyed, oddly leonine-looking at this stage, for their muzzles are short; above all, not quarrelsome among themselves as dog pups so often are, and brimming with adulation toward adults. The pups besieged their big meat-giver with feverish love pats and kisses. They thronged his head, sat on their haunches and threw both arms around his neck as far as they would go. They kissed his face and gave him love pats around the mouth with huge soft paws. They even kissed the inside of his mouth if he opened it. All their attentions were oriented to Trigger's head.

"Looks like they just tingle all over when they even touch him," said Cris. Their soft excitement reminded me of nothing so much as baby water ouzels, fluttering vibrissimo after being fed, so that the enchanted parent rushes for more food to repeat the delicious excitement.

LOIS CRISLER, *Arctic Wild*

BELOW: A mother plays with her black-phase pup. Carl R. Sams II/Peter Arnold, Inc. OPPOSITE: Scruffy, a low-ranking pack member, often played the same role as Mowat's "Uncle Albert," minding the pups when the pack was off hunting and enjoying their attentions. Jim Brandenburg.

UNCLE ALBERT, PUP SITTER

The sixth morning of my vigil had dawned bright and sunny, and Angeline and the pups took advantage of the good weather. Hardly was the sun risen (at three a.m.) when they all left the den and adjourned to a nearby sandy knoll. Here the pups worked over their mother with an enthusiasm which would certainly have driven any human female into hysterics. They were hungry; but they were also full to the ears with hellery. Two of them did their best to chew off Angeline's tail, worrying it and fighting over it until I thought I could actually see her fur flying like spindrift; while the other two did what they could to remove her ears.

Angeline stood it with noble stoicism for about an hour and then, sadly disheveled, she attempted to protect herself by sitting on her tail and tucking her mauled head down between her legs. This was a fruitless effort. The pups went for her feet, one to each paw, and I was treated to the spectacle of the demon killer of the wilds trying desperately to cover her paws, her tail, and her head at one and the same instant.

Eventually she gave it up. Harassed beyond endurance she leaped away from her brood and raced to the top of a high sand ridge behind the den. The four pups rolled cheerfully off in pursuit, but before they could reach her she gave vent to a most peculiar cry.

The whole question of wolf communications was to intrigue me more and more as time went on, but on this occasion I was still laboring under the delusion that complex communications among animals other than man did not exist. I could make nothing definite of Angeline's high-pitched and yearning whine-cum-howl. I did, however, detect a plaintive quality in it which made my sympathies go out to her.

I was not alone. Within seconds of her *cri-de-coeur*, and before the mob of pups could reach her, a savior appeared.

It was the third wolf. He had been sleeping in a bed hollowed in the sand at the southern end of the esker where it dipped down to disappear beneath the waters of the bay. I had not known he was there until I saw his head come up. He jumped to his feet, shook himself, and trotted straight toward the den—intercepting the pups as they prepared to scale the last slope to reach their mother.

I watched, fascinated, as he used his shoulder to bowl the leading pup over on its back and send it skidding down the lower slope toward the den. Having broken the charge, he then nipped another pup lightly on its fat behind; then he shepherded the lot of them back to what I later came to recognize as the playground area.

I hesitate to put human words into a wolf's mouth, but the effect of what followed was crystal clear. "If it's a workout you kids want," he might have said, "then I'm your wolf!"

And so he was. For the next hour he played with the pups with as much energy as if he were still one himself. The games were varied, but many of them were quite recognizable. Tag was the standby, and Albert was always "it." Leaping, rolling and weaving amongst the pups, he never left the area of the nursery knoll, while at the same time leading the youngsters such a chase that they eventually gave up.

Albert looked them over for a moment and then, after a quick glance toward the crest where Angeline was now lying in a state of peaceful relaxation, he flung himself in among the tired pups, sprawled on his back, and invited mayhem. They were game. One by one they roused and went into battle. They were really roused this time, and no holds were barred—by them, at any rate.

Some of them tried to choke the life out of Albert, although their small teeth, sharp as they were, could never have penetrated his heavy ruff. One of them, in an excess of infantile sadism, turned its back on him and pawed a shower of sand into his face. The others took to leaping as high into the air as their bowed little legs would propel them; coming down with a satisfying thump on Albert's vulnerable belly. In between jumps they tried to chew the life out of whatever vulnerable parts came to tooth.

I began to wonder how much he could stand. Evidently he could stand a lot, for not until the pups were totally exhausted and had collapsed into complete somnolence did he get to his feet, careful not to step on the small, sprawled forms, and disengage himself. Even then he did not return to the comfort of his own bed (which he had undoubtedly earned after a night of hard hunting) but settled himself instead on the edge of the nursery knoll, where he began wolf-napping, taking a quick look at the pups every few minutes to make sure they were still safely near at hand.

His true relationship to the rest of the family was still uncertain; but as far as I was concerned he had become, and would remain, "good old Uncle Albert."

FARLEY MOWAT, *Never Cry Wolf*

WHAT'S IN A GAME?

The three wolf pups shuffled out of their den, one by one, and plopped onto their haunches with a kind of sweet canine gracelessness. . . . They tramped around the den site, schlepping their way through the days, bumbling into each other, and often tripping over their own oversized paws. They nuzzled each other with their little pug noses, bit faces and ears, and licked each other all over. In mock assaults, they even laid ambushes for one another, acting out playful rivalries as they pounced and sent each other rolling into the den, pencil-thin tails wagging furiously. They were irresistibly clumsy and, unable to stay away from each other, alive with body contact. For hours each day, they would sleep, lounging on top of each other in a rich puppy pile of bluish-gray fur. . . .

Like a play on the stage, the play of the pups was also a text to be read. Their play was anything but aimless. It was filled with meaning. . . . In addition to developing distinct personalities, these wolf pups were also learning a complex vocabulary of gestures and postures for expressing their status relative to each other.

One of the pups, for example, was bigger than the others, easily identifiable by a bold white star on its chest. A leader, it was always the first one to emerge from the den in the morning. One morning it poked out of the den but paused at the mouth for ten minutes, until the others appeared too. Then it padded off down a small trail into nearby grass. The other two followed. It chewed some grass . . . attacked an unsuspecting moose bone, disappeared into some spruce to the left of the den, and reappeared on a small ridge behind the den. Here, it sat down and scratched an ear, the quintessence of puppiness. . . .

The starred pup suddenly began to get worked up with anticipation, spotting an opportunity. Pawing the ground, its rear end and little tail wagging in growing excitement, it looked like a dog eager for its owner to throw a ball. And then? A sudden spring, bowling [a] smaller, more timid littermate snout over tumbling tail into the den.

The triumphant pounce was only one of several ways the starred pup expressed its superiority over the others. Frequently, it would mount the other pups from the side, front paws on their backs, in a posture of dominance that biologists call "riding up." The other pups would respond with the classic pose of submission—head lowered, ears back, tail curled between hind legs. The starred pup would also assert itself by "standing across" another pup, which would curl on its back, stomach up, tail tucked between its legs.

CHARLES BERGMAN, *Wild Echoes*

Charles Bergman's Wild Echoes: Encounters with the Most Endangered Animals in North America *is a collection of powerful and highly personal reports on many of our endangered species, including wolves. An active environmentalist, Bergman has written for* Audubon, Smithsonian, *and* National Geographic *magazines.*

Young pups tussle over a pine cone prize. Adult wolves as well as pups often play with objects. Jim Dutcher.

MEAT BY MAGIC

That night about eleven o'clock, when the sunlight was rosy on the mountains across the lake, Trigger and Lady came trotting over the shadowed tundra from a kill across the lake. At the foot of the mesa they paused. Trigger buzzed the male ptarmigan that hung out down there. Lady went to look at the wolverine. When I called she looked up and started up with surprising alacrity and speed. But at the top she looked at me as if she had forgotten I was there.

She evaded my hands and leaped into the pen, uttering the strong whine which we knew by now was the wolf "puppy call." I started into the cabin but Cris called me back in a soft urgent voice.

"Look there. She gave them her meat." All the puppies were in a bunch, eating. The long-legged young wolf whimpered gently to them. She lay down and the puppies toddled and climbed over her.

At this juncture Trigger arrived. He glanced the situation over. We did not wonder what he would do; we didn't know enough to suppose he would do anything. He stepped to [the dog] Tootch, tied near the pen. Just out of reach of her bared fangs, with an expression of such bashful sweetness that it made us smile, he dumped before her his load, the contents of his stomach—about two or two and a half pounds of fresh red meat. I pushed it a foot closer so that the justly baffled dog could reach her present.

The wolves presently fell asleep near the recipients of their gifts, Trigger near Tootch, Lady near the pups. But Cris and I stood forgetting to move.

"Never underestimate little Lady," said Cris. "You said she wasn't mature as a parent and Trigger was, but she fed the pups."

What impressed Cris was wolf logistics. "They've got an ideal way of carrying their meat. In their stomachs. They can run and smell and chase things along the way, and nobody could tell they were taking meat to a den."

I was impressed by the good condition of the meat; it could have come from a market counter. Did wolves inhibit digestion?

An adult wolf regurgitates for a pup. The ways wolves greet each other as adults, licking and nibbling the muzzles of alpha animals, is an outgrowth of pup behavior, when these actions stimulate the disgorging instinct. Scot Stewart.

. . . But it was not these points that held us motionless in the gray shadow of the mountain. Full and clear at last had been stated the great theme of feral generosity. Lady had given to pups no kin of hers, Trigger to a dog that more than once had bitten his muzzle.

It always does us good, says Thoreau, "it even takes the stiffness out of our joints, and makes us supple and buoyant, when we knew not what ailed us, to recognize any generosity in man or Nature." From now on, for years to come, we were to see wolves concerned and eager to give the choicest food they could get not to wolf pups, for there were none, but to any indifferent dog pups they could reach. And always I felt a touch of wonder.

LOIS CRISLER, *Arctic Wild*

OLD ONES

▼▼▼▼▼▼

Wild wolves that live ten years are considered quite old, and the oldest known captive wolf lived to age sixteen. Older wolves that can no longer hunt effectively may become the lowest-ranking pack member, trailing behind and living off the remains of kills; or the others may allow it to go on traveling and feeding with them. (If a former alpha wolf, how it is treated may depend on how it once treated its packmates.) Barry Lopez, finding an old female with blunted canines, wondered why she was still with her pack: "I could not shake the idea that what she contributed was the experience of having done so many things. She was one, I thought, who knew where to go to find caribou." Roger Caras tells another story of an old one:

END OF THE TRAIL

On another day, in another part of their range, an aged female limped soulfully into their lives. She was beyond the breeding age, no longer of interest to an unattached male, and obviously widowed, for she had once been a magnificent animal. Obvious too was the fact that she was an animal of great skill, a creature in harmony with her world, for she had survived into arthritic old age

without help. . . . She had outlived those with whom she had joined, those whom she herself had created with the magic art of her inner body. Gray now and very old, yet proud, she appeared one day—near where the silver she-wolf and her two cubs feasted on a pronghorn that had been taken only because old age had come his way as well—and sat watching at an acceptable distance. Although obviously half starved and wild to join the feasting, she did not move toward the kill. The silver she-wolf, meanwhile, circled the kill several times as her cubs fed, keeping her eyes always upon the stranger . . . [then] allowed the sad old creature to approach the carcass. . . . When the silver trotted away from the kill, her cubs with her, the old female limped along behind.

The addition of the old female to their family unit did not unduly affect the cubs, although now there was sometimes less food than before. Unable to hunt for herself, her gait slow and most uncertain, her teeth broken and worn, the old hag had asked for and had been granted care. She was fed for three months without question or trouble. Then one night she moved off quietly, rested her great, gray head on her swollen front paws, closed her clouded yellow eyes and slept; and in her sleep she slipped easily away and rejoined the legends from which she had once arisen.

Whether she became a figure on a totem pole along the northwest coast of the continent, whether she became a legendary figure who would find and gently rear human children, or whether she would become the dreaded man-killer whose only pleasure was in the cries of her human victims, mattered little to her. To whichever legend she was assigned, however it was recorded—in skillfully sculpted wood or spoken word alone—she was a wolf that had come and gone, lived and died, and hence was part of a living, self-reproducing legend. . . .

ROGER CARAS, *The Custer Wolf*

THE STEPPENWOLF
▼▼▼▼▼▼

The Wolf trots to and fro,

The world lies deep in snow,

The raven from the birch tree flies.

But nowhere a hare, nowhere a roe.

The roe — she is so dear, so sweet —

If such a thing I might surprise

In my embrace, my teeth would meet,

What else is there beneath the skies?

The lovely creature I would so treasure,

And feast myself deep on her tender thigh,

I would drink of her red blood full measure,

Then howl till the night went by.

Even a hare I would not despise;

Sweet enough its warm flesh in the night.

Is everything to be denied

That could make life a little bright?

The hair on my brush is getting grey.

The sight is failing from my eyes.

Years ago my dear mate died.

And now I trot and dream of a roe.

I trot and dream of a hare.

I heard the wind of midnight howl.

I cool with the snow my burning jowl,

And on to the devil my wretched soul I bear.

HERMANN HESSE, *Steppenwolf*

OPPOSITE: "Wolf," painting by Ken Carlson, 1988. LEFT: Timber wolf pauses during a ridge traverse. Stephen J. Krasemann/DRK Photo.

WOLVES AT PLAY

▼▼▼▼▼

Everyone who has watched wolves for any length of time has re-marked on their lifelong readiness for play. Pups play with each other, of course, and with tolerant older packmates, but adults are almost as likely to wake out of a snooze with mischief on their minds. Observers marvel, in fact, that as hard as wolves must work to get their food, they flagrantly expend calories in romping.

Wolf games include tag (the most common, as chasing may be their deepest-rooted instinct); wrestling matches; charge-and-tack-le; pouncing on each other from ambush or while one wolf is sleeping; and "keep-away," teasing pursuers with a stick, a stolen hat, or whatever seems desirable at that moment. Lois Crisler's wolf Lady learned to filch a handkerchief from her husband's pocket and run "flaunting it as a trophy for Trigger to chase." They also bring each other gifts or toys for play.

Wolves' boundless curiosity about every detail of their envi-ronment compels them to investigate and take apart any novelty—as humans who have lived with them quickly learn! David Mech and photographer Jim Brandenburg watched as a wild pack on Ellesmere Island methodically dismantled their tent camp, and barely saved a red sleeping bag from the intruders' teeth.

Wolves even play toss-and-catch; Barry Lopez writes that he "once saw a wolf on the tundra winging a piece of caribou hide around like a Frisbee for an hour by himself." And though wolves only reluctantly go into the water after prey, researchers from Durward Allen's team "saw 4 wolves romping, wrestling and engaged in a water fight. . . . [O]ne wolf was throwing water on the others using his paw as a paddle."

Much of wolves' play has practical roots—sharpening reflexes, keeping fit, and so on—but few would question that they seem to take vast pleasure in play and bring to it the same intensity as they do to social affairs or hunting.

HOLIDAY ON ICE

As I stood within the trees, I heard the high-pitched barking of wolves coming from the northeast. . . . [They] were on the ice of one of our largest beaver ponds. . . . Although visibility wasn't great, I had no difficulty seeing the eight gray-fawn wolves that were dashing about over the ice, at times bunching up, on other occasions spreading out over an area of some four hundred square feet. The wolves were playing! Using the field glasses to confirm my first impression, I was immediately able to determine that a definite game was in progress. Seven of the wolves were chasing a large individual, clearly the pack leader, each trying to make body contact with him. The Alpha was dashing about wildly, at one moment running at full speed, at another coming to an abrupt, sliding stop that swiveled his hindquarters, much as an automobile skids around when braked abruptly on a slippery surface. The result of this maneuver was that the big wolf turned about, sliding sideways. This caused the pursuers to run right past him, all of them sliding also as they tried to stop in order to turn and continue the chase. Recovering his balance, the leader would then charge into the rearmost of his

ABOVE: *Young gray wolves bump and jostle each other in play. Peter McLeod/First Light.* OPPOSITE: *Three-way tug of war with a piece of deer hide. Jim Brandenburg.*

pursuers, hitting it with his chest and sending it rolling over and over, skidding helplessly on the snowy ice. When this happened, the seven chasers would bark shrilly, including the one that had been bowled over, as though registering their pleasure and amusement. Then the whole show began over again. . . .

I watched those wolves for seventeen minutes. They ran, skidded, rolled, and leaped over the ice in complete abandon, remaining in more or less the same part of the pond and behaving, it seemed to me, like children newly let out for recess.

R. D. LAWRENCE, *In Praise of Wolves*

DIVERSIONS

Hunkering down to make myself as small as possible, I wormed my way into the rocks and did my best to be unobtrusive. I need not have worried. The wolves paid no attention to me, if indeed they even saw me. They were far too engrossed in their own affairs, which, as I slowly and incredulously began to realize, were at that moment centered around the playing of a game of tag.

It was difficult to believe my eyes. They were romping like a pair of month-old pups! The smaller wolf (who soon gave concrete evidence that she was a female) took the initiative. Putting her head down on her forepaws and elevating her posterior in a most undignified manner, she suddenly pounced toward the much larger male whom I now recognized as my acquaintance of two days earlier. He, in his attempt to evade her, tripped and went sprawling. Instantly, she was upon him, nipping him smartly in the backside, before leaping away to run around him in frenzied circles. The male scrambled to his feet and gave chase, but only by the most strenuous efforts was he able to close the gap until he, in his turn, was able to nip her backside. Thereupon the roles were again reversed, and the female began to pursue the male, who led her on a wild scrabble up, over, down, and back across the esker until finally both wolves lost their footing on the steep slope and went skidding down it inextricably locked together.

When they reached the bottom they separated, shook the sand out of their hair, and stood panting heavily, almost nose to nose. Then the female reared up and quite literally embraced the male with both forepaws while she proceeded to smother him in long-tongued kisses.

The male appeared to be enduring this overt display of affection, rather than enjoying it. He kept trying to avert his head, to no avail. Involuntarily I felt my sympathy warming toward him, for, in truth, it was a disgusting exhibition of wanton passion. Nevertheless he bore it with what stoicism he could muster until the female tired.

FARLEY MOWAT, *Never Cry Wolf*

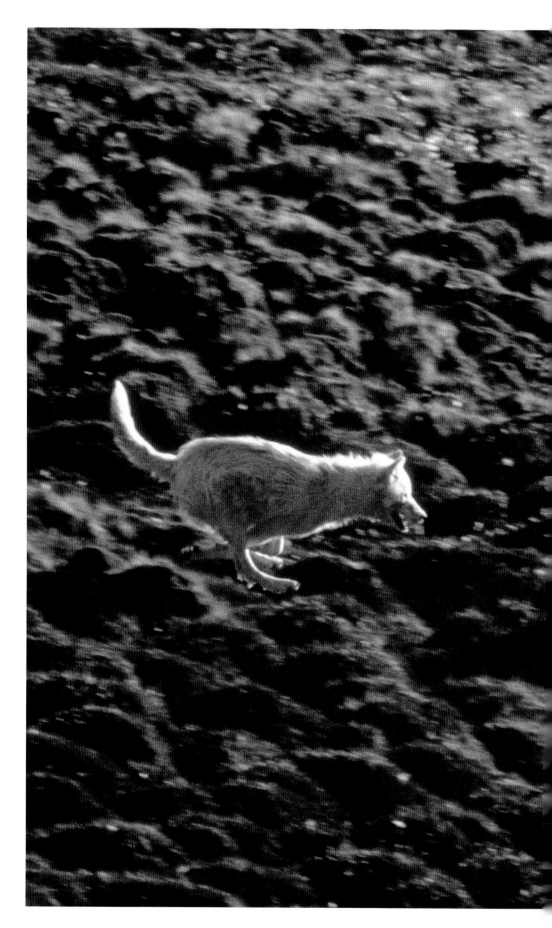

Evolution has been a matter of days well-lived, chameleon strength, energy, zappy sex, sunshine stored up, inventiveness, competitiveness, and the whole fun of busy brain cells.

EDWARD HOAGLAND,
Red Wolves and Black Bears

What but the wolf's tooth whittled so fine
The fleet limbs of the antelope?

ROBINSON JEFFERS

Like all wild creatures, the wolf can be truly understood only in relation to its world, the ecosystem of which it is a part. The wolf is shaped—both as a species and as individuals—by the landscapes it inhabits, their climate, winds, seasons, soils, terrain features, and plant life; and by the other animals it has shared those places with, from microbes to woolly mammoths. And, as the preeminent predator in the northern world, the wolf

The Wolf's World

has played a vital role in the evolution of the large hoofed mammals we so admire—the deer, caribou, elk, moose, mountain sheep, and arctic oxen. They grew strong and fleet to outrun it; they developed systems of communication and defense to thwart it. Over shorter spans of time, either predator or prey may gain a temporary advantage; over the long haul, each needs the other to survive and thrive. Wolves are woven into their world in many ways besides predation. In their wide travels, they spread the seeds of plants that cling to their furry coats. That same fur is used by hawks and other birds to line their nests. They have forged a special relationship with the raven, which scouts for prey and takes its turn at the kill when the wolves are done. Pups learn their trade by testing the wits of small rodents. Wolves borrow dens from foxes and lend them to porcupines; and they coexist in various ways, from tolerant to hostile, with other northern carnivores: bear, wolverine, fox, lynx, and mountain lion. The only fellow predator they haven't yet come to terms with is the human.

THE MEANING OF WHOLENESS

On a frozen morning more than a decade ago I intersected a set of prints entirely new to our home range. They read wolf. *Canis lupus.* Once as abundant and widespread as early humans throughout North America—and the rest of the northern hemisphere—wolves were almost completely eradicated south of Canada by early in this century. They have since reestablished a population of about thirteen hundred in the northern Great Lakes region. Just one other part of the United States outside Alaska has a known breeding group today. That is the North Fork of the Flathead, which already harbors one of the Lower 48's best surviving grizzly populations.

To say that wolves have established themelves in the North Fork sounds too assured. The reality is this: in 1978, the year those tracks cut the corner of our property, a single black wolf was seen just across the border in British Columbia. At first hardly anyone paid much attention. Although wolves were scarce throughout that southern region of Canada, a few small packs still live in the spine of the Rockies toward Kootenay, Yoho, and Banff national parks, which lie about a hundred miles north. And wolves are long-legged travelers. So it was not really unexpected when some drifted across the border. They usually came alone, like this one, and they never seemed to stay long. Or if they did, they never seemed to live long. Most of the sightings of wolves in Montana over the decades involved a wolf shot, snared, or poisoned.

The black wolf hung around the North Fork border for another year, then dropped out of sight just as a research project to study a possible wolf recovery got underway. Come spring, however, the biologists captured a gray, eighty-pound

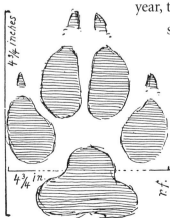

PRECEDING SPREAD: Grey wolf in early fall foliage. Wayne Lankinen/Valan Photos.
OPPOSITE: Gray wolves in fall landscape, Alaska. Tom and Pat Leeson.

A fundamental issue revolves around wolves. Are we really out to conserve wildness? Or only the pieces that suit us? To the extent that we pick and choose pieces, wildlife communities will reveal that much more about the temporary goals of human communities and that much less about the holistic workings of nature. How, then, shall we ever understand creation?

DOUGLAS CHADWICK, *The Kingdom*

European gray wolf, Børas Sanctuary, Sweden. Mattias Klum.

picked berries. She avoided human footprints and ski trails, reversing direction when she happened upon them. In the next fifteen months she visited Montana once, near Kishinena Creek. As far as anyone knew, she was always alone.

Those were the raw data. To the handful of us locals who had taken an interest in her as a kind of shadow neighbor, the data didn't seem to make her all that much more real. A wolf's intelligence, like our dogs' and our own, is essentially social. The wolf survives best in packs because the hoofed prey it depends upon are smart, sensitive, and socially alert as well—and often bigger, faster, and stronger than a single wolf. What was it really like, then, to be a lone, eighty-pound female trying to keep alive in our valley? How did it feel in the gut? In the mind? What did it mean to have a song, an old tune, going round in her head, but never a chorus? What were her chances here? All we had

female in the same area. They gave her a Kootenay Indian name—Kishinena—after the bright tributary draining from British Columbia through the northwest tip of Glacier National Park, and they began following her with the help of a radio collar.

Kishinena moved with the game, at times traveling deeper into Canada toward the North Fork headquarters. She ate moose, beavers, snowshoe hares, ground squirrels, mice, voles, and spruce grouse. That was how the sign read. She might have eaten elk, mule deer, and whitetails too. She scavenged, running down the scent of leftover meat, as often as she killed. And in summertime she also

to go on was this skin-and-bones outline.

Researchers followed Kishinena through another winter. Her track remained a solitary line even when blood on the snow indicated that Kishinena was in heat. She was already middle-aged. I held little hope that she would ever see offspring. Then another winter, another breeding season alone. Always alone. And always, there were men visiting these woods who plumb hated wolves, or thought they were supposed to. Sure enough, [soon] rumors filtered through the valley that she had been done in. Shoot, shovel, shut up. The usual deal.

Then the black wolf reappeared. In the moist, packed snow of spring details of the paws became clear. One foot of the black wolf was missing a toe, most likely left in someone's steel-jawed trap. This told us something we already knew: the black wolf was a survivor. Together, his tracks and the female's wound through the country. Later in the spring, Kishinena bore seven pups in a den just within British Columbia. They grew up, most of them, and became a functional group operating on both sides of the border. Called the Magic Pack—partly for its ability to suddenly vanish from human ken for long periods and then materialize just as unexpectedly, and partly for the fact that it existed at all—it soon began denning in Glacier.

From this beginning the little group should have expanded into a larger one, then divided into several different groups with various leaders, or alpha wolves. It did just that, but more slowly than anticipated. Members were shot from new logging roads pushed into the once-remote corner of southeastern British Columbia. Some were trapped. Still others dispersed to unknown countrysides. In order to protect habitat critical to the wolf's recovery on the United States side from harmful developments, it was necessary to establish that there was, in fact, a recovering wolf pack there. Yet money for the research project ran out. A solitary scientist named Diane Boyd kept the tracking work alive, often funding it out of her own pocket. As Kishinena had done for so long, as as the pack was doing now, she endured from day to day. . . .

It has been a dozen years now since I first saw those wolf tracks near home. I have seen more since, and heard wolves howl from across the river. So they are around, still trailing signs and songs behind them. But I could not tell you where they are going, or when—or even if—they will ever be able to return as an integral part of the ecosystem.

I wish I knew.

DOUGLAS CHADWICK, *The Kingdom*

Wildlife biologist Douglas Chadwick has joined the ranks of leading nature writers with his acclaimed books A Beast the Color of Winter (*on the mountain goat*), The Fate of the Elephant, *and* The Kingdom: Wildlife in North America. *He travels widely on assignment for* National Geographic *and other magazines, and lives in Montana near the edge of Glacier National Park, wild country to which wolves are slowly returning.*

Gray wolves stretch their legs in a game, Montana. James D. Markou/Valan Photos.

LUPINE LANDSCAPES

▼▼▼▼▼▼

Wolves once were key members of nearly every North American ecosystem, from the Gulf Coast wetlands to the primeval forests of the Northwest. Today they are viable only where humans do not compete too heavily for land resources and game, and we must piece together from scanty evidence their former place in other landscapes.

All around the northern hemisphere, local wolf populations and subspecies adapted to the prevailing conditions: they became smaller and lighter of coat in more southerly climes, and hunted in smaller packs because the prey animals were less large and formidable than those farther north. In the arctic, by contrast, wolves reach their largest size and tend to be white-coated, the better to blend with their snow-and-ice background.

In some places wolf packs stay more or less put within established territories where they hunt year round. Elsewhere—in the subarctic caribou range and the Great Plains in the days of the buffalo—they migrate along with the herds. Their diet can be limited almost entirely to the meat of one or two large ungulates, or it can include small mammals, fish, and even berries. Dens are most often burrows in sandy soil or glacial ridges called "eskers," but wolves will use what's available: an abandoned beaver lodge or dam, hollowed-out tree bases, fallen trees, or rock caves. They often take over and enlarge dens dug by foxes.

Compared to the plants and other creatures that compose a wild community, wolves are always among the least numerous members: one wolf for every ten square miles is a high density. Combined with their shyness, this makes the chance of seeing a wolf very slim, even in places where they thrive. Today there are all too many North American landscapes where a person could roam for a lifetime and never even hear a wolf—where they persist only in the imagination, as in the Southwest sketch by James Burbank that follows. Elsewhere, people are working to return wolves to landscapes—such as the Yellowstone region—where they have lived in the past and have a rightful place.

Arctic wolf atop the rock overhang where the pack's den is located, Ellesmere Island, Canada. Jim Brandenburg.

THE HIGH ARCTIC

The high Arctic setting in which the wolves play out the intricacies of their lives is as beautiful as it is severe. The lack of winter daylight, the bitter cold and the desert-like aridity combine to make Ellesmere an extraordinarily difficult place for life to gain a foothold. Over millions of years, however, a stalwart crew of species has managed to survive and establish a food chain that eventually winds its way down the wolf's alimentary canal.

There are abundant lichens, those strange, often multi-colored amalgams of fungus and algae that conspire to eke out a collaborative living on bare rocks. The acids produced by this symbiosis leach into a stone's surface, and over time, boulders begin to break down to sand and soil. A variety of grasses and sedges can, in turn, find cracks in which their root systems can proliferate, further expediting the breakdown of rock. . . .

The tiny Arctic willow, a true perennial, is the only tree living on the island today, but it is dwarfed by various flowering plants which can grow to a relatively towering ten inches high. As the wolf puppies grew older, I often witnessed them sniffing these flowers—poppies, mainly—that blossom in a brief, erratic explosion during warm weather.

Insects exist on Ellesmere in all the typical groups seen in more moderate climes, from moths to bumblebees to mosquitos. . . . The wolves had their own ways of dealing with the mosquitoes. While the pups generally retreated to the den, the adults would light out for the windiest hillsides they could find, hoping the air flow would provide relief. On still days, when the situation was close to unbearable for me, the wolves took the attacks stoically. They curled up in tight balls with the tails looped protectively over their noses and slept, reflexively twitching their tails all the while. On such days, I greatly envied their hides and equanimity.

Birdlife on Ellesmere consists of a few species living year-round in the Arctic and a larger number of species spending summers there. The rock ptarmigan is perhaps the best example of the first group. This plumpish white bird survives the winter thanks in part to its great feathered coat; even the ptarmigan's feet are feathered. . . .

The list of migratory birds on Ellesmere includes Arctic terns,

"The Moon and The Wolf," by Susan A. Point (Coast Salish), 1991.

ivory gulls, snowy owls, snow buntings, ruddy turnstones, red knots, gyrfalcons, and Arctic loons. While all are fascinating birds, none so captured my imagination as the Arctic tern, a black-headed bird with sharply angled wings and a tail with twin points. Every year, this bird flies 24,000 miles from Ellesmere to Tierra del Fuego, the longest migratory route known. It lives most of its life in constant daylight, alternating between the 24-hour days of the far north and the far south. . . .

Ellesmere Island was also home to a variety of fish and aquatic animals. The Arctic char, which is related to trout and salmon, has ben described as the best-tasting fish in the world. The wolves regularly patrolled the beaches near the den hoping to find char washed ashore. . . .

Large sea mammals also live in the waters off Ellesmere. White beluga whales swim in smallish groups in the inlets, and one day I watched about 200 narwals, the unicorn of the sea, herding offshore. The wolves must dream of the day when one of these leviathans will wash up on the beach.

On the east side of the island, walruses abound. Seals were also common. According to the weather station personnel, the wolves sometimes stalked the seals that lounged on the ice. Though I did not see this myself, I was told that the wolves worked in pairs, the first one pacing back and forth to distract the seals, the second sneaking up to pounce from behind. . . . Hunting Arctic hares [also] might be expected to lend itself to the pairs approach, but I never saw the wolves go after them in anything but a random, every-wolf-for-itself kind of way. . . .

The other major mammalian predator of Arctic hares is the Arctic fox, which ironically is smaller than its prey. These foxes are beautiful white animals that for some reason, probably competition, seem to be utterly despised by the wolves. Once, Midback spied a fox, quickly caught and killed it, and brought it back to the den as one of many trophy toys she gave the pups. . . .

Curiously, the wolves never seemed to eat foxes, though they ate almost anything else that moved. Their favorite prey species were the large grazing mammals, primarily musk oxen and caribou. One variety of the latter, the so-called Peary caribou, was especially delightful. These whitish, elfin creatures seemed to be characters straight from a fairy tale. They derive their name from the famous explorer, who along with other explorers almost wiped the species out by using it for food during expeditions. . . .

At the pinnacle of the Ellesmere food chain are the large predators: wolves, polar bears and humans—three occasionally competing species whose interactions are not always harmonious. . . . Polar bears . . . do roam through wolf country at times. A fight between a single wolf and a single bear would almost certainly favor the bear. Given even a small pack of wolves, though, the odds would change quickly. . . .

A few [wolves] are killed each year on Ellesmere, primarily by Inuit hungers who can sell the luxurious pelts for $300 apiece. . . . [But] wolves have more than people to worry about. For instance, a

host of parasites can enervate and sicken them. Wolves are also extremely vulnerable to injuries, and because they are so dependent on speed for hunting, a broken bone can be devastating. . . .

Not long before I left Ellesmere, I traveled to a remote section of the island where scientists had discovered the remains of a grove of giant redwood trees dating back some 50 million years. Numerous carbonized stumps marked the spots where trees once towered. Though the climate had certainly grown colder over the millennia, Ellesmere's position relative to the equator has changed very little. What fascinated the scientists was the question of how such trees could have survived, since they stood unshrouded in darkness for nearly half the year. Life somehow finds a way.

So does death. Not far away from these stumps, the scientists were also disinterring fossilized mollusk shells, the jaw of a giant lemur and teeth from a crocodile. If one is dealing with a long enough time frame, it seems that extinction is more the rule than the exception. I found myself wondering how soon it will be before all that remains of the wolf is a smattering of skulls covered by sand.

JIM BRANDENBURG, *White Wolf*

Jim Brandenburg has been photographing and writing about wolves for many years. He realized a dream when, in the mid-1980s on assignment for National Geographic, *he discovered a wolf pack on Ellesmere Island in the Canadian arctic. Never hunted, they were relatively unafraid of humans, and gave Brandenburg an unparalleled opportunity to document the daily lives of wild wolves. He spent several months shooting them in the course of several visits, and his resulting book,* White Wolf, *is a classic of wildlife photojournalism.*

ABOVE: *Rock ptarmigan chick, Ellesmere Island. Jim Brandenburg.* OPPOSITE: *The arctic fox, pure white against winter's snow, turns dark gray in summer. Jim Brandenburg.*

SOUTHWEST HIGHLANDS

Seen to the east from the Sonoran plateau that extends for miles in a gently sloping plain to the Rio Grande, the Sandia Mountains resemble a giant tortoise forever frozen in stone. This geological reptile rises ominously above the sere desert landscape dotted with dust green pinion, juniper, yellow-flowered chamisa, and the twisted spidery arms of cholla cactus.

For the Tewa Indian village of San Juan, eighty miles to the north, these mountains are called Oku Pin (Turtle Mountain). . . . At 6 A.M. on a day early in September, I'm the only hiker headed north on the Rincon Ridge section of the Piedra Lisa trail that leads up the northeast flanks of Oku Pin. Even this early, it is already beginning to get hot. I trace a route over a small sub-ridge toward the shelter of Juan Tabo Canyon, where a trickle of water flows through willows, elders, and granite boulders worn smooth by centuries of wind.

From my cool sanctuary I spy the barren heights of 8,000-foot Rincon Peak to the west extending in a bow that comprises the front leg of the ancient tortoise—Rincon Ridge—my goal for today's walk. I stare at fluted spires and walls of stone fired pink by morning sun. A buzz of insects and my rasping labored breath penetrate the silence as I once again begin my ascent.

Soon I am among giant Ponderosa pine and gambel oak reading signs of this mountain's life in limestone and shale escarpments deposited some 300 million years ago by an ancient Pennsylvanian sea. . . . After negotiating several switchbacks, at about 8,500 feet I make ridgetop among spindle fir. I gaze east to Mount Taylor, and fifty miles away see the looming basalt tower called El Cabezon ris-

Mexican wolf, Canis lupus baileyi, *with its distinctive face markings. Tom and Pat Leeson.*

ing 2,000 feet from the desert floor. I scan the dusty burnt umber plateau of the Rio Grande Valley broken by a thin green slash of meandering river. . . . Here I am content to consider a hawk as it darts in and out from spires and buttressed aretes, listening to my heart thump. I attend to that moment between inhalation and exhalation where stillness resides. . . .

Without warning, somewhere below a branch snaps. I whirl around. There on a bald flat a thousand feet above the creek a large gray wolf emerges from surrounding trees, eyes burning as he scans his territory. His pelage mottled dun, another smaller wolf emerges cautiously from surrounding trees. Finally a third wolf pads with nonchalance and ease into the gathering light. For a moment these three inspect this unprotected prominence and sniff the wind, noses held high, eyes slightly closed.

At some hidden signal a great jostling and bumping of wolf bodies ensues as the two latter wolves smile and touch noses with the first in an enthusiastic greeting full of wolf affection and good humor. With great dignity the first wolf breaks from his fellows. Lifting his leg, he urinates to mark this place with his scent. In imitation, his companions follow suit, lifting legs, micturating and scratching the earth once or twice. In an instant they are gone, vanished forever. . . .

Only in my imagination do wolves emerge from these mountains where once they roamed. The Mexican wolf, grizzly, pronghorn antelope, elk, and even the prairie dog disappeared from the Sandia Mountains long ago.

JAMES C. BURBANK, *Vanishing Lobo*

ISLE ROYALE WOODLANDS

Isle Royale [Michigan] has a growing season of about five months, May through September. The first flower of spring is the skunk cabbage, whose purple-striped spathe may be seen, even in late April, poking through holes in the ice of wet bottomlands. A few days of warming sun will bring out hepaticas on south slopes, clusters of bloom ranging from white to blue and rose. Marsh marigolds spring from the muck along watercourses. . . .

Summer comes with a rush after mid-June. It is a time of drying, toughening, massive plant growth, mosquitos, black flies, and big squashy toads in the trail dust. Among old-growth conifers there are resinous smells and a sultry midday quiet of which the hesitant semi-warble of the red-eyed vireo becomes a monotonous part. . . . High and out of view, the black-throated green warbler speaks eternally of "sweet, sweet, Susie!". . .

The blossoms of June become a set of fruit by July. Then we know whether the crop will be large or small. Some Juneberries are already ripe; many of them are borne near the ground because moose took all the twigs above last winter's snow line. . . . The fruits of July and August include a new crop of bearberries, wintergreen, bunchberry, currants, red elderberry, red-osier dogwood, squashberry, sarsaparilla, beadlily, baneberry, twisted-stalk, northern commandra, and many others. No doubt all of these are taken by birds and some by foxes, squirrels, and mice. . . .

During the growing season, at least part of the time, the sun has beamed its energizing rays over land and water. . . . In about 5 months energy has been stored that, for the most part, must operate the entire ecosystem during the rest of the year. . . . From October to May, most plants are largely or totally dormant, and animal life is living on seeds, fruits, and the vegetative parts of plants that grew and developed when they could. Some animals eat the plants directly: birds, woodmice, red squirrels, hares, muskrats, beavers, and moose. Higher in the pyramid of life, and fewer in number, are the secondary consumers, the animals that eat the animals that eat the plants: hawk, raven, weasel, mink, fox, and wolf.

DURWARD L. ALLEN, *Wolves of Minong*

Gray wolf, northern Montana woods. Erwin and Peggy Bauer/Bruce Coleman, Inc.

A CLOSER LOOK

▼▼▼▼▼▼

Wolves interact with their environment in countless small ways. The winds carry scents to them; the sound of breaking branches may lead them to a moose. The young wolf that stops to sniff a puffball daisy may get its nose tickled and sneeze, scattering seeds to the breeze. Packs tend to use grassy areas as summer nurseries for growing pups, in part because they harbor lots of mice, and the grasses they lie upon may also be chewed and swallowed as a purgative. The seed of yet another plant may lodge in a wolf's ear, permanently harming its equilibrium.

Young wolves' curiosity and verve leads them to make playthings of just about any inanimate object that can be chewed, chased, tugged on, or tossed around—a pine cone, a piece of birchbark or old hide, a deer antler or leg bone. Their curiosity about new substances and smells can also lead them into traps, unless a more experienced wolf warns them off.

Wolves use terrain details and vegetation to their advantage in hunting—stalking from cover, scouting from heights, chasing a deer out onto frozen lakes where it is more vulnerable, or towards an impassable windfall. To ease the work of traveling through deep snow, they often trot in a caribou's trail rather than break their own. And to avoid bothersome clouds of mosquitos, arctic wolves have learned to hang out on windy slopes or lingering snowfields where the air is colder and the insects less thick.

Even the wolf's final products link it to other lives in its world. Ravens, besides getting in on wolf kills, enjoy picking tidbits out of their scats. And a fascinating example of parasitism is a certain tapeworm that lives in moose organs. Ingested by wolves eating moose kills, it is eliminated with their droppings and transferred to vegetation, which is eaten by another moose, which in turn becomes infected—and thus more likely to be caught by wolves.

NEW TOYS

One day, Mech and I were near the den watching the mother wolf and her pups with our binoculars when we heard a commotion back at our camp. Looking back, we saw several of the pack members circling our tents. Discovering that we were not in them, the alpha male stuck his head inside a porthole window, grabbed a red nylon mummy-style sleeping bag and dragged it out. He and his buddies were about to tear it to shreds when Mech and I did the only thing we could think of to save our property—we started to bark.

Barking is a sign of alarm to wolves. Coming from so close to the den, our woofs and snorts had a predictable effect. The happy marauders instantly dropped the sleeping bag, their faces etched with alarm, and ran full speed to the den to make sure everything was okay. We, in turn, high-tailed it back to our camp, retrieved the sleeping bag and began strategizing as to what we might do to frustrate future incidents of lupine curiosity and imperialism.

JIM BRANDENBURG, *White Wolf*

SEEDS OF LEARNING

The black wolf stood by her first patch of newly opened dark-pink daisies, acquainting herself with them. She brushed her nose across them, raised her paw and touched them. Long afterward we were to glimpse other young wolves acquaint themselves in this way with newly opened flower patches.

A wolf's curiosity is impersonal. It goes beyond food and fear.

Lady patted her first puffball, sprang back and sneezed, then patted it again. She ran curiously to where I was picking and eating the first sour blueberries. I mashed a few, she licked them, watched attentively while I picked and gave her more. Then she picked and ate a few berries for herself. Wolves have to learn.

But those incidents had connection with food. Pure impersonal fascination with the unknown showed on the morning she first met ice. She stood examining the ice in her water pan, touching it with her paw. Even after I poured water over it, she reached her paw through the water and stroked that novel satin underneath.

LOIS CRISLER, *Arctic Wild*

ABOVE: *Gray wolf reflected in an autumnal stream. Jim Dutcher.* OPPOSITE: *Wolf pups, about four months old, explore some high ground in Canada. Jack Couffer/ Bruce Coleman, Inc.* LEFT: *Illustration of wolfbane, Aconitum species, also known as monkshood—a lovely but deadly European plant that got its name and fame as a poison bait for wolves. (One early writer described it as "Aconit that Killeth Woolfs.")*

FUR FOR A NEST

[Biologist] Robert Stephenson recalls one morning being out with Bob Ahgook, one of his Nunamiut friends, searching for a den. They were traversing a hillside when suddenly Ahgook stopped and pointed to a faint trail about four inches wide in some moss and lichen. By twisting his head to get the right angle of illumination and peering intently, Stephenson was able to make out a depression in the moss.

"Wolf trail," said Ahgook, scanning the slope above them. Suddenly a white female, who had been sleeping 150 feet up the slope, stood up and stared at them, then turned, quickly ascended an escarpment, and disappeared. In the silence that followed a bird landed on a rock near where the wolf had been, moved around a few moments, then flew away.

"She has a den up there, see that?" said Ahgook.

"See what?" asked Stephenson.

"Where that robin landed, picked up some wolf hairs, and flew away? That would be a good sleeping place, maybe very close to a den."

Stephenson recalled later that even though he had seen the bird it was so quick, so far away, he did not know it was a robin and would never have seen the wolf hairs in its beak. When they had climbed up to the spot it proved, indeed, to be a sleeping place. The female's den was a hundred feet away. Ahgook said as the wolf departed that he saw she had shed hair around her mammae, which meant she was very close to giving birth. . . .

BARRY LOPEZ, *Of Wolves and Men*

A PUP COMES OF AGE

Near where the wolves lay there was a heap of rotting wood. Melting snow had left little pools in cracks and dents that helped the process of decay. On this rich garden there grew spicy tufts of the velvet-stemmed collybia, the tangy early mushroom of springtime and dead wood. The sticky, reddish-yellow caps with their tawny margins and the firm, velvety stems arose from death but heralded new life and beauty. Attracted by the aroma of the collybia but surely immune to its true beauty were two spicebush swallowtails. Relatively rare so far west, these four-inch butterflies skidded low to the ground, changing from blue to green in iridescent waves of living light as the sun's intensity was filtered and changed by the foliage overhead. Softly coming to rest near the mushrooms, they had become the focal point of another's attention.

The thirteen-lined ground squirrel was nearly a foot long, although four to five inches of that length consisted of unimpressive tail. As the name implies, his body was marked with thirteen lines, yellowish-white alternating with tones of chestnut, the darker punctuated with white spots. . . . He was as beautiful as he was nervous: a shadow, a dart, a flicker, a spot of life as he stalked the swallowtails. His great oval eyes saw all within immediate range—but they had missed the larger scale.

And thus the wolf cub came closer, not only to the squirrel but to the knowledge that life was not to be easy. Here was food—prey—that had to be taken; and although being a wolf might be the grandest miracle of all, it was not necessarily enough. You had to be a skilled wolf to survive, not just a wolf. . . .

[T]he wolf cub's presence was quickly sensed. With a sharp little squeak and a sudden spring-like action, the squirrel leaped away, spun around and, on his hind legs, faced his foe. He was a burrower, not a climber, and without his burrow he would have to find another hiding place or stand his ground. He looked about. There were no hollow logs, no piles of stones, no mounds of forest debris. . . . No, it was there—in that glade where the sun fell in shafts and painted stripes on the ground—that the mature, lifewise, thirteen-lined ground squirrel must face the immature, clumsy cub. The outcome was by no means certain.

When the rodent cried out and inconveniently leaped away

from the spot where he could easily have been taken, the wolf cub, in surprise and confusion, stood up to his full height. Despite himself, as much as he wanted to be a wolf, the best he could do at first was cock his head to one side and whine. He had not faced such determination before, nor had he ever seen so small an animal rear up, face him, and scold so loudly. It was all rather confounding. . . .

[W]ithout regard for tactics that he would one day know and use as a matter of course, the wolf cub moved in on the ground squirrel. Stiff-legged, a little hesitant, somewhat intimidated by the constant flow of invective that was being heaped upon him in such shrill tones, Lobo began his approach. His first fateful mistake was in letting curiosity get the better of his kill-instinct: as Lobo pushed his snout forward to smell his foe, the ground squirrel, not at all interested in the fine distinction between this indignity and a fatal thrust, fastened himself to Lobo's upper lip and felt his teeth meet in the middle. With a yapping shriek, the wolf leaped backward, outraged, shaking his head and striking at his face with his paws. The ground squirrel lost his grip and hit the ground, rolled, righted himself, and again faced his foe on his hind legs, scolding furiously. . . .

Wary now, alert to the danger inherent here in the foe, Lobo began feinting in the classic manner of the wolf. First he would make a brief, short rush and then suddenly pull up short, leaving the adversary confounded and increasingly less certain of itself. . . . Finally, as Lobo made his thrust, the sense and caution of an animal who had already survived one hostile year gave out and the squirrel charged the wolf. Alert now to the teeth of rodents, Lobo sidestepped quickly, turned and brought his great paw down on the squirrel's back.

The little animal twisted within his own skin and cruelly lacerated the cub's right front paw, causing more blood to flow.

The two foes quickly resumed their opposing positions, the ground squirrel on his hind legs, dancing to and fro, the wolf cub circling around him, haunch high, forelegs to the ground. Now, however, the cub was forced to stop from time to time to lick his damaged right front paw. During one such hesitant moment, the rodent grasped an opportunity—returning to his four feet, he streaked past the wolf up the rise toward some thicker wood. . . .

OPPOSITE: *"Flight of the Shaman," by Jessie Oonark, 1970. The artist was a member of the Baker Lake community, Northwest Territories.* BELOW: *Wolf pup in a standoff with a skunk. Ernest Wilkinson/Animals Animals.*

When the rodent turned his back on the cub, however, he had already made his fatal mistake. Even with his injured paw, the cub was fast enough. In two bounds, still awkward and seemingly more frisky than deadly, he overtook the squirrel. With the advantage of coming up from behind his foe, away from those slashing incisors, he quickly closed his teeth, felt the satisfaction of penetrating living flesh, and held the dead squirrel in his teeth by the time they met in the middle. A single well-placed snap had crushed out its life and made the wolf cub the victor. A career was launched there that day.

ROGER CARAS, *The Custer Wolf*

DEN DETAILS

Located well away from the rocky bed of St. George Creek in a hanging treeless meadow . . . dug by foxes during some long-past time, the den was set twelve feet deep beneath the meadow's skin of powdery, acid soil. Slanting downward for almost eight feet through glacial debris, it turned at right angles to the main passageway before ending abruptly in a cul-de-sac only slightly larger than the small wolf. The den had no other entrances or exits. The soil surrounding the den chamber itself consisted of powdered rock fines, and because of its elevation and origin, was free of permafrost. As such, it was dry, a fact which long ago made the site acceptable to those who used it.

The floor of the den was littered with use-worn pebbles and small sticks, but was devoid of bones and other debris. It was a place of total darkness, to be used by scent and feel alone. . . .

Above ground, the den's mouth was hidden among the nodding tufts of wiry sedges and porous slab rock that covered the entire dome, and was nearly invisible.

JAMES GREINER, *The Red Snow*

ABOVE: *Pups crawl out the back door of the Ellesmere Island den; most have only one entrance. Jim Brandenburg.*
OPPOSITE: *The yearling male Scruffy and his young charges near the den's main entrance. Jim Brandenburg.*

DISCOVERING A DEN

In den hunting, one must turn detective and use every clue available. Unfortunately some of the clues may only serve to give one a false notion of the location. Seeing wolves, if one is fortunate enough to see them, may be suggestive. In the morning, wolf travel is likely to be in the direction of the den, and in the evening away from it. But if the wolf happens to be twenty miles from home when seen, the observation is of little use and may be misleading. Much wolf travel is miscellaneous and irregular, and one can easily get erroneous notions and become more and more puzzled and confused. Seeing a wolf resting somewhere is especially suggestive, for it may be lying at the den. Tracks are always helpful.

I was much interested in a bit of woodcraft that an Indian from the upper Tanana River used in finding dens. He said that at first when he hunted for wolf dens he did not know where to hunt, but in time he learned more about animals and now knew where to look. . . . Once, in winter, he saw spruces barked by porcupines. The next spring, when he and his brother were searching for wolf dens, he returned and, pointing to the porcupine sign on the trees, said to his brother, "Probably a den over there." They went to the porcupine barking he had seen in winter, and there was a wolf den as he had suspected. His reasoning: he knew that the porcupine that barked the trees had to have a shelter and thought that maybe the shelter was a wolf den.

This bit of ecology fitted into my own experience, for I found a wolf den that a porcupine had used in winter and many willows nearby that the porcupine had barked. . . .

After a fall of snow about the middle of May, I saw wolf tracks on the broad gravel bar of East Fork River directly in front of the little log cabin in which I was camped. The tracks led both up and down the river. Since there was no game upstream at the time to attract the wolves, it appeared that some other interest, which I hoped was a den, accounted for the movement that way. I followed the tracks for a mile or more to a point where they climbed a bluff bordering the river bar, and there I surprised myself and a black wolf, a male. He ran off about a quarter of a mile into a ravine and howled and barked at intervals. Then, following tracks going out to the point of the bluff, I found the den. As I stood four or five yards from the entrance, the female furtively pushed her head out of the burrow, then, on seeing me, withdrew. But in a moment she came out with a rush and galloped part way down the slope, where she stopped a moment to bark. She loped away and joined the male, and both parents howled and barked from the nearby ravine until I left.

ADOLPH MURIE, *A Naturalist in Alaska*

PREDATOR AND PREY

▼▼▼▼▼▼

Ecologically speaking, the wolf is one of the "animals that eat the animals that eat the plants"—more succinctly, a predator, shaped over eons for its role at the top of the food chain. The wolf and the large herbivores it eats are an example of "coevolution," each species changing and improving in response to advances in the other that give it an edge.

An axiom of natural selection is that predators improve the gene pool of prey species by taking the weak, the old, the sick, and the too-numerous young—not because it's the "right" thing to do, but because they are the easiest to catch. This is mostly true, though if wolves can bring down an animal in its prime, they will. Another time-honored belief is that wolves are born knowing what is prey, but observations do not always bear this out. Lois Crisler's young wolves, for example, acted fearful of caribou on first sight.

Many have noticed that, at a certain point in the encounter between predator and prey, there is a moment of eye contact, a look that seems to pass between them. Some have interpreted it as a moment of decision, the prey animal accepting its fate. Barry Lopez calls this the "conversation of death" and compares it with the Native American concept of an animal "giving" itself to the hunter—a gesture for which it is honored and thanked. This is a speculative realm, but Native hunters may have come to such beliefs in part from watching how prey animals, still capable of defending themselves, instead surrender to wolves.

What is a wolf's prey? Large hoofed mammals are the mainstay, and wolves need such prey to survive

in the long term. In various parts of North America, the chief species may be deer (white-tailed or mule deer), caribou, elk, or moose; less often mountain sheep (bighorn and Dall sheep) and goats. In historic times, buffalo were major wolf prey until they were wiped out by settlers; the speedy pronghorn were occasionally taken.

Without doubt, wolves also kill livestock. As David Mech says tersely, "Where man has substituted his domestic animals for wild ones, wolves have made a similar substitution in their diet." The key factor is opportunity: where deer and other wild prey are thinned by habitat loss and human hunting, and livestock are introduced, wolves will take the easy option. This, in essence, is the reason for the wolf's eradication from much of its former range. Even so, wolves do not kill livestock at every opportunity; many seem not to recognize domestic animals as prey.

Wolves can and do subsist partly on smaller prey, especially in summer: beaver, squirrels, mice and other rodents, hares, mink, muskrat, birds, fish, lizards, snakes, even insects and worms can figure in their diet. Young wolves hone their skills on small prey before graduating to the full-scale hunt.

But large ungulates are what they were made for. As it happens, deer and their relations are also favored targets of human sport hunters. The roots of wolf biology lie in early attempts to determine the impact of wolf predation on game animals, and hunting interests still influence research being done today. The "balance of predator *(continued page 108)*

OPPOSITE: Kills freeze quickly in the northern winter and may be used for several weeks. Jim Brandenburg. ABOVE: "Timber Run," painting by Tim Jessell, 1991.

HUNTING SONG OF THE SEEONEE PACK
▼▼▼▼▼▼

As the dawn was breaking the Sambhur belled
    Once, twice, and again!
And a doe leaped up, and a doe leaped up
From the pond in the wood where the wild deer sup.
This I, scouting alone, beheld,
    Once, twice, and again!

As the dawn was breaking the Sambhur belled
    Once, twice, and again!
And a wolf stole back, and a wolf stole back

To carry the word to the waiting pack,
And we sought and we found and we bayed on his track
    Once, twice, and again!

As the dawn was breaking the Wolf Pack yelled
    Once, twice, and again!
Feet in the jungle that leave no mark!
Eyes that can see in the dark—in the dark!
Tongue—give tongue to it! Hark! O hark!
    Once, twice, and again!

RUDYARD KIPLING, *The Jungle Book*

and prey" is another subject of mythmaking: it was once assumed that wolves simply decimated game herds, given the chance, and must therefore be expunged. Later game management studies fostered the idea that predators and prey always remain in perfect balance.

The reality seems to be that, in some places, at some times, wolf predation does lower game populations—often in combination with hard winters and overgrazing by populations that grew too large in the absence of predators or hunting. It's hard to know how things would work out in a system entirely unaltered by man, because so few exist. Among the things we do know is that predator-prey cycles must be tracked over many years, because so many variables are involved—and that where human "needs" include sport hunting and livestock raising, there will be pressure to control wolves.

Rocky Mountain goats, a nanny and her kid. Superb rock climbers and well-armed with sharp horns, adult mountain goats rarely become wolf prey, though young are sometimes taken at lower elevations in their range. David C. Fritts/Animals Animals.

ESKIMO CREATION TALE

In the beginning there was a Woman and a Man, and nothing else walked or swam or flew in the world until one day the Woman dug a great hole in the ground and began fishing in it. One by one she pulled out all the animals, and the last one she pulled out of the hole was the caribou. Then Kaila, who is the God of the Sky, told the woman the caribou was the greatest gift of all, for the caribou would be the sustenance of man.

The Woman set the caribou free and ordered it to go out over the land and multiply, and the caribou did as the Woman said; and in time the land was filled with caribou, so the sons of the Woman hunted well, and they were fed and clothed and had good skin tents to live in, all from the caribou.

The sons of the Woman hunted only the big, fat caribou, for they had no wish to kill the weak and the small and the sick, since these were no good to eat, nor were their skins much good. And, after a time, it happened that the sick and the weak came to outnumber the fat and the strong, and when the sons saw this they were dismayed and they complained to the Woman.

Then the Woman made magic and spoke to Kaila and said: "Your work is no good, for the caribou grow weak and sick, and if we eat them we must grow weak and sick also."

Kaila heard, and he said, "My work is good. I shall tell Amorak [the spirit of the wolf], and he shall tell his children, and they will eat the sick and the weak and the small caribou, so that the land will be left for the fat and the good ones."

And this is what happened, and this is why the caribou and the wolf are one; for the caribou feeds the wolf, but it is the wolf who keeps the caribou strong.

As told to FARLEY MOWAT, *Never Cry Wolf*

THE ADVANTAGE OF SURPRISE

Downslope, and visible only because of slight head movements, were several sets of dark antlers above the contour of the clearing. The black wagged his tail slowly, its tip brushing his mate's nose. She edged closer to his side. The rain had stopped during their slow approach to their final positions among the bog tufts below.

One of the caribou, a gaunt cow among several that occupied the clearing's upper half, stood slowly to shake the rain from her ash-colored back. . . . Seemingly satisfied, the old cow belched deeply, then stood staring downslope into the darkness of the hillside, blissfully unaware of the presence of the two wolves that had now closed the distance between them to less than fifty yards. . . .

The first weak light of false dawn was filtering through the overcast as the big black felt the wind with his broad nose one last time. Then he bunched his powerful hind legs under his belly and hitched his body forward. The coolness that ran along the side of his muzzle was an almost undefined reminder that the air currents on the slope still favored his position. Now, however, the time for watching was over, and with a quick

From the film production of Never Cry Wolf. *Photo © The Walt Disney Company.*

glance over his shoulder at his mate, he launched himself from concealment.

Both wolves erupted from their vantage point running flat to the ground, tails held low, and at full speed. Little sound attended the charge as they hurtled downslope into the caribou. During the first fleeting seconds, the gray bitch veered away at a slight angle, her fifteen-foot leaps eating up the distance between her and the now lunging caribou. Both gravity and surprise were allies of the wolves, and placed the caribou at a critical disadvantage.

The small tundra clearing became a scene of instant bedlam. Within the space of the wolves' first appearance, a chaos of blurred movement had erupted, punctuated by the sounds of clicking hooves, wheezing grunts, and the tearing of wet moss and willow roots as blunt hooves splayed and slashed in the panicked frenzy of attempted escape.

A fleeing calf, its nose held high, bleated in terror as the momentum of the gray bitch's final vaulting leap carried her past the floundering animal, causing the old wolf to miss her best opportunity at a quick kill. . . . The black wolf was luckier. In full stride, he launched his own leap while still ten feet away from a barren cow that had, like the calf, hesitated almost imperceptibly to change direction. The same maneuver that spared the calf spelled doom for the cow as the 140-pound wolf crashed into her rib cage just behind her shoulder. The collision caused her to pitch sideways and stumble.

In a blur of motion too fast to see, the black switched direction, his jaws clamping shut over the cow's muzzle, enveloping it in his mouth. Then, using his bulk and strength as a lever, the big wolf dragged the hapless cow to a stop, forcing her head downward into the soft moss. . . .

Having missed in her own first lunge, the gray bitch cut her pursuit short, and two long bounds carried her to her mate's side. Without pause, she ran her own muzzle beneath the cow's neck where she took a firm grip on its throat. . . . Closing powerfully, the gray bitch felt the brittle cartilage of the caribou's windpipe collapse. Minutes later, the cow's eyes rolled and her legs stiffened spasmodically as death came by suffocation.

JAMES GREINER, *The Red Snow*

THE WOLVES AND THE DEER

The Wolves had a feast on a prairie at the mouth of Skeena river. They invited the chiefs of the Deer to the feast. The Deer who had been called came. Then they sat down on the prairie face to face with the Wolves. The Wolves said to the Deer, "You on the opposite side, begin to laugh." But the Deer did not agree. They said, "You shall laugh first." The Wolves replied, "Now we will laugh. Ha, ha, ha, ha, ha! Now you must laugh, you on the other side." Then the Deer laughed:

"M, m, m, m, m! Now you laugh again, Wolves." Then the Wolves laughed again: "Ha, ha, ha, ha, ha!" Now the Deer were afraid when they saw the large teeth of the Wolves.

The Wolves said, "Now, you on the other side, you shall laugh again. Don't keep your mouths closed when you are laughing. Nobody laughs like that. You must open your mouths as far as possible when you are laughing. Now do so. Try as hard as you can. Don't be afraid to open your mouths." Thus spoke the Wolves. "Now laugh." Then the Deer laughed again: "Ha, ha, ha, ha, ha!" They opened their mouths wide. They had no teeth. When the Wolves saw that they had no teeth they attacked them, and they bit them all over. Then they devoured the Deer. Only a few of the Deer succeeded in escaping. For this reason the Deer are afraid of the Wolves.

Tsimshian tribal story

ONE CHASE AMONG MANY

Wolf watchers have sometimes constructed a scene of wolves encountering prey from tracks left in the snow, as in this account of an unsuccessful chase.

Sun struck the wolves as they lay in the snow hollow beneath a jack pine's sagging branches. The smoke-colored female opened one eye, blinked, then opened the other. Slowly she raised her head and sniffed the still air. She yawned hugely, then rose and stretched each leg in turn. She was hungry.

There was a flicker of motion on the shore of the lake below. The female froze as a deer walked out onto the lake. Perhaps it was only a change in her breathing that wakened the male, but it was as though an electric current had passed through the snow. His eyes snapped open, his nostrils quivered, and he drew his legs beneath him. The deer stopped and looked back over its shoulder as another deer tiptoed out of the forest. Haltingly the pair turned to walk along the shore toward the waiting wolves. When they were thirty yards away, the female leaped forward. In four strides she was at top speed, back flexing, rear legs reaching past the front as they stretched, grabbed, and whipped the snow into a mist that showered the male as he slowly overtook her. . . .

The deer didn't hesitate; by the time the female had completed her first stride, they were bounding for the trees. They reached the forest edge in five bounds, while the wolves took eight. The snow was deep in the forest, deep enough to cover the logs and rocks that the deer leaped over with ease, leaving a trail of elongated craters. The male could not quite leap from one crater to the next; after each bound he floundered in chest-high snow. The sounds of the deer grew fainter as he lunged, but their scent hung in the air.

The female took the lead. Her mate had broken trail, so she was still strong, and they soon closed in on their quarry. The wolves burst into a clearing. Each lunge was now a separate effort. One of the deer stood on the other side, stretching its neck to browse.

Rested, the deer bounced away, still chewing its mouthful of spruce tips. Lurching to a halt, the wolves stood panting, watching with unblinking eyes as its tail wig-wagged away into the trees.

ROGER PETERS, *Dance of the Wolves*

OPPOSITE: Hopi kachina figures representing deer (left) and wolf (right). Photo by Jerry Jacka. ABOVE: White-tailed deer three bucks on alert. Len Rue, Jr./Animals Animals.

Nature does not care whether the hunter slay the beast or the beast the hunter. She will make good compost of them both, and her ends are prospered whichever succeeds.

JOHN BURROUGHS

Photographer Jim Brandenburg and biologist David Mech got a close-up look at the Ellesmere Island pack hunting musk oxen. The great beasts can usually hold off attacking wolves as long as they stay in a defensive circle, with the calves inside. But if they break and run, as in this case, the wolves have a good chance of bringing down a calf. Here the alpha male, Buster, is at his quarry's heels. Another wolf will grasp the calf's nose and then several gather to finish the kill.
Jim Brandenburg.

I do not think it is possible to truly understand even one leg muscle of one elk in the absence of wolves. Not a single leap of a single deer, nor any traverse of any mountain goat across a winterbound cliff wall. The size and endurance of hoofed beasts on this continent; their speed, coordination, and quicksilver reactions; their social structure and communication abilities—wolves sang these things into their present form.

DOUGLAS CHADWICK, *The Kingdom*

THIS PAGE: *Agility, experience, and persistence come into play when a wolf encounters the badger. With its impressive set of teeth and jaws, this large, feisty rodent can hold off a single wolf for a long time, if it doesn't turn its back. Tom Brakefield.* OPPOSITE: *"White Wolves Attacking a Buffalo," by George Catlin, 1832-1833.*

THE HEAVEN OF ANIMALS
▼▼▼▼▼▼

Here they are. The soft eyes open.
If they have lived in a wood
It is a wood.
If they have lived on plains
It is grass rolling
Under their feet forever.

Having no souls, they have come,
Anyway, beyond their knowing.
Their instincts wholly bloom
And they rise.
The soft eyes open.

To match them, the landscape flowers,
Outdoing, desperately
Outdoing what is required:
The richest wood,
The deepest field.

For some of these,
It could not be the place
It is, without blood.
These hunt, as they have done,
But with claws and teeth grown perfect,

More deadly than they can believe.
They stalk more silently,
And crouch on the limbs of trees,
And their descent
Upon the bright backs of their prey

Make take years
In a sovereign floating of joy.
And those that are hunted
Know this as their life,
Their reward: to walk

Under such trees in full knowledge
Of what is in glory above them,
And to feel no fear,
But acceptance, compliance.
Fulfilling themselves without pain

At the cycle's center,
They tremble, they walk
Under the tree.
They fall, they are torn,
They rise, they walk again.

JAMES DICKEY

115

FELLOW CREATURES

▼▼▼▼▼

Although at one time or another wolves have probably killed and eaten "every kind of backboned animal that lives in [their] range," as David Mech says, many of the creatures they share space with are not really prey but cohabitants.

Bears—black, grizzly, or polar—overlap with wolves in many places. While the two animals do not directly compete for prey, they do quarrel over the right to feed at existing kills, and sometimes bears invade a pack's denning area, drawing a spirited response. The outcome of such meetings—depending on the number of wolves present and the age of the parties involved—is usually that one or the other is driven off. Only an unwary wolf fails to dodge away from a bear's lunge.

Coyotes, though close relations, are not warmly treated by wolves—except in the former range of the red wolf, where the two crossbred (this does not otherwise happen). The more adaptable coyote has replaced the wolf throughout the eastern and southwestern states.

Foxes and wolves have no mutual fondness, but they do trade favors: wolves often appropriating fox dens and foxes raiding wolf food caches—a trick they seem especially clever at. Wolverines, minks, and other small carnivores will sneak in for a few bites from a wolf kill when the pack is away; the strong and resourceful wolverine may even try to sever and make off with a hefty haunch. Lynx, the beautiful and secretive cats of the north, have a passionate antipathy to wolves, described by Jack London in a memorable sequence from *White Fang;* they will take each other's young at times. The traditional dog-versus-cat relationship seems to prevail equally in the wild: Lois Crisler's captive wolves in Colorado once kept an angry mountain lion treed for the better part of a day.

Wolf kills provide winter forage for the gamut of northern meat-eaters, including a number of birds. Of these, the wolf's most notable associate is the raven. Both Native and scientific watchers have observed raven flocks attending wolf kills, feeding at carcasses, and in some cases apparently cluing wolves to the whereabouts of prey. These two social creatures also seem to have invented their own game to while away the down times. A raven will land a few feet from a resting wolf and wait, or waddle closer, or dive and pester it—then flap out of range as the wolf leaps. The birds almost always win, but both seem to enjoy it.

LEFT: Canada lynx pads across the snow, Montana. Daniel J. Cox/Natural Exposures. OPPOSITE: Grizzly bear (Ursus arctos) *standing in scrub willow, Alaska. Victoria McCormick/Animals Animals.*

bounded off an old kill as the wolves arrived. The fox was practically shaken to pieces, as is usual.

This shaking of medium-size animals by big carnivores has a practical purpose. Not only is it damaging to the victim, but it prevents the attacked animal from doubling back and inflicting wounds on the head of its assailant. A small dog shakes a rat for the same reason.

In some chases the fox has an advantage; it can sail away over soft snow at times when the wolves are floundering. Rolf saw a chase abandoned after only 75 yards on 28 January 1975. On 2 February at the east end Rolf and Don saw part of the east pack in hot pursuit of a fox across Hidden Lake. But when another group of the pack appeared, the chase was forgotten in favor of a greeting ceremony. . . .

We have two records of foxes probably eaten by wolves, although the evidence is circumstantial. In another case, the pack of 10 killed a fox on Malone Bay, and Rolf and Don collected the carcass. A day later they saw a trailing wolf come along and carefully investigate the bloody snow. Before the plane left the loner was seen to roll in the spot three times. Evidently there is something about a fox. . . .

DURWARD L. ALLEN, *Wolves of Minong*

WOLVES AND FOXES

We think of the fox as a "follower" of the wolf because the wolf is so obviously a winter provider. Seldom do we locate a moose carcass that is not, sooner or later, visited by foxes. A kill site seems to be a zone of relative tolerance among local foxes, and 3 to 5 can often be counted at once. The most anyone ever saw was 10.

Wolves have only a casual interest in foxes. It is sometimes observed that a couple of wolves using a kill will take no notice of a fox or two that will be curled up nearby, day after day, awaiting a chance to feed. When wolves are hunting, the chance flushing of a fox is likely to mean a sudden sporting chase and a kill. In 1960 Dave and Don saw the big pack snatch up a fox that

ABOVE: Illustration by Fritz Eichenberg from the old tale of Reynard and Isengrim. In stories dating back to the twelfth century, Reynard the fox (representing a clever peasant hero) and Isengrim the wolf (the dull-witted nobles in this allegory) carry on a feud in which Isengrim is constantly duped by the tricky Reynard. RIGHT: Red fox, the most common North American species. Steven T. Krasemann/Peter Arnold, Inc.

WOLVERINE WAYS

It was our fate in Alaska to deal most with the animals we had least expected even to see—grizzlies, wolves, now wolverines. We had had a few priceless glimpses of wolverines in the wilds—a wolverine with caribou, a wolverine braving Cris, even a set-to between a wolf and a wolverine, a strangely temperate affair, for the wolf had used not fangs and fury but fast footwork to head off the wolverine from her den.

[The Crislers arranged with some Eskimos to receive and care for a trapped wolverine, so they could observe and photograph it until its wounds healed enough to be released. They were awed by the efforts it made to escape from the sturdy pen they built, her husband commenting:]

"He uses his whole body as prize and wedge. Makes you think of a bee when it's excited and stinging you; it just jumps on you and doubles all up. He tried to pull a rock and he strains on it like a man, till his body quivers. He works with his whole body—teeth, claws, chest, head. He uses his whole body as a lever or pry. . . . He's not intelligent like the wolves, but he's so aggressive and determined."

"Brave and strong and busy," said the old Eskimo wolverine song. Every word was confirmed. [Friends of ours] had seen a wolverine perform a nearly incredible feat: it dragged off a moose ham over its shoulder. We did not doubt it.

LOIS CRISLER, *Arctic Wild*

RENARD THE BOTANIST

Stanley Young relates "an interesting legend" (probably among Native Americans, though he doesn't specify) about foxes using the squill plant or sea onion *(Urginea maritima)* as a protective measure against wolves. "It was believed that if a wolf tread upon the flower of the squill, it became torpid in time and could not bend its head back. Hence, the fox, to protect itself in wolf country, would strew the squill flowers in the wolf's runway to produce the desired effect." Begging the question of the fox's intellect, Young notes that certain Native Americans used the pulverized bulbs of this same plant to induce a toxic swoon in fish, which then floated to the surface to be easily caught.

The harmony inhabiting all living things is what attracts our interest, and it would be utterly unscientific, if not downright dishonest, to deny this. A strictly objective description or illustration of an animal or plant departs from the truth in one crucial respect if the beauty of the living organism itself is not made evident.

KONRAD LORENZ, *The Year of the Graylag Goose*

Above: This wolverine on a frozen river in Montana wears the defiant expression typical of its kind. Daniel J. Cox/Natural Exposures

GRIZZLY EVENTS

As a rule, grizzlies and wolves occupy the same range without taking much notice of each other, but not infrequently the grizzlies discover wolf kills and unhesitatingly dispossess the wolf and assume ownership. The loss is usually not a serious matter to the wolves, for if food is scarce the kills will generally be consumed before the bears find them. In the relationship existing between the two species, the wolves are the losers and the meat-hungry bears are the gainers.

When the bears take possession of a kill in the presence of wolves, they are much harassed, but they are so powerful that the wolves must be careful to avoid their strong arms. The wolves must confine their attack to quick nips from the rear. But the bears are alert, and usually the wolves must jump away before they come near enough for even a nip.

At the East Fork wolf den were observed two bear-and-wolf encounters. The first one, which took place on June 5, I did not see, but it was reported to me by Harold Herning. A female grizzly with three lusty two-year-old cubs approached the den from downwind. They lifted their muzzles as they sniffed the enticing smell of meat, and advanced expectantly. They were not noticed until they were

almost at the den, when the four adult wolves that were at home dashed out at them, attacking from all sides. The darkest cub seemed to enjoy the fight, for he would dash at the wolves with great vigor and was sometimes off by himself, waging a lone battle. (On later occasions I noticed that this cub was particularly aggressive when attacked by wolves.) The four bears remained at the den for about an hour, feeding on meat scraps and uncovering meat the wolves had buried. During all this time, the bears were under attack. When the pillaging was complete, the bears moved up the slope.

ADOLPH MURIE, *A Naturalist in Alaska*

LEFT: *Wolves sometimes fish for themselves but often wait to steal scraps from the better-equipped grizzly. Katmai National Park, Alaska. Johnny Johnson/DRK Photo.* ABOVE: *"Bear and Wolf," by Patrick Amos, 1992.*

THE BANQUET TABLE

As the first day slipped by, the impulse to feed excessively quickly passed, and the wolves rested more, always within a short distance of the carcass, which by now bore little resemblance to its original shape and size. As some of the pack dozed in the weak warmth during the brief days that followed, other members left the river to hunt on their own. The black and his buff son were, as a result, absent for periods of up to a half day. The pack's stay at the kill was a short one despite the hunger each wolf had brought to the Tatlanika, and as the pack moved on, others moved in to gain their expected share of what remained. Ravens, Canada jays, chickadees, several short-tailed weasels, and a solitary, orange-throated pine marten fed while the pack dozed or was absent. The marten, a weasel-like tree dweller, was drawn to the carcass more by simple curiosity than were the others, and his feeding was a game as he dodged the rushes of the pups. Boldest of all were the white-collared Canada, or gray, jays, and they often fed wing to shoulder with the wolves, who ignored their presence.

The fastidious vixen had quickly become a regular at the kill. She possessed the uncanny ability to determine when the wolves were well fed, and at such times she advanced cautiously to snap up a small frozen chunk of meat and then retreat quickly with it to the willows that bordered the spruce at the bar's edge. On several occasions, the gray bitch's pups chased her, but such pursuits were a game as they were with the dark-furred marten. Mostly the pups tolerated the fox, as did the rest of the wolves.

JAMES GREINER, *The Red Snow*

Mountain lions (Felis concolor) *are often treed by wolves. Jim Dutcher.*

WOLF AND LION

[In Pueblo mythology] Wolf and Mountain Lion were considered to be companions and . . . they visited each other constantly and talked about hunting. Wolf was thought to make his kills rather directly and easily. Mountain Lion could not run as swiftly, and did not kill as many as Wolf. He sang a song and sprang on his prey, while Wolf pursued his quarry and never gave up the chase.

In one story, Mountain Lion and Wolf held a contest to see who was the greater hunter. Wolf chased some deer without fatigue, but Mountain Lion hid himself and waited until the deer that Wolf was chasing passed his hiding place. Then he sprang out and quickly dispatched the deer. This happened several times and Wolf was left to gnaw the bones and other leavings of Lion's kills. [It may be that] Wolf's lesser position in Pueblo mythology was due to wolves that could often be observed cleaning up lion kills.

JAMES C. BURBANK, *Vanishing Lobo*

TXAMSEM AND THE WOLVES

In the myths of the Tsimshian, a people of south coastal Alaska, Raven (whose name is Txamsem) is a greedy trickster who pursues an epic series of adventures, like Coyote in southwestern tales. One day as he is wandering in the woods, hungry and lonely, he comes upon the house of Chief Wolf and his people, who welcome him and feed him for several days on roasted dried salmon, mountain goat, venison, bear, geese, and so on. They even fix him a bag of provisions when he leaves for his next adventure, in which he is wounded in the belly by Chief Grouse. Txamsem returns to the wolves, who sniff his bloody wound with interest but listen sympathetically to his tale and continue to give him rich meat and fat. Not content with this generosity, Txamsem follows some young wolves on a hunt and conceals their kill under hemlock branches, scheming to keep it for himself. When found out, he claims to have been just guarding it from robbers—but at their next feast, the wolves do not speak to him.

Adapted from FRANZ BOAS,
Tsimshian Mythology

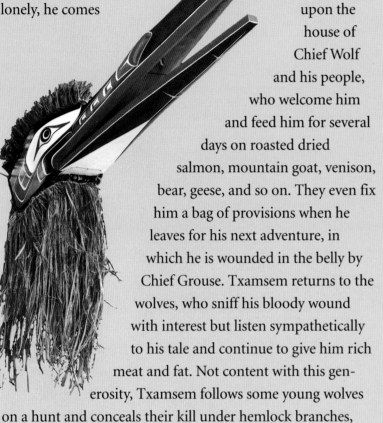

"Hamatsa Raven," painted mask by Kwakiutl artist Bruce Alfred. Photo by Trevor Mills.

RAVEN PLAY

Trigger stood down on the river, his back toward the bank. He was wagging his tail and watching a raven hopping around him. Finally, it hopped right across in front of his nose. Four more ravens joined it, alighting near the wolf. They were initiating the young wolf into the fraternity of the lonely tundra. He stood and turned and stepped gently among them, wagging his tail. When Lady ran down from the kill she was rougher and the ravens flew up. . . .

Many a time after this we saw wolves and ravens fraternize. Why had the ravens—which, according to Dr. Konrad Lorenz, have the highest mental development of all birds—chosen to teach friendliness to the wolves? Of course the wolves helped them. Both are predators or scavengers. Wolves make kills; ravens eat on them. And it is remotely possible that ravens help wolves. Circling over a dead caribou they could reveal its location.

But to us it looked as if the ravens and wolves just liked each other's company; it pleased them. Maybe it entertained them. "Maybe they get lonesome," said Cris. It is lonely on the big tundra. A fabulous incident is told by Mrs. Olaus Murie. A raven liked to nestle in the box with her Siberian wolfhound and puppies; it was smothered accidentally.

LOIS CRISLER, *Arctic Wild*

SCOUTS AND SCAVENGERS

We had a flock of seven ravens that year, large, coal-black birds that arrived daily between 4:00 and 4:30 P.M. to spend about half an hour talking to each other and to our rangy cubs.

[One] afternoon while I was socializing with Tundra and Taiga, they turned away from me and ran to the north end of the pen, their noses raised and their ears pricked forward as they detected an influence hidden from my senses. . . . After some moments of fruitless vigil, I was about to turn away and leave the enclosure when I heard the faint cawing of ravens. Now Taiga whined softly and Tundra pawed at the fence wire. The raucous calls grew louder but were still distant, and the sky remained empty. I waited, alternately watching the wolves and the sky; presently I saw the first raven as it flapped over the trees. It was followed by the other six.

As the birds neared the enclosure, they started to call more frequently. The wolves began to dance, whining to each other and rising on their hind legs, one sometimes climbing on the other so that the passenger's back legs were off the ground and its front legs had to move at twice the normal rate to keep up with the haphazard pacing of its companion. This behavior always denoted excitement. . . .

The wolves separated when the ravens dropped below the tree-tops and approached us. Now the cubs sat on their haunches and watched the birds until they flew over our heads in disorderly formation, losing height rapidly just before they alighted on nearby trees. Tundra and Taiga trotted toward the landing area, arriving there just as the ravens started to call, at which the young wolves began to howl rather discordantly and to pace back and forth.

A wolf keeps a wary eye on ravens gathering at a kill, northern Minnesota. Jim Brandenburg.

I was no stranger to such interspecies communion, having learned . . . that ravens could lead me to wolf kills, sometimes after the hunters had eaten and left the scene, on other occasions while the wolves were actually feeding. The first time this happened, I was surprised to see that the birds were sharing the meat with the hunters and were tolerated by the adult wolves, but charged by the untutored yearlings, who were eventually to learn that their tactics were never rewarded by success. Quite the contrary! Ravens are hardy, daring, and highly intelligent birds, always ready to steal anything edible that is not actually inside the mouth of a predator. . . . Beyond this, as I have observed a number of times, ravens appear to act as scouts for wolves by congregating near prey animals, calling loudly and excitedly. It may be that the birds have learned that there are times when an old or injured deer or moose is dying, or has already died, and will thus offer them a sumptuous meal; or it may be that the birds are deliberately advertising the presence of prey in the hope that the wolves will respond and make a kill, after which the ravens drop down from the trees to take their share. . . .

Sooner or later, all wolves learn to accept the ravens when these are sharing a kill, but during their first year of life, the young hunters acquire wisdom the hard way after the wily birds have stolen many choice morsels from them.

R. D. LAWRENCE, *In Praise of Wolves*

MYSTERIES OF WOLF ECOLOGY

▼▼▼▼▼▼

In no single place have the biology, habits, and ecological role of wolves been so intensively studied as on Isle Royale, Michigan, an island near the upper end of Lake Superior and since 1940 a national park. The native moose herd on Isle Royale (Minong to the Ojibwas) was world-famous and protected, but suffered heavy losses in the 1930s due to overpopulation and overbrowsing. Then—probably in the severe February of 1949—a few wolves found their way across the lake ice from the Ontario shore and started a breeding pack on Isle Royale, setting in motion the longest ongoing study of predator-prey relationships ever conducted. Its director was Durward Allen, and his research team included several later notables of wolf biology: David Mech and Rolf Peterson. Allen's Wolves of Minong *remains a readable classic, with surprisingly modest conclusions about what "wolf truths" science is capable of determining.*

A main problem of scientific studies in natural communities is that important changes can sometimes be witnessed only at long intervals. They happen under conditions that represent a continuum of variations; they involve causes that are unknown or even unsuspected. Our only approach in appraising such things is to observe and record what we see. As records accumulate, they reveal aspects that are repeated or which seem to conform to some pattern.

A weakness of ecological research in its first 50 years has been the short-term approach. Those time-consuming weather trends, plant successions, and things we do not know about are poorly evaluated in the three or four years it commonly takes to produce a doctoral thesis. Thesis jobs are immensely valuable, because they can be financed as convenient units, and the students must give their all. Degree candidates are inspired by an immediate goal. For a period that cannot be stretched too far, they live at subsistence level and gamble their wives, their fortunes, and their sacred honor.

In [the Isle Royale] project we had it both ways by running students in relays on manageable segments of the long-range study. At intermission time there was always a good reason for taking off on a new start. It is for the best that the program worked out as it did.

If I had called a halt at 10 years and done my writing according to that period of remarkable stability, the story would have been convincing. We had proved wolves to be amazingly selective and consistent in their killing and feeding habits. It was evident that they almost never killed a moose in that 1-to-5 age class. Of course, any generation included a few weaklings, but the wolves got most of those as calves. Up to that time, the information from other studies, usually concerning wolves that fed on deer, seemed to bear out our Isle Royale findings.

To plump up the account, we could have asserted with confidence that wolves cleaned up one kill before they went on to another; they did not indulge in excess killing. Our findings proved that wolves were almost entirely carnivorous. Unlike foxes, they did not eat fruit. [And] wolves had strict social controls on their own numbers. When the population spurted up a bit, it quickly dropped back to that magic number, a wolf per 10 square miles.

By way of contrast, what would have been the conclusions if we had begun this work in 1969, the advent of years of deep snow and many changes? What if we had followed it through to 1976 and then stopped? Again we would have had a consistent record.

Aside from a heavy calf kill, we would have said there was little age discrimination in the predation on moose by wolves. They took young animals about in proportion as these occurred in the population, just as they did the older less numerous moose. A habitat condition—heavy overbrowsing of the winter range — resulted in wolves killing malnourished calves and other moose beyond their needs and only half cleaning up the remains. In a summer of plenty, they ate fruit. Around rendezvous in 1975, more than a quarter of the scats contained fruit. It was plain poppycock that wolves would not build up beyond one animal per 10 square miles. Give them enough food and they would increase to twice that number. . . .

The research on Isle Royale exemplifies a kind of scientific inquiry that should be carried on through many decades and many changes in weather and vegetation. In reality it is one of those continuous searches into the unknown that has no foreseeable end.

DURWARD L. ALLEN, *Wolves of Minong*

Gray wolf in the North Woods. Alan and Sandy Carey.

Of all the native biological constituents of a northern wilderness scene, I should say that wolves present the greatest test of human wisdom and good intentions.

PAUL L. ERRINGTON, *Of Predation and Life*

For every wolf running wild in the Montana mountains, the highlands of northern India, or the Minnesota lake country, another wolf lives in the mind of the rancher, villager, or weekend camper. Most often, especially in the past, this wolf is savage, cruel, and cowardly, bloody of fang and insatiable of appetite. In some places and times, he is no less than a familiar of the devil. This wolf, we have begun to realize, is not a true image of the

The Wolf of Dreams and Nightmares

animal but a reflection of something we fear in ourselves. More than any other creature, wolves stand for what is wild in nature, what humans have tried to corral and control ever since we left off hunting our food and turned to growing grains and tending flocks. As predators living at the edge of pastoral communities, wolves were justly feared—especially in Europe where wild and cultivated lands lay close together. Efforts to banish them began in classical times, and only a few wolves linger in western Europe. The Europeans who settled the New World brought their wolf hatred with them, mounting a brutally effective campaign that nearly eradicated them from the contiguous U.S. But respect and admiration for wolves persist in native cultures that have have hunted near them since prehistory, and still do. Their views, along with our growing awareness of ecological relationships and the right of all creatures to a place on earth, are slowly reshaping our picture of the wolf. New images are appearing in literature and art that reflect an emerging sense of kinship with brother (or sister) wolf. If wolves and people still cannot live together, we may yet find ways and places to let wolves live on their own.

127

A WILDNESS IN THE SOUL

▼▼▼▼▼▼

The wolves had dug their den into the crest of a small ridge in a dense stand of spruce trees. We meandered toward the den site, keeping to the thin line of one of the many wolf trails, past several lifeless beaver ponds and through the wet underbrush. High in the Alaska Range, the soggy clouds hung off the sides of the surrounding peaks like wet clothes, loose and heavy. We emerged from the dark spruce into a clearing where the wolves had trampled the dirt around their den into a hard pack. A small hole in the ground, the opening of the den looked like a dirty mouth puckered into a belch, and around the mouth was scattered the gnawed litter of former meals — four beaver skulls from the nearby ponds, moose bones well chewed by teething pups, an antler, a ram's horn from a Dall sheep, duck feathers.

Though the wolves were gone, and though there was a calm in the darkness of the shaded den site, it took little imagination to feel the intimations of ferocity and passion in the marks of the fangs on these bones. I found myself thinking not of comfortable domesticity but of Francisco Goya and his painting *Chronos Devouring His Children* — an image of savagery and hunger. And I realized, for the first time, that one aspect of living in time and nature is to live with hunger. . . . I found an image of wolves at this den site that could not be easily domesticated, some threat always hovering on the edges of our lives, on the borders of our consciousness. The wolf has long been an image of this frightening hunger, both in nature and in the human spirit. In *Troilus and Cressida*, Shakespeare looked inside and found "appetite, an universal wolf," that devours "all universal prey."

Instead of facing this dark aspect of the wolf and other animals, we have in this country and this century worked to domesticate nature. Both scientists and environmentalists have contributed. Scientists, by working to reduce animals to rational and objective terms, to numbers and formulae and laws; environmentalists, by making nature into a mirror of our middle-class, comfortable culture, a realm of tidy homes and nurturing families.

In both cases, we remain alienated from some deep and primal power in the wolf, a power not accessible to reason and not necessarily comfortable to culture. As I stood by the mouth of the wolves' den, I felt stirrings of this power.

I had come to this wolf den with Danny Grangaard, a biological technician for the Alaska Department of Fish and Game. We had been helicoptered deep into the Alaska mountains, to a place too remote and rugged for a regular plane. Danny was taking part in a long-term study to gain a scientific understanding of the relationships between wolves and their prey. . . .

The wolf has always evoked powerful passions in humans. Very few Americans, for example, have ever seen a wolf, yet the animal lives in all our imaginations. Every animal wears a double face: It is both creature and symbol, fact and analogy. Seeing a wolf as an animal, as Danny was trying to do in this study, tells what the wolf is: It helps us see the wolf rationally, objectively, with a certain kind of distance. Seeing a wolf as a symbol tells us what it means: It helps us see the wolf imaginatively, often with a confusing intimacy.

The symbol shows the wolf that lives inside, and much that it reveals is not only cultural but personal. It connects us to our childhood dreams, to our most basic needs and desires, and to the demonic.

In a strange way, the images of hunger around the den did not frighten so much as exhilarate me. Looking at the mouth of the den, I could feel the wolf inside. Like Alice in Wonderland, I had an impulse to crawl in and see the pups — an irresistible urge to see the wolf face-to-face, to confront the beast in its den.

Danny said he thought it would be all right. I grabbed a flashlight and dropped to my hands and knees. The hole was only 14

inches wide. I could barely fit through. Still, I wormed my way in up to my hips. The burrow dropped straight down and then angled hard right. It was crowded inside; my arms were cramped, I was barely able to reach ahead and shine the light. The dirt walls were wet, dripping, stinking of wolf piss and damp fur. In the beam of the flashlight, about 7 feet away from me, three wolf pups cowered in the far corner of their den, a protoplasmic pile of bluish-gray fur.

One brownish ear, I remember, was crushed against the top of the den. A couple of huge rust-colored paws poked out from the pile, precise owners unknown. The pups had small snouts on adorable faces, giving only faint hints of the fangs to come. Their eyes reflected a dull blue from the flashlight, expressionless and completely impersonal, inhuman.

The pups growled at me in low, menacing tones, the snarling edge of the unknown. Those throaty growls were the fiercest threats I've ever heard.

This was as close to the pure experience of the alien and the wild as I have ever come in nature, as raw as the bones the wolves themselves had chewed. These wolves were untamable. Facing them in their den, I found myself at the borders of the irrational, staring in awe at its power.

The wolves in the den — a world beyond reason and culture.

I thought later of one of La Fontaine's fables, of the wolf that preferred a life of hunger in the wild to the well-fed life of a dog wearing a collar. At some barely accessible level, this is the wolf that lives in the American psyche, part of the fabric of our daily language:

> Hunger makes the wolf.
> We wolf down our food.
> The wolf at the door.
> We cry wolf.
> A man who loves women and sex? A wolf, of course.

ABOVE: *The big bad wolf of legend, early illustration for* Little Red Riding Hood. PAGE 126: *Black phase wolf. Art Wolfe.* PAGE 128: *The werewolf, lithograph after a tableau by Maurice Sand, 1857.* PAGE. 129: *Gray wolf young in the den, Alaska. Art Wolfe.*

These images unconsciously shape the way we see wolves; most of them are full of fear, defined by hunger and sex and a sense of intrusion. Fantasy is always a precondition for our perception of reality. The wolf in our imagination describes an interior landscape of fearful and alien impulses, projected onto the beast beyond.

But there is more to this wild wolf.

When we are crazy, on the edge of madness or uncontrollable passion, then what? In that irresistible urge for freedom and that unrestrainable wildness, we howl with the wolves at the moon.

Such wildness wears a horrifying mask too. One manifestation is lycanthropy, which once was considered a medical condition. Overcome by melancholy, a person could be transfigured into a wolf; stealing into cemeteries and churchyards at the dark hour of midnight, the afflicted person digs up corpses like a wolf. It is a gruesome association of death and hunger and the travesty of the sacred.

The mistake is to take all this literally. It is psychology. A man-wolf, or werewolf, might howl fearfully, but the fur is not really on the outside. The more horrifying fur grows beneath the skin, creepy and itching, felt invisibly.

Here—in the human soul—is the second true wilderness. Animals like wolves can give us some of that wild energy that William Blake called "the opposite of reason." The wolf den, and the experience of crawling into it, evoked for me this deeper layer of meaning. We all have the right to construct our own meanings out of our experiences in nature: Nature is not only an objective world but also a world we create.

More is at stake in saving a wild wolf than we realize. We need to save both the literal and the symbolic creatures. Part of the reason so many animals are endangered, in this rational and empirical age, is precisely that we have forgotten the two faces of every creature. We have forgotten what animals mean.

I don't want to settle for only half the animal. Already, we are learning to accept diminished beasts and diminished selves. In facing those wolf pups in the den, I entered nature in a new way, engaged and passionate.

CHARLES BERGMAN, *Wild Echoes*

Gray wolf, black phase. Michael Francis/The Wildlife Collection.

THE WOLF IN US
▼▼▼▼▼▼

The paw-print of a two year old Alaskan timber wolf,
   canis lupus pambasileus
      is the same size as the face
Of a three month old human child.
We humans fear the beast within the wolf
   because
We do not understand the beast within ourselves.

GERALD HAUSMAN, *Turtle Island Alphabet*

IN THE BEGINNING

▼▼▼▼▼

It was perhaps two million years ago that early bands of hunter-gatherers and wolves first met on the Eurasian steppes, and some wolf relative was surely known to early hominids in Africa as well. It's likely that these people saw wolves hunting the same hoofed animals they sought themselves, and—consciously or not—used some of the same tactics. They may have found wolf dens and, being omnivores, taken pups for food. Sooner or later, they kept and raised one for a companion.

Ethologists have found many similarities in the social organization and hunting styles of wolf packs and prehistoric peoples. In fact, George Schaller and others believe that wolves are a better model for early human development than primates. Both are carnivores native to open savannahs rather than dense forests. Both are highly intelligent, live in small groups, pursue social hunting of large game, and share food with the group (rare among primates).

ABOVE: Hunter, by Frank LaPena (Wintu-Nompitom), 1992. BELOW: Ojibway petroglyph of wolf, northern Minnesota. Scot Stewart.

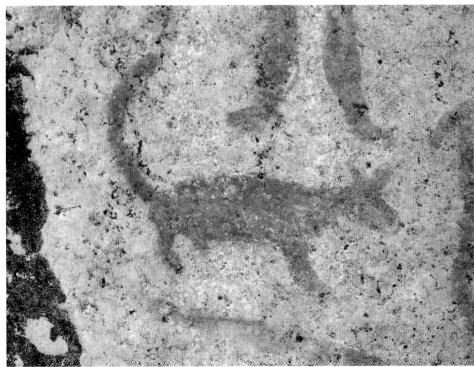

Both operate from a home base, range over large territories in search of food, and divide labor into hunters and nonhunters (among wolves, not by sex but by age and ability). And both wolves and humans spend about the same proportion of their lives as infants and subadults, requiring a long commitment by parents and pack.

If early people now and then ate a wolf, the wolves no doubt returned the favor. As one writer says, "It is not hard to imagine these efficient carnivores attacking an occasional lone ape-man and hauling him off in those long-gone times before humans were really human"—especially before humans invented the weapons that made wolves so wary of us later. So respect, recognition, and fear must have been mingled in primitive man's regard for wolves, as they are in native cultures still.

HUNTERS IN COMMON

The caribou-hunting tactics of wolves in the Brooks Range and those of the Nunamiut *were* similar. And similarity in hunting technique in the same geographical area was found elsewhere. Wolves and Cree Indians in Alberta maneuvered buffalo out onto lake ice, where the big animals lost their footing and were more easily killed. Pueblo Indians and wolves in Arizona ran deer to exhaustion, though it might have taken the Pueblos a day to do it. Wolf and Shoshoni Indians lay flat on the prairie grass of Wyoming and slowly waved—the one its tail, the other a strip of hide—to attract curious but elusive antelope close enough to kill. And if we have made the right assumptions at Paleolithic sites in North America such as Folsom, early man killed mammoths in the same mobbing way wolves did, because men did not yet have extensions of themselves like the bow and arrow. They had to get in close with a spear and stab the animal to death.

BARRY LOPEZ, *Of Wolves and Men*

Three-month-old pup wrestles with a rack of antlers. Ernest Wilkinson/Animals Animals.

THE PRIMEVAL STALK

The Naskapi people of Labrador hunt caribou as described below by anthropologist Georg Henriksen. The sequence is strikingly close to the way wolf packs stalk herds of large prey:

The hunters quickly shuffle away from camp. . . . [They] walk at a fast and steady pace, keeping up the same speed hour after hour. When from a hilltop the men spot caribou some miles in the distance they set off at a brisk pace. . . .

No words are spoken. Half running, every man takes the wind, weather, and every feature of the terrain into account and relates it to the position of the caribou. Suddenly one of the men stops and crouches, whistling low to the other men. He has seen the herd. Without a word the men scatter in different directions. No strategy is verbalized, but each man has made up his mind about the way in which the herd can best be tackled. Seeing the other men choose their directions, he acts accordingly.

GEORG HENRIKSEN, *Hunters on the Barrens*

CONVERGENT EVOLUTION

About 100,000 years ago, human beings first invaded the northern regions of Eurasia in a big way, hunting the largest of herbivores, primarily those inaccessible to wolves by reason of immense size and strength. In those days, the north was inhabited by a variety of elephants, rhinoceroses, and other creatures whose sheer mass and might permitted them to graze unconcerned among such formidable predators as the wolves and great cats that shared their inhospitable habitats. . . . It remained for a carnivorous creature who could circumvent such vast strength to invade the giant-herbivore-hunter econiche, and man was the one to do so.

[T]hus, in the beginning, humans and wolves probably shared the tundra forests of Eurasia amicably enough, their econiches rarely overlapping enough for direct competition between them to take place. Fleeter and with more endurance in the chase then their human counterparts, wolves concentrated their diet on deer and the like (as they now do), while human beings preyed intensively on the easily captured giants.

[T]he human invasion of the north marked the rapid decline of the giants, so that the advance of man coincides precisely with the rapid extinction of the northern giants throughout the world. . . . The large-mammal fauna remaining in cool parts of the world in the last few thousand years largely comprises those mammals which by means of speed, secretiveness, or sheer aggressiveness were able to circumvent the wiles of Stone Age hunters.

Now, it happens that just such mammals are the preferred prey of wolves, so that we mark a period between about 30,000 and 10,000 years ago during which human beings were forced by their own excesses to begin competing with wolves. We are still seeing this competition throughout both Eurasia and North America as our kind, improving the efficiency of its deadly hunting methods, mops up the last of the great wild herds of game. This contest between wolf and human, in which the sounds of modern firearms are underscoring the last sorry chapters, has resulted in one of the most intimate symbioses of disparate species known to us, a relationship strikingly reflected in our history, folklore, and biology.

JOHN C. MCLOUGHLIN, *The Canine Clan*

CLASSICAL WOLVES

▼▼▼▼▼

As people and wolves advanced into historical times, their relationship took on darker shadings. In far northern realms, and elsewhere that hunting cultures persisted, the wolf continued to be admired as a fellow successful predator and often invoked as a totem; wearing a wolf skin or head was thought to confer the creature's power. But in more southerly lands, where hunting gave way to herding and agriculture, the wolf's bad reputation was well on the way to being established by pre-Roman times. Greek and Roman writers including Aristotle, Levy, and Plutarch wove accounts of its ferocity into their narratives. Both Homer (800 B.C.) and the Bible give us allegories of the wolf and lamb as enemies. And it was in ancient Greece that the wolf first had a bounty put on its head.

There are intriguing exceptions, though—especially in Greece, which was settled by immigrants from the north. The god Apollo appears as a wolf in some of his manifestations; he is called "wolf-born" because his mother, in the form of a wolf, was guided by wolves to the island of Delos (where she gave birth to him) for protection from the jealous wife of his father Zeus. The Lyceum

at Athens was probably a temple to the wolfish Apollo; the issue is unclear because the same Greek word, *lukos*, means both "light" and "wolf."

In southern Egypt, the city of Lycopolis had a wolf (probably the small Arabian wolf or even a jackal) as its beast-god. The most famous wolf myth of all—the suckling of Romulus and Remus by a she-wolf—comes from Rome. From classical times, too, come the first werebeast legends, which probably arose from the totemistic practice of dressing in the skins of animals.

In Teutonic myths the wolf displays its greatest power and ferocity, in the dual role of companion to the gods and world destroyer. Ironically, this was the wolf image that a modern-day mythmaker—Adolph Hitler—appropriated as one of the totems for his Third Reich.

LYCAON'S CURSE

A legendary Greek king named Lycaon is said to have tamed the wild province of Arcadia and begun the worship of Zeus there. Later, Lycaon and his fifty-odd sons neglected their sacred observances, so Zeus, disguised as a humble laborer, visited Arcadia to check up on them.

The impious sons suspected the ruse and persuaded their father to serve their guest a welcoming meal containing human entrails. In his fury Zeus overturned the table and struck Lycaon and the sons with his thunderbolt, turning them all into wolves. The youngest, Nuktinos, whom the others had murdered for the feast, he restored to human life. (In another version of the story, Lycaon's actions are slightly more justified, because Zeus had seduced his daughter Callisto).

In ancient Athens any man who killed a wolf had to bury it by subscription.

JAMES FRAZER, The Golden Bough

OPPOSITE: *"Two wolves tearing at a ram,"* *Greek figurine, 6th century B.C.* LEFT: *"Romulus and Remus Suckling the Capitoline Wolf," by Peter Paul Rubens.* BELOW: *Engraving of Lycaon changed into a wolf by Zeus, anonymous.*

Not yet appeased, Zeus rained down a flood that drowned all but a few Arcadians. It is said that those survivors later practiced ritual human sacrifice to the gods. Shepherds were served a meal like the one given to Zeus, and "the one who found human entrail in his bowl ate it, howled like a wolf and, leaving his clothing hung on an oak, swam across a stream where he remained in a desolate region as a werewolf for nine years." (Barry Lopez) He turned human again if he ate no human flesh in that time.

Adapted from PLINY, Historia Naturalis

Homo homini lupus
   "Man to man is a wolf"

Lupus pilem non mentem
   "The wolf changes his hair but not his
      nature"

Ovem lupo committere
   "To entrust the sheep to the wolf"

In bocca al lupo!
   "Into the mouth of the wolf," modern
      Italian equivalent of "Break a leg!"

Rough play among European wolves, Sweden. Mattias Klum.

THE WOLF-BRED TWINS

Romulus was the legendary founder of Rome, the son of Mars by Rhea Silvia, daughter of Numitor, King of Alba Longa. He was exposed in the wild at birth with his twin brother Remus, by his great-uncle Amulius, who had usurped the throne. The twins were suckled by a wolf and brought up by a peasant named Faustulus, and his wife Acca Larentia. Romulus founded Rome in 753 B.C. but quarrelled with Remus, whom he slew. In 716 he was carried to heaven in a chariot of Mars and worshipped as the god Quirinus.

It is generally accepted that today that in most historical legends there is some grain of truth. However, it is not possible . . . that the twin babies could indeed have been suckled by a she-wolf. What, then, is the truth of the story, or is it pure myth? The most probable suggestion made is that Faustulus and Acca Larentia were wolf-cult people and regarded as wolves or werewolves by their neighbors.

[To which that sixteenth-century pragmatist, Edward Topsell, adds, "I rather think it was a harlot than a wolfe that nursed those children," referring to the double meaning of lupa—*wolf and whore.]*

RICHARD FIENNES, *The Order of Wolves*

"Wolves drawing the chariot of Mars," illustration in Splendor Solis, c. 1600.

WOLF GIANTS OF THE NORTH

The hugest, fiercest, most powerful wolves of legend are found in Nordic mythology. Odin, chief of the gods, was accompanied into battle by two wolves named Geri and Freki. To see a wolf and raven together was a good omen for success in war; thus Wolfram (*wolf-hrahen*, "wolf-raven") was a great warrior's name. The Norns, or Germanic fates, also kept wolves as companions. And one of the Nordic giantesses, Hyrrokin, rides astride an enormous grey wolf with a snake for a bridle; Barry Lopez relates that when she "arrived at the funeral of Balder, four Berserker struggled to hold her wolf in check. . . ."

The wolf that looms largest in Norse legend is the giant Fenris-wolf, a terrible agent of destruction. Fenris was the offspring of Loki, the trickster god, and a giantess; his siblings were the dread Midgard serpent and Hel, goddess of the underworld. Odin raised Fenris at Asgard, the gods' stronghold, to be a loyal companion, but as he grew ever larger and fiercer, the gods feared him. The only one who could approach was Tyr, who fed him each day. (Up to this point the story strangely echoes the experience of some people who have tried to raise wolves.)

Odin determined to bind Fenris to the earth to prevent trouble, but Fenris snapped the strongest chains ever forged. Finally the gods sent for a magic rope spun by dwarves, thin as spider's silk and made of all the earth's mysteries: mountain roots, the sounds of fish breathing and cats walking, the spittle of birds, and so on. Fenris was suspicious and insisted that Tyr place his hand in his mouth while the rope was fitted; when the wolf realized he was trapped, he closed his jaws and severed Tyr's hand.

Fenris was fated to remain bound until doomsday, precipitated when Loki brought about the death of Balder, the best of the gods. At *Götterdämmerung*, the powers of evil were unleashed; the sun and moon were engulfed by wolf-giants whose jaws dripped blood. The Midgard serpent filled the air and waters with venom, and Fenris was freed from his bonds to join the climactic battle against the gods, his great mouth flashing fire. He swallowed Odin, and was himself slain by Odin's son Vidor. In the end the world was

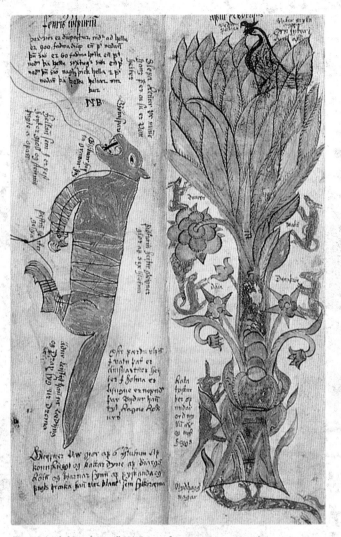

"Fenris and the Ash-tree," miniature from quarto manuscript.

consumed by fire—but from its ashes a new world and a new race of human beings arose.

Today the Fenris story may suggest something about the dangers of trying to cage and restrain the earth's wild forces. Also, it's useful to recall that older cultures did not segregate the powers of creation and destruction, but often incarnated them in one being. In any event, the old Norsemen clearly honored the wolf's strength and sagacity, as shown by the names they gave their kings: Beowulf (war-wolf), Berthewolf, Wulfstan, Wulfred, and Ceowulf, among others.

Adapted from various sources

A BEAST FROM THE MEDIEVAL MIND

▼▼▼▼▼

The dominant image of the wolf in western folklore—the ravening beast that takes human lives, the cruel and cowardly slayer of innocent livestock—is a product of medieval Europe. In this gloomy and fearful time, when wars and plagues ravaged the population, when nobles preyed on the weak, when pagan beliefs were being stamped out by a church that saw heretics behind every tree, it was easy to blame a mysterious and powerful creature for many misfortunes.

There is some truth in the wolf that we inherited from the fevered reports, religious tracts, and fairy tales of medieval Europe. In many regions, wolf habitat overlapped with pasture and farmland, and livestock became convenient prey. Wolves were known to scavenge corpses abandoned on battlefields, evoking shivers of horror. In hard winters, they ventured close to towns and cities, prompting panic, and no doubt an occasional woodsman or shepherd wandering in wild country was attacked.

If not all the lurid accounts of wolf mayhem on humans can be disproved, most can be seriously questioned. Based on contemporary records, wolves almost never regard humans as prey. Investigators believe that most of the European reports of wolves killing people involve either rabid animals or feral dogs, often larger and less predictable than wolves.

But the demonizing of wolves went beyond a practical response to a dangerous predator. For many reasons—their elusiveness, intelligence, and identification with the wild woods—wolves took on a supernatural stature, became an icon of all that was vicious, uncivilized, and unholy. The Church, always in need of vivid metaphors, promoted the comparison of wolves preying on sheep with Satan preying on innocent souls. Christianity assumed into its mission subduing the wild, and by killing wolves, as Barry Lopez notes, "Man demonstrated his own prodigious strength as well as his allegiance to God. . . ."

Kill wolves they did, for any reason and by many means. They were trapped and shot by gamekeepers and local militias; hunted for sport with hounds bred for the purpose. Vast tracts of wooded habitat were cut down or burned. Rulers set bounties, such as the Scottish king who "ordaint that the slayer of one wolf have ane ox to his reward." Landlords schemed to have their lands cleared of wolves by making it a condition of obtaining a lease.

By the late nineteenth century wolves were virtually gone from the western European countries, and the focus of the long war against them had shifted across the Atlantic.

MYTH OF THE MARAUDER

Throughout the ages, even in the prehistoric world, whilst his howling athwart the stillness of nature and night struck fear into the heart of primaeval man crouching far back in the dark retreat of some cold rough cave; further down the centuries when he was known as the savage plunderer and swift pitiless marauder of the shepherd's grazing flocks, not sparing to attack child and maid or even the solitary wayfarer by the wood; nearer yet, what time the red glare of his eyes across the drear plain of unflecked snow in the cold steely moon has paralyzed some lone leash of travellers, and the plunging horses made with terror break into a frenzied gallop, . . . all down the vistas of dateless centuries the wolf has ever been the inevitable, remorseless enemy of man, and few animals indeed has the world's fancy, nay, the experience and dearly purchased knowledge of our forefathers, invested and surrounded with so many gloomy superstitions and beliefs that are horribly real and true.

The distinctive features of the wolf are an unbridled cruelty, bestial ferocity, and ravening hunger. His strength, his cunning, his speed were regarded as abnormal, almost eerie qualities, he had something of the demon, of hell. He is the symbol of Night and Winter, of Stress and Storm, the dark and mysterious harbinger of Death.

In Holy Writ the wolf is ever the emblem of treachery, savagery, and bloodthirstiness. . . .

MONTAGUE SUMMERS,
The Werewolf

OPPOSITE: "Du loup et de sa nature," from Le Livre de la Chasse, *by Gaston Phébus de Foix, 16th-century French manuscript.* ABOVE: *1881 magazine illustration of a "wolf-charmer," an old French legend probably linked to werewolf myths.* RIGHT: *18th-century engraving of the Beast of Gévaudan, anonymous.*

BIOLOGICAL MAYHEM

From studies of the available literature dealing with wolves in Europe, . . . one gains the strong impression that the majority of attacks on humans were made by rabid animals, both full-bred wolves and wolf-dog crosses. The late Dr. C. H. D. Clarke, who for years was head of the Fish and Wildlife Division of Ontario's Ministry of Natural Resources, certainly believed that rabies was the principal cause of attacks in Europe. In a manuscript entitled *Beast of Gévaudan*, he said: "Down the long list of recorded attacks by wolves, it becomes clear that the Russian baron in his troika is folklore, but the rabid wolf is grim fact. The pattern is universal. The famous wolves of medieval song and story were all rabid. . . ."

A number of factors probably contributed to the spread of rabies among European wolves. In the first place, wolf wilderness areas that had come under the influence of large human populations had been drastically reduced, or eliminated altogether. Where the wolf packs had once lived and hunted relatively undisturbed, human villages and towns had burgeoned, forests had been cleared, domestic livestock had multiplied; so had dogs and cats. Starving wolves began feeding on cattle and sheep, pursued by hunters and their dogs. . . . In such a climate, the rabies virus began to thrive, first attacking domestic dogs; then, because it is probable that no wolf is totally immune to the disease if exposed to it frequently enough, the wolves became seriously affected. Huge wolf-dog hybrids began to appear and these, rabid or not, attacked people. The two that are described in Dr. Clarke's manuscript terrorized the regions of Vivarais and Gévaudan, France, from 1764 to 1767. . . . These two predators killed sixty-four humans and attacked more than a hundred. . . . Both killers were much larger than those wolves generally found in that area of Europe. Descriptions of color and skull measurements have been preserved, and these, added to the size of the animals, caused Dr. Clarke to believe that they were not purebred wolves, but wolf-dog crosses.

R. D. LAWRENCE, *In Praise of Wolves*

WOLF AND SAINT

There is an old story about a wolf in Gubbio, Italy, involving Saint Francis. The wolf had been threatening the villagers and Saint Francis was trying to get the animal to desist. He and the wolf met one day outside the city walls and made the following agreement, witnessed by a notary: the residents of Gubbio would feed the wolf and let him wander at will through the town and the wolf, for his part, would never harm man nor beast there.

Beneath the popular, anecdotal appeal of this story is a common allegory: the bestial, uncontrolled nature of the wolf is transformed by sanctity, and by extension those identified with the wolf—thieves, heretics, and outlaws—are redeemed by Saint Francis's all-embracing compassion and courtesy.

Medieval men believed that they saw in wolves a reflec-

tion of their own bestial nature; man's longing to make peace with the beast in himself is what makes this tale of the Wolf of Gubbio one of the more poignant stories of the Middle Ages. To have compassion for the wolf, whom man saw as enslaved by the same base drives as himself, was to yearn for self-forgiveness.

BARRY LOPEZ, *Of Wolves and Men*

ABOVE: "The Wolf of Gubbio," painting by Luc Olivier Merson, 1877, France.
LEFT: "Shepherds putting a wolf to flight," Greek manuscript, 479 A.D.

THE CHASE
▼▼▼▼▼▼

We rustled through the leaves like wind,

Left shrubs and trees and wolves behind;

by night I heard them on the track,

Their troop came hard upon our back,

With their long gallop which can tire

The hound's deep note and hunter's fire:

Where'er we flew they followed on,

Nor left us with the morning sun;

Behind I saw them scarce a rood,

At daybreak winding through the wood;

And then through the night had heard
their feet,

Their stealing, rustling step repeat.

GEORGE GORDON, LORD BYRON,
from *Mazeppa*

Group howl in snowy woodlands. Peter McLeod/First Light.

THE WOLVES OF CERNOGRATZ

Wolves feature in several short stories by Saki, who wrote gracefully and pointedly about the foibles of the nineteenth-century bourgeoisie. In "The Wolves of Cernogratz," a nouveau-riche baron and his wife unwittingly employ as a governess an elderly survivor of the noble family whose castle they have acquired. The old lady unexpectedly speaks out at dinner when the Baroness scoffs at an old legend about wolves in the castle woods. Europe's aristocracy often reserved for themselves the privilege of hunting wolves; here the wolf's howl is a compliment reserved for those of noble birth.

"It is not when anyone dies in the castle that the howling is heard. It was when one of the Cernogratz family died here that the wolves came from far and near and howled at the edge of the forest just before the death hour. There were only a few couple of wolves that had their lairs in this part of the forest, but at such a time the keepers say there would be scores of them, gliding about in the shadows and howling in chorus, and the dogs of the castle and the village and all the farms round would bay and howl in fear and anger at the wolf chorus, and as the soul of the dying one left its body a tree would crash down in the park. That is what happened when a Cernogratz died in his family castle. But for a stranger dying here, of course no wolf would howl and no tree would fall. Oh, no."

There was a note of defiance, almost of contempt, in her voice as she said the last words.

H. H. MUNROE, *The Complete Works of Saki*

Wolves have roamed the forests, steppes, and tundra landscapes of Russia since long before it was a nation, and have a large place in its folklore. According to James Frazer, the Chukchee natives of northeastern Siberia hold a festival when they have killed a wolf, at which they cry, "Wolf, be not angry with us! It was not we who killed you, it was the Russians. . . ." Theodore Roosevelt hunted wolves in Russia, where it was an aristocratic pastime; the elegant borzoi is the Russian-bred wolfhound. And the nomadic tribesmen of south-central Russia still hunt wolves by falconry, using a special type of eagle.

A common ingredient of Russian fiction is the winter journey by troika across the frozen plains, pursued by vast wolf packs; this image was imported to the American midwest by Russian immigrants and appears in a famous scene from Willa Cather's *My Ántonia*. Krilov, the prolific Russian fabulist, began his career adapting the fables of Aesop and La Fontaine, and later created his own using the familiar animal characters of Wolf, Fox, and so on. Many had strongly patriotic themes, such as the following, in which the wolf represents the hated invader Napolean, and the huntsman the wily old general Kutuzoff, a Russian hero.

A big grey wolf did come out of the forest.

THE WOLF IN THE KENNEL
▼▼▼▼▼▼

A Wolf, that thought into a fold to creep
    By night, mistakenly did leap
Into a kennel, and could not get out.
    At once arose a fearful rout,
Scenting the bully grey, the baying pack
    Would break through all to fight;
The whippers in "A thief! up, up lads!" shout;
    The doors are closed with ready kick;
And all the kennel is a hell of noise and fright.
    With sticks some thither run;
    Others snatch up a gun:
"A light! a light!" they cry. "Twas brought, and there
    Our wolf sat, huddled 'gainst the wall,
His tail into the corner pressed, bristling his hair,
Chattering his teeth, and in his eyes a glare,
As if with them he could devour them all.
But, seeing that no sheep now stopped his way,
    And that the reckoning came at last
    For those, on which he'd broken fast
    So oft, our trickster 'gan to pray
    For parley and for peace:
"My friends, what cause is there for all this riot?
'Tis I, your friend of old and comrade quiet,
Come in good will to let all quarrels cease;
Let bygones be forgot, and general concord reign,
And I engage, not only no flock to touch again,
But for it 'gainst all others myself my teeth to use,
    And on my oath of Wolf I swear,
        That I . . ."—"Good friend, forbear,"
    Broke in the huntsman, "to abuse
    Thyself! No greyer than my own thy hair,
    And long thy wolfish nature have I seen;
    Hence this my rule hath always been:
    Not otherwise a peace to make
    With any wolf, but when I take
    His skin from off his back."
And on the Wolf at once let loose the eager pack.

IVAN ANDREYEVITCH KRILOV, *Fables*

Illustration by Warren Chappell, 1940, for Peter and the Wolf, *a children's book by Serge Prokofieff based on his musical composition.*

"Attacked by the Wolves," painting by Nicolas Wassilievitch Orloff, c. 1900, Russia.

A RUSSIAN IMMIGRANT'S TALE

The wolves were bad that winter, and everyone knew it, yet when they heard the first wolf-cry, the drivers were not much alarmed. They had too much good food and drink inside them. The first howls were taken up and echoed and with quickening repetitions. The wolves were coming together. There was no moon, but the starlight was clear on the snow. A black drove came up over the hill behind the wedding party. The wolves ran like streaks of shadow; they looked no bigger than dogs, but there were hundreds of them.

Something happened to the hindmost sledge: the driver lost control—he was probably very drunk—the horses left the road, the sledge was caught in a clump of trees, and overturned. The occupants rolled out over the snow, and the fleetest of the wolves sprang upon them. The shrieks that followed made everybody sober. The drivers stood up and lashed their horses. The groom had the best team and his sledge was lightest—all the others carried from six to a dozen people.

Another driver lost control. The screams of the horses were more terrible to hear than the cries of the men and women. Nothing seemed to check the wolves. . . . The little bride hid her face on the groom's shoulder and sobbed. Pavel sat still and watched his horses. The road was clear and white, and the groom's three blacks went like the wind. . . .

At length, as they breasted a long hill, Peter rose cautiously and looked back. "There are only three sledges left," he whispered.

"And the wolves?" Pavel asked.

"Enough! Enough for all of us."

[The next sledge to fall victim was that of the groom's father. The groom tries to leap after them. He is restrained, but this gives Pavel—whose horses are tiring—an idea.]

Now his middle horse was being almost dragged by the other two. Pavel gave Peter the reins and stepped carefully into the back of the sledge. He called to the groom that they must lighten—and pointed to the bride. The young man cursed him and held her tighter. Pavel tried to drag her away. In the struggle, the groom rose. Pavel knocked him over the side of the sledge and threw the girl after him. He said he never remembered exactly how he did it, or what happened afterward. . . .

Pavel and Peter drove into the village alone, and they had been alone ever since. They were run out of their village. Pavel's own mother would not look at him. They went away to strange towns, but when people learned where they came from, they were always asked if they knew the two men who had fed the bride to the wolves.

WILLA CATHER, *My Ántonia*

THE DEVIL'S DOG

This excerpt from a twelfth-century bestiary translated by T. H. White summarizes many of the medieval superstititions about wolves—for example, the notion that if a wolf looks upon someone, his power of speech will disappear. The wolf's link with the devil endured for centuries; in Robert Browning's poem "Ivan Ivanovitch," the lead wolf is called, "Oh that Satan-faced first of the band!"

The devil bears the similitude of a wolf: he who is always looking over the human race with his evil eye, and darkly prowling round the sheepfolds of the faithful so that he may afflict and ruin their souls.

That a wolf should be born during the first thunder of this month of May symbolizes that the Devil fell from heaven in the first motion of his pride.

Moreover, since this creature keeps its strength in its fore parts and not in its backward parts, it signifies that this same Satan was at first forward among the angels of light and was only made an apostate by the hindward way.

Its eyes shine in the night like lamps because the works of the devil are everywhere thought to seem beautiful and salubrious, by darkened and fatuous human beings. . . .

ABOVE: *In a 15th-century Greek miniature illustrating Aesop's* Fables, *a hero slays a wolf under the dog constellation of the Canicule.* BELOW: *Running wolves. Stephen J. Krasemann/DRK Photo.*

Because a wolf is never able to turn its neck backward, except with a movement of the whole body, it means that the Devil never turns back to lay hold on repentance.

Now what on earth can a man do, from whom the Wolf has stolen away the strength to shout and who even lacks the power of speech and consequently cannot get the help of distant people? If he is able to do anything, let him drop down his clothes to be trampled underfoot and take two stones in his hands, which he must beat together. Seeing this, the Wolf, losing the courage of his convictions, will run away; and the man, saved by his own ingenuity, will be as free as he was in the beginning.

Now all this is to be understood in a spiritual manner. . . . For what can we mean by the Wolf except the Devil, what by the man except sin, what by the stones except the apostles or other saints or Our Lord himself? All the prophets have been called stones of adamant. And he himself, Our Lord Jesus Christ, has been called in the Law "a stumbling block and a rock of scandal." . . .

T. H. WHITE, *The Bestiary: A Book of Beasts*

THE WOLF WHO WOULD BE A MONK

Once upon a time there was a Wolf who had heard great things about the clergy in monasteries, and how they did very little work, lived easy and had lamb for dinner. So he decided to be a religious. His friends told him that he would have to go through the proper training for this, which would mean going to the abbey school for his education. He did so, and there was a schoolmaster there who had to teach him his alphabet. The master had a birch and Wolf had a pointer with which he had to pick out the letters. They got over A, and they got over B. It was hard going. Then they arrived at the third letter. "What does that stand for?" asked the master. Poor Wolf, who thought that this might surely be it at last, cried out enthusiastically: "Lamb!"

But they only turned him out, on the score that he was a humbug.

T. H. WHITE, *The Bestiary: A Book of Beasts*

*ABOVE: "Wedding party attacked by wolves,"
1894 French lithograph. RIGHT: "Le loup et
l'agneau," engraving by Jean Baptiste Oudry,
c. 1750, illustration for La Fontaine's fable
The Wolf and the Lamb.*

THE WEREWOLF CULT

▼▼▼▼▼

From classical drama to to the romances of Shelley and Stoker to contemporary fantasy writers, the werewolf has been a potent metaphor for the beast in man. Were-legends exist around the world: there are were-jaguars in South America, were-hyenas in Africa, were-bears in Scandinavia, and were-foxes in Japan. In shamanistic cultures, the phenomenon of shape-shifting expressed power and mystery but not necessarily evil; later it took on specific associations with the demonic and with uncontrollable urges of murder and lust.

The term lycanthropy (from the legend of Lycaon) denotes a psychotic condition in which the victim goes on all fours, howls, eats raw meat, and may commit violence (usually to himself). In the Middle Ages, the existence of werewolves was unquestioned and those who exhibited such symptoms were executed like witches. A Down's syndrome child, with its flattened features, was thought to be the offspring of a werewolf. The Church took all this very seriously; as late as 1961 the clerical scholar Montague Summers produced a whole book treating werewolves as fact.

Most modern renditions of werewolves in fiction and film have defanged the beast, depicting werewolves as the helpless agents of supernatural or psychological forces. In *The Howling* they are under the spell of a cultlike leader; in Whitley Strieber's *Wolfen*, they lurk in the ruins of New York tenements, taking revenge for the desecration of sacred Indian burial grounds. Like other wolves, they will assume whatever form the human mind of a certain time and place requires.

PROFILE OF A WEREWOLF

[A] werewolf is a human being, man, woman or child (more often the first), who either voluntarily or involuntarily changes or is metamorphosed into the apparent shape of a wolf, and who is then possessed of all the characteristics, the foul appetites, ferocity, cunning, the brute strength, and swiftness of that animal. . . . Were-wolfery is hereditary or acquired; a horrible pleasure born of the thirst to quaff warm human blood. . . . Masqued and clad in the shape of the most dreaded and fiercest denizen of the forest the witch came forth under cover of darkness, prowling in lonely places, to seek his prey. . . .

The werewolf loved to tear raw human flesh. He lapped the blood of his mangled victims, and with gorged reeking belly he bore the warm offal of their palpitating entrails to the sabbat to present in homage and foul sacrifice to the Monstrous Goat who sat upon the throne of worship and adoration. His appetites were depraved beyond humanity. In bestial rut he covered the fierce she-wolves amid their bosky lairs. . . .

MONTAGUE SUMMERS, *The Werewolf*

LOUPS-GAROUS
▼▼▼▼▼▼

It was late when I arrived at Dr. Glosspan's office.

Overhead, the replenished moon

Rode high, spending itself

Upon the acquiescent earth.

He was none too pleased to see me. Indeed,

As he explained, under the glare of the framed vellum and
the framed sheepskin,

He had agreed to do so only to explain again

How impossible it was

For him to take me as a patient —

His work-load was already so heavy,

Dr. Glosspan said. I seized his cold, reluctant hands

And poured out my plaints and pleas.

I told him how I was tortured by dreadful dreams

Of running, naked, on all fours

Swiftly, fleetly, through the endless woods and fields —

And all the rest of it — the chase, the quarry, the hazard,
and the blood.

Oh, the blood! Oh, the blood!

Scarcely had I begun to realize

That the hand I held had a hairy palm, when

Dr. Glosspan groaned.

We watched each other's faces push out to muzzles

And our teeth grow long and white and sharp

And hair grow thick and grey on all our changing limbs.

Together we slipped from alien clothes and,

Laughing, laughing, howling, growling, we leaped

Through the open window

To run forever through the endless woods and fields

Beneath the festering fullness of the moon:

The chase, the hazard, the quarry, and the blood.

Oh, the blood! Oh, the blood!

AVRAM DAVIDSON

OPPOSITE, TOP: "Wolf and man-wolf," drawings by Charles Le Brun, 17th century. BOTTOM: "The Werewolves," illustration from The Book of Were-Wolves, 1865. RIGHT: 16th-century portrait of the "hairy man," Petrus Gonsalvus, anonymous (German school).

Even a man who is pure in heart
And says his prayers by night
May become a wolf when the wolfsbane blooms
And the autumn moon is bright.

Ancient Gypsy rhyme

THE WILD CHILD
▼▼▼▼▼

Amid the darkness of our historic conflict with wolves, there have been glimpses of a different, happier relationship: the image of a human child abandoned in the wilderness, nurtured by a mother wolf and adopted by the pack. Romulus and Remus is the seminal western story on this theme, but like other wolf myths it crops up in many places.

The existence of wolf-raised children is based on cases of lost or abandoned children who displayed behavior similar to lycanthropy—walking on four limbs, howling, rejecting speech, attacking their keepers. The most likely explanation (and reason for their abandonment) is that they were autistic or schizophrenic; such children, as Barry Lopez points out, are strongly drawn to dogs and might possibly take refuge in a wolf den. And people knew that wolves—despite other failings—were good parents.

The best-known cases of feral children were Victor, the Wild Boy of Aveyron, whose story François Truffaut told in the film *The Wild Child*, and Amala and Kamala, twins rescued from a cave outside Calcutta by a Reverend J. A. L. Singh and raised in his orphanage. No proof of a specific link with wolves exists outside the Reverend's diary, however. The most famous fictional wolf child also came from India: Mowgli of Kipling's *The Jungle Book*. Barry Lopez relates the tale (circa 1845) of a wolf girl in Texas, orphaned at an isolated ranch and spirited away by wolves, with whom she was later seen; this too is probably apocryphal.

What's important in these stories is not their literal truth but what they say about our dreams of a benevolent wolf. Especially today, "we seem to want forgiveness from wolves," as Lopez says—to stretch our constricted, fear-based conception of them to encompass their complexity, their loyalty, their capacity for tenderness.

"We found her wandering at the edge of the forest. She was raised by scientists."

LEFT: *Drawing by W. Miller,* © *1993* The New Yorker Magazine, Inc. ABOVE: *Still photo from* The Wild Child, *a film by François Truffaut,* © *1970 by United Artists.* OPPOSITE: *Mowgli's fate is debated by the wolf council, illustration by André Collot for* The Jungle Book, *1937.*

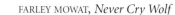

"Something is coming uphill," said Mother Wolf, twitching one ear. "Get ready."

The bushes rustled a little in the thicket, and Father Wolf dropped with his haunches under him, ready for his leap. Then, if you had been watching, you would have seen the most wonderful thing in the world—the wolf checked in mid-spring. He made his bound before he saw what he was jumping at, and then he tried to stop himself. The result was that he shot up straight into the air for four or five feet, landing almost where he left ground.

"Man!" he snapped. "A man's cub. Look!"

Directly in front of him, holding on by a low branch, stood a naked brown baby who could just walk—as soft and dimpled a little atom as ever came to a wolf's cave at night. He looked up into Father Wolf's face and laughed.

"Is that a man's cub?" said Mother Wolf. "I have never seen one. Bring it here."

A wolf, accustomed to moving his own cubs can, if necessary, mouth an egg without breaking it, and though Father Wolf's jaws closed right on the child's back not a tooth even scratched the skin as he laid it down among the cubs.

"How little! How naked, and—how bold!" said Mother Wolf softly. The baby was pushing his way between the cubs to get close to the warm hide. "Ahai! He is taking his meal with the others. And so this is a man's cub. Now, was there ever a wolf that could boast of a man's cub among her children?"

"I have heard now and again of such a thing, but never in our Pack or in my time," said Father Wolf. "He is altogether without hair, and I could kill him with a touch of my foot. But see, he looks up and is not afraid."

RUDYARD KIPLING, *The Jungle Book*

I [asked] Ootek if he had ever heard of the time-honored belief that wolves sometimes adopt human children. He smiled at what he evidently took to be my sense of humor, and the gist of his reply was that this was a pretty idea, but it went beyond the bounds of credibility. . . .

A human baby put in a wolf den would die, he said, not because the wolves wished it to die, but simply because it would be incapable, by virtue of its inherent helplessness, of living as a wolf. On the other hand it was perfectly possible for a woman to nurse a pup to healthy adulthood, and this sometimes happened in Eskimo camps when a husky bitch died. Furthermore, he knew of at least two occasions where a woman who had lost her own child and was heavy with milk had nursed a wolf pup—husky pups not being available at the time.

FARLEY MOWAT, *Never Cry Wolf*

THE WOLF OF FABLE AND FAIRY TALE

▼▼▼▼▼▼

In children's stories we are more likely to find someone's idea of how the world should be than how it really is, or a lesson slipped between the lines of a lively narrative. So it is with tales featuring wolves, both old and new. In the fables of Aesop, La Fontaine, and Krilov the wolf's stereotyped character flaws—greed, stupidity, treachery, self-justification, and bullying—are used to draw morals about our own foibles. Or he provokes some other undesirable behavior, such as lying ("The Boy Who Cried Wolf") or boasting ("The Kid and the Wolf"). An exception is a Japanese tale in which a boy removes a bone stuck in a wolf's throat, and the grateful wolf brings him a gift of a pheasant (scaring the boy's friends when he appears).

Little Red Riding Hood is, of course, the archetypal warning of what can befall someone who strays off the path in the deep dark woods. Most interpreters agree that the wolf represents sexual temptation, and that the tale is meant to keep pubescent girls from flaunting their sexuality.

Later writers, notably Rudyard Kipling and Jack London, portrayed wolves more sympathetically. London emphasized their courage and loyalty (in

contrast to some of his human characters), and Kipling their family and tribal affections, but both showed man as the ultimate master and implied that the wolf could be "saved" only when socialized.

Current juvenile fiction uses wolves in various ways. Sometimes they are "rehabilitated" by performing a kind act—totally unrelated to real wolf behavior—for a human. Some stories reflect our longing for kinship and contact, such as Whitley Strieber's *Wolf of Shadows*, where wolves adopt a human mother and child and lead them to safety after a nuclear holocaust. In a delightful revisionist *Three Little Pigs*, a convict wolf claims that his crimes were totally misunderstood. And in *Julie of the Wolves*, a primitive (Eskimo) culture and wolves are favorably contrasted with technological society. So while they offer more positive and fully drawn images of wolves, children's stories continue to reflect the psychic and social agendas of our times.

RIGHT: *French Canadian hooked rug depicting the La Fontaine fable "The Wolf and the Crane," c. 1930-1950.*
OPPOSITE: *Illustration by Ed Young, from* Lon Po Po: A Red Riding Hood Story from China, *1989.*

THE WOLF AND THE SHEPHERDS
▼▼▼▼▼▼

A Wolf once prowled outside a fold, and thence

On peeping through the fence,

Saw that upon the best sheep of the flock

The Shepherds quietly were feeding,

And that the dogs lay round unheeding;

So off he muttering went, feeling a spiteful shock:

"Ye would have made, my friends, a nice ado,

Had I done this instead of you!"

IVAN ANDREYEVITCH KRILOV, *Fables*

THE WOLF AND THE CRANE

A wolf, in gorging himself upon some poor animal he had killed, had got a small bone stuck in his throat. The pain was terrible, and he ran up and down beseeching every animal he met to relieve him. None of the animals, however, felt very sorry for the wolf, for, as one of them put it, "That bone which is stuck in the wolf's throat might just as well be one of mine."

Finally the suffering wolf met the crane. "I'll give you anything," he whined, "if you will help me take this bone out of my throat."

The crane, moved by his entreaties and promises of reward, ventured her long neck down the wolf's throat and drew out the bone. She then modestly asked for the promised reward.

"Reward?" barked the wolf, showing his teeth. "Of all the ungrateful creatures! I have permitted you to live to tell your grandchildren that you put your head in a wolf's mouth without having it bitten off, and then you ask for a reward! Get out of here before I change my mind!"

Aesop's Fables

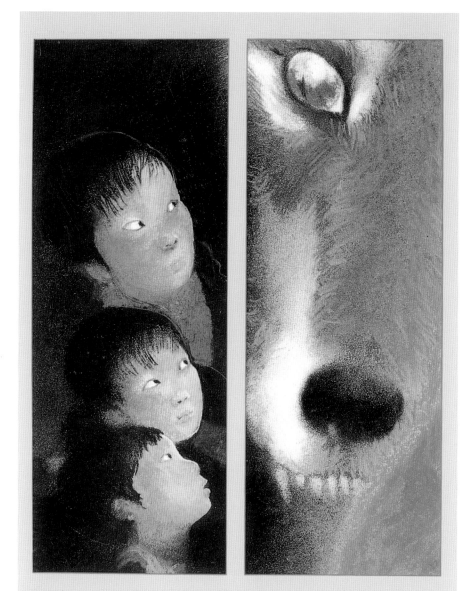

In a Chinese version of the Little Red Riding Hood story called Lon Po Po, *a wolf notices the mother depart on a visit to the grandmother, and disguises himself as the old woman to deceive the children—who discover his ruse and outwit him.*

Shang [the eldest] listened through the door. "Po Po," she said, "why is your voice so low?"

"Your grandmother has caught a cold, good children, and it is dark and windy out here. Quickly open up and let your Po Po come in," the cunning wolf said.

Tao and Paotze could not wait. They shouted, "Po Po, Po Po, come in!"

At the moment he entered the door, the wolf blew out the candle.

"Po Po," Shang asked, "why did you blow out the candle? The room is now dark."

The wolf did not answer.

ED YOUNG, *Lon Po Po*

A DREAM OF WOLVES

In an essay entitled "The Occurrence in Dreams of Material from Fairy Tales," Sigmund Freud recounts the childhood dream of a patient he calls the Wolf-man. The child was born, curiously, on Christmas Eve, 1886, in western Russia to an upper-middle-class family. He grew up maladjusted, and in psychoanalysis Freud traced his infantile neurosis through a boyhood dream that, Freud felt, derived in part from the child's having been frightened by the wolves in Red Riding Hood and other children's stories.

In the dream the boy is lying in bed at night. He is looking out over the foot of his bed through casement windows at a row of walnut trees. It is winter and the old trees are without leaves, stark against the snow. Suddenly the windows fly open and there sitting in a tree are six or seven wolves. They are white, with bushy tails, their ears cocked forward as though they were listening for something.

The boy awakes screaming.

Freud's analysis has not much to do with wolves, but the boy's dream is surely as eerie, as surreal, a vision of wolves as exists in any fairy tale.

BARRY LOPEZ, *Of Wolves and Men*

ABOVE: *"The wolf become shepherd," lithograph by Jules David for* The Fables of La Fontaine, *c. 1850.* RIGHT: *Illustration by Lane Smith from* The True Story of the 3 Little Pigs, *by A. Wolf (as told to Jon Scieszka), 1989. In this update of the classic, the wolf offers his side of the story, insisting that he merely called on the pigs to borrow a cup of sugar and accidentally "sneezed" their houses to bits.* OPPOSITE: *Illustration by Jessie Wilcox Smith for "Little Red Riding Hood," 1911.*

We know that the folklore was exaggerated, that generally [wolves] don't attack man, which is a relief, but we treasure the stories nonetheless, wanting the woods to be woods.

EDWARD HOAGLAND, *Red Wolves and Black Bears*

JESSIE WILLCOX SMITH

Bruno Bettleheim, in The Uses of Enchantment, *is among many who have looked at the tale of Red Riding Hood and the wolf in sexual terms, the wolf representing the id, or the potentially destructive part of our nature that lures us off the safe path. It also offers a lesson about the loss of innocence:*

Little Red Riding Hood is universally loved because although she is virtuous, she is tempted; and because her fate tells us that trusting everybody's good intentions which seem so nice, is really leaving oneself open to pitfalls. If there were not something in us that likes the big bad wolf, he would have no power over us. Therefore, it is important to understand his nature, but even more important to learn what makes him attractive to us. Appealing as naiveté is, it is dangerous to remain naive all one's life.

BRUNO BETTLEHEIM, *The Uses of Enchantment*

"A HOWLING WILDERNESS"
▼▼▼▼▼▼

The Europeans who carved out the first settlements in the New World found a land of apparently boundless resources. But along with the fat deer and the wealth-bearing beaver, they also found their old enemy, the wolf. Like the indigenous people who inhabited North America, taking game and fish as needed, following herds and raising their young, wolves represented a dangerous obstacle in the path of Manifest Destiny.

Wolves were numerous throughout the eastern forests and did pose a hazard to livestock on isolated farmsteads (though feral dogs did much of the killing they were blamed for). The continent's first wolf bounty was imposed in 1630 by the Massachusetts Bay Colony, and in 1717 enough wolves were still around that Cape Cod residents considered building a fence clear across the peninsula to keep them out. But by the end of the eighteenth century wolves had retreated to remote areas, and the battle lines had moved west.

It was on the Great Plains that the wolf wars reached a climax of slaughter. In the 1800s, wildlife of all kinds was abundant; the vast buffalo herds supported wolves as well as the Plains tribes and countless scavengers. When buffalo corpses began to pile up as skin hunters took their fill, wolves discovered they could get an easy meal by following the hunters, who in turn began poisoning the carcasses.

Everyone killed wolves: farmers, ranchers, trappers, professional wolfers, sporting travelers, and government agents. The weapons were guns, traps, snares, and especially strychnine (when buffalo ran out, other baits were used). Thousands of native fauna, dogs, and even children died in the wholesale poisonings. Some wolves avoided capture for years, and legends sprang up around these "renegades." But their doom as a population was sealed when cattle replaced the buffalo as primary grazers on the plains; a whole new economy was at stake in ridding the country of wolves.

From our perspective, it may be difficult to understand the hate that many felt toward wolves. North America was a vaster wilderness than the settlers had ever seen or dreamed, and their fearful response was proportionately strong. Wolves, as ever the running, breathing symbol of hostile nature, bore the brunt.

Wolves *would* be more of a loss to us than some exotic mouse, because they epitomize the American wilderness as no other animal does, and fill both the folklore of childhood and that of the woods. . . .

EDWARD HOAGLAND, *Red Wolves and Black Bears*

There is little hope of [the wolves'] utter destruction, the Countrey being so spacious, and they are so numerous, travelling in the Swamps by Kennels: sometimes ten to twelve are of a company. Late at night, and early in the morning, they set up their howlings and call their companies together, at night to hunt, at morning to sleepe; in a word, they may be the greatest inconvenience the Countrey hath. . . .

WILLIAM WOOD, c.1650
New England's Prospect

PRECEDING SPREAD: *Timber wolf and farmlands, central Canada. Thomas Kitchin/First Light.*
ABOVE: *"A wolf had not been seen in Salem for thirty years," painting by Howard Pyle, 1890.*

DEBATING GRAY WOLF

In 1929 William T. Hornaday, a naturalist and former director of the New York Zoological Park, wrote a book called Wild Animal Interviews, *in which he purports to let wild creatures speak for themselves. Though an avowed wildlife supporter, his "interviews" reveal much about the author's prejudices—especially in his dialogue with the wolf.*

"I refuse to be cross-examined. I hate you!"

Big and savage Gray Wolf snapped his defiance at me through the bar-work of a perfectly good cage; and it almost wrecked my poise.

"What's the matter with me?". . .

"I've been told some of the mean things you have printed about me. You blame me for killing my food, and put big bounties on my head, and yet you are a killer yourself. All the men who blame me are worse killers than I am, and you can't deny it. I never kill just for fun!. . ."

"Well, Lobo, you can suit yourself about answering questions," I snapped back, "I just thought that in view of your off-color reputation, and the hundreds of thousands of dollars that Congress appropriates every year to kill you off on the cattle ranges, you might like a chance to make a statement for publication. . . ."

"Well, you know perfectly well that I kill and eat hundreds of the prairie-dogs that spoil the cattle ranges, and thousands of those gray ground-squirrels that eat up the farmers' crops umbrageous."

"There's something in that," I admitted. "It saves some government poison."

"And I help the cattle-men in getting rid of starved and frozen cattle that otherwise would poison the air. . . . In all these years your humane society never gave us any credit whatever for putting out of their misery the maimed, the halt and the blind among the herds of buffalo, elk, antelope and deer. We have saved an awful lot of helpless animals from dying lingering and painful deaths, have we not? . . .

I observe, near all gangues of Buffalow, wolves and when the buffalow move those animals follow, and feed on those that are too pore or fat to keep up with the gangue.

MERIWETHER LEWIS, 1804

"Landscape with Herd of Buffalo on the Upper Missouri," 1833 watercolor by Karl Bodmer. A white wolf scouts the herd from a promontory in the foreground, a common sight when Bodmer was depicting the American West.

"And now look at this greatest service of all. Who is it, I ask you," pursued Wolf, "who puts pep, stamina, and the savvy of the trail into the pampered domestic dogs of the North, and produces the best, the bravest and finest sled dogs in the world? Northern wolves, sir, and nobody else! . . . *Woo'-o-o-o-o-oh!*"

"Lobo, perhaps you are partly right about that, — for once in your life. . . . And now, Wolf," I went on, "I have listened to your testimony in your own behalf, and I am going to show you the seamy side of yourself. In the first place, you are the most savage and most cruel game and stock killer of all North America. Your taste is so finicky that usually you scorn to eat any meat that you have not killed yourself; but you have been known to murder sixty-five sheep in one night. . . ."

"Why," he snarled, "I learned that from the sportsmen! More than half of them kill all they can, don't they?"

"Never mind about that. I'm talking now about what you do. You are too brave. You travel about too much. You have been known to travel from fifty to sixty miles in one night, — for your own devilish purposes, of course. You are not content with killing colts and calves that you can eat up, but you kill big, fine steers and heifers, ready for the market. . . ."

"You think you are mighty smart, don't you," snarled Lobo, sarcastically.

"Lobo, I think that you are the meanest and the cruelest animal of all North America, and if I could do it I would exterminate all of you but one pair. You and your mates and litters, and your scouts and packs, are much too expensive for people who sometimes consume beef and mutton. And speaking of 'services,' and 'credit,' Lobo, I think you have boundless nerve."

At that Lobo stared at me in stupefied surprise, glared a few glares, then turned, and slowly marched off back stage in unspeakable disgust.

WILLIAM T. HORNADAY, Wild Animal Interviews

THE END OF RAGS

The professional wolfers who hunted down the last wolves on the western plains gained respect for their quarry's intelligence, strength, and courage. Despite the terrible nature of their work, some came to feel a bond with the creatures who had eluded them for so long. The story of Rags, the most intensively hunted wolf in Colorado, has such an ending:

ABOVE: *"Moonlight Wolf," painting by Frederic Remington, c. 1909.* RIGHT: *"The Leader of the Pack," drawing of the famous outlaw wolf Lobo of Currumpaw, by Ernest Thompson Seton, c. 1895.*

There was no question. It was Rags [in the trap]. Big, brawny, ragged in coat, rangy in body, potential death to any living thing that might cross his path except a superior killer, he stalked away, hunting freedom by escape.

The drag caught. . . on a tiny twig in the trail. One more step would take the big wolf clear of this futile obstruction. One lunge would crack a branch many times as tough as the one that held the drag.

But he did not move. For a long moment he stood immovable, looking ahead to the open trail. Then slowly he turned his great wedge head. His red tongue lolled from the fatigue of the fight he had made. His gray eyes sought those of Caywood.

Then slowly, ever so slowly, he turned. He faced Caywood. Their eyes met. Held. With no hurry, with no expression of fury, the big gray started a slow, measured step back toward the hunter. The drag hook came loose from the twig. It rattled, twisting in the trail. There was nothing for it to catch on and impede that stalking walk of the big killer. . . . The unbelievable had happened! Caywood, wolfer supreme, was being stalked by his catch!

Then there came a great wave of relief. He had almost forgotten the gun he held in his hands. The turning of the wolf, so unlooked for, so unusual, had held his attention completely.

He brought up the rifle. His thumb sought the hammer. He pulled it back. *It did not catch!*

Frantically he pulled at it again. The first try had been as good as this second. The hammer would not stay back. It slipped under his thumb.

Seventy-five yards away Rags had turned. His measured steps had not retraced more than twenty-five feet of that distance. He was still coming in that unhurried, slow walk, so deadly, so like an inevitable Nemesis bearing down on the hunter. . . .But still there was that forty-, no, thirty-foot space between Caywood and the old loner.

A strange new vision came flashing fleetingly to Caywood. A vision of a lonely, heart-hungry old wolf, without mate, yearning for some fondling touch, perhaps the kindly caress of his arch enemy, the trapper. The vision was stalking down that trail toward him. Something, something tremendous, indefinable, about Rags caught his attention and held it for the flash of a great understanding.

Could Rags have acknowledged his defeat? Was the old wolf coming to the hunter because he knew that Caywood was master? Was heart-hurt and loneliness driving Rags to stake his life while seeking the friendship of the outdoor soul that lived in big Bill Caywood? . . .

Twelve feet—no, ten—with traps clanking, the determined, unhurried wolf was coming.

For what? Forgiveness, company, sympathy, release, recognizing Bill Caywood, wolfer, outdoorsman, kindred spirit, as his master? Could he be coming seeking release from the trap, sympathy for the injured paw?

Or was it murder, revenge, the final summation of the hate he had held for years against man? Was there blood lust in that wolf heart, deep boiling spirit of revenge against the man who had trapped him, deprived him of liberty?

The flash of fang, those steady eyes, that clanking, unhurried tread!

With all his understanding of the wild and its inhabitants Caywood could not tell whether Rags came seeking friendship or was stalking along that trail intent on killing.

Not an instant remained to speculate, to try to analyze the emotion throbbing through the heart of Rags. Bill Caywood yanked, yanked as he had not before at the hammer on the 25-35! It clicked! Held!

Eight feet! Just eight feet left between Rags and the man who had mastered him.

A snap! Quick, sharp, spitting death! The bullet had but scant distance to go.

Quivering, struggling still to come on, Rags slumped in the trail, a bullet through his heart!

For a long moment Bill Caywood stood in the trail, staring down on the jerking body of the great wolf. One instant there whipped through him keen, agonizing regret. The next he was thanking his lucky stars that the bit of a splinter from the stock of the gun had not held that trigger from catching when he made the last frantic pull.

Life flickered feebly in Rags, the lonely killer's eyes looked up at the man in front of him. . . . In the last shaky effort the great gray form raised itself, incumbered by the gripping tentacles of death, weighted with the traps of steel, and tried with the last flow of strength before his life finally slipped away, to reach the feet of wolfer Caywood, his master. Almost with his quivering nose touching Caywood's boot he fell, quivered, stiffened.

"You poor old devil!" cried Bill huskily as he stooped impulsively. "You poor, lonely old murdering devil!"

STANLEY P. YOUNG, *Last of the Loners*

We reached the old wolf in time to watch a fierce green fire dying in her eyes. I realized then and have known ever since, that there was something new to me in those eyes—something known only to her and to the mountain. I was young then, and full of trigger itch; I thought that because fewer wolves meant more deer, that no wolves would mean a hunter's paradise. But after seeing the green fire die, I sensed that neither the wolf nor the mountain agreed with such a view.

ALDO LEOPOLD,
A Sand County Almanac

In the days of peaceful moods,
    they wandered and hunted.
In the days of need or greed,
    they warred and loafed.
Beneath the lazy sun, kind winds above,
    they laughed and feasted.
Through the starlit night, under the moon,
    they dreamed and loved.
Now, from the wind-beaten plains,
    only their dust rises.

GREY COHOE, from *"Ancestors"*

BROTHER WOLF

▼▼▼▼▼▼

In earlier days, Native peoples all over this continent shared habitat with wolves and pursued similar lifeways. Both lived in relatively small groups, depended on hunting game (often migrating with the herds), observed territories, and used sign language. Seeing that wolves were skillful and resourceful hunters, shared food with the entire pack, and held strong family loyalties—qualities these people valued and required for their own existence—they honored the wolf in their folklore, magic rites, and sacred observances.

In many Native American creation myths, an animal helps pile up mud to create the earth; often it is a wolf. In a Cree version, Wolf carries a ball of moss around the raft bearing those who survived a great flood, until the earth reforms.

The Plains tribes—especially the Cheyenne, Pawnee, and Blackfeet—told stories of "wolf helpers" who guide lost or outcast people through strange country, feeding and protecting them.

Leading warriors and chiefs often took wolf names, and a famous warrior corps of the Cheyenne were the Wolf Soldiers. This tribe (known

to themselves as the Tsistsistas) also held a ceremony in which the hunting camp was made holy by rituals featuring dancers in wolf dress. On the Northwest coast, the two great clan divisions were the wolf and raven. The wolf was considered a spirit helper, and the Makah wolf ritual was a great masked festival.

Southwestern peoples, farmers as well as hunters, had more ambivalent views. The Navajo Wolf Way, in which purified hunters took on the power of wolves, was once a major ceremony. But the Navajo also believe in witches—"skinwalkers"—that take the form of wolves and do harm. These shapeshifters are not wholly evil but instead disturb the world's balance, which can be righted through the proper ritual. In a Hopi kachina dance, a wolf dances beside a sheep in a reconciliation ceremony.

Underlying all Native American wolf lore is the knowledge that life is based on taking life, and hunting therefore is a sacred act. As a supreme hunter, Wolf was often invoked and rarely killed, except if it posed a clear threat or for ceremonial use of its skin. Indian peoples today still cherish their kinship with Wolf and find parallels in their experience as native survivors.

WOLVES

▼▼▼▼▼▼

Once shy nomads from Pacific slopes
to fireweed meadows and tide flats,
they would call us from our longhouses
with their white-throated song.
When the wind returned the seven breaths
the snowfall yelped from dawn to dusk.
The hunters in our family always waited
like shadows to hear our brothers'
winter count take us back to the deer,
the running beauty striking off their hooves.

DUANE NIATUM *(Klallam)*

OPPOSITE: "*Kawadelekala*," by Frances Dick (Kwakiutl), 1986. ABOVE: *Gray wolf, Yukon Territory, Canada. Jack Couffer/Bruce Coleman, Inc.*

AN HONORABLE NAME

In Alaska, the Tlingit Indians in their Na-dene language called many chiefs of many fine houses by the name of wolf: in the Star House *(Qotxanaxa)* the chief was called *Yakwan,* Swimming Wolf. In *Tcak kudi,* Eagle's-nest House, the chief was *L!ex* or Gray Wolf; in *Tcal,* or Halibut House, the chief was *Datxiagutc,* which meant Wolf Walking Around a Person. . . . Others were *Datlketsate* (Stomach of a Wolf); *Yanaxnawu* (Swimming Wolf); *Stuwaqa* (Named from a Wolf); *Andeci* (Many Wolves Howling About the Town);

Q!aleq (Red-mouthed Wolf); *Saxa* (Named from a Wolf's Cry); and *Yandjiyitgax* (Hungry Wolf Crying for Food). To these peoples the wolf was the embodiment of many desirable traits—skill, craft, understanding, inventiveness, strength, courage. Thousands of children were named for the admired predator.

ROGER CARAS, *The Custer Wolf*

HOW THE WOLF RITUAL BEGAN

The wolf ritual of the Northwest tribes (called Klukwalle by the Makah, Klukwana by the Nootka) is their most important ceremony, equivalent to the Sioux Sun Dance or the Navajo Night Chant. Dramatizing old legends with colorful dances and masks and chants, it is meant to transmit the wolf's power and bravery to initiates. (Where real wolves still linger in the region, they sometimes answer the ritual howls.) This story tells how the Nootka version came about.

A long time ago, a young woman of the tribe, with three companions, was walking outside the village. They were going to a place called To-mak'cluh to look for *ah-et's'l,* a small plant whose roots they used for food. During the journey a Wolf went trotting across their path, strong and sleek, and scarcely noticing the girls. The young woman said: "How handsome he is! I wish my husband, when I marry, could be as strong and as fearless." At nighttime the women went to sleep, and the Wolf came in. (The Wolves know everything and read the minds of human creatures.) The girl did not know he had come, but the Wolf woke the sleeping girl, and told her he was going to take her with him. Opening her eyes, she saw a fine young man standing before her. . . .

The young woman went with the Wolf to his home in the mountain, and was there a long time. Two sons were born, who grew up to be half Wolf and half man. The old father of the girl, meanwhile, did not know where his daughter had gone, and was greatly troubled. At her home they tried everywhere to find her, looking in vain in all sorts of places, until they grieved for her as dead. In the Wolf country the oldest son, grown to be a man, asked his mother why he looked different from the people around him (the Wolves). The mother told him that he came from another place, and that there, far from where the Wolves live, dwelt her own father. Then the son asked her when she was going home, because he wished very much to see what it was like there. So the woman told her

husband that their son would like to see his grandfather. He finally agreed, but before they went, as a gift to his wife, the Wolf began to teach the woman about the Klukwana [the wolf ritual], which they had there. It was the Chief of the Wolves that the woman had married, and all the Wolves came to the Chief's house to have Klukwana.

When she had learned all about it, the Wolves came to take her away to her own village. They brought her to her father's house at night, and waited behind the other houses but did not come near. The woman went in to wake her father, and began talking to him of the daughter he had lost, though she kept hidden who she was. She said she herself had a Wolf husband, and that she had with her two sons. . . . The woman also told her father many things about the Wolves, and that the villagers must not do anything when the Wolves howled, or try to harm them. Instead they must try to learn from them. . . .

The old father had been much grieved because his daughter was dead, but he did not know her because it was nighttime, and she was much changed after so many years. But at last she revealed herself to him and told him that now she was going to have a "song" of her own as a sign that the Wolves had brought her back and by which he might know her again. *[The father gathered his people and told them of his daughter's return. They heard the wolves outside and began to beat on long boards and sticks. The wolves howled four times and departed.]*

Then the woman taught her father all about Klukwana, and the secrets she had learned from the Wolves as to their power and strength. After she had taught him all the songs and all the dances, the father began the Klukwana, and later taught the rest of the tribe all that his daughter had learned from the Wolves.

ALICE ERNST,
The Wolf Ritual of the Northwest Coast

Native group in ceremonial dress with large carved wolf dishes, taken in 1911 at the Kwakwaka'wakw village of Memquimlees on Village Island, British Columbia. Photo by C. F. Newcombe.

NAVAJO WOLF WAY

During late fall before the first full moon in December, Navajo Wolf Way was planned. The northwest New Mexico sky shone brilliant blue. The air was crisp and chill. In preparation for mating season the deer were fat and sleek. Each day those volunteers who had chosen to participate in ritual hunting according to Wolf's Way untied knots made in a string to mark the time before departure day arrived. . . . [On that day] As afternoon shadows quickly lengthened, four men entered the [sweat] lodge.

Songs to invoke the assistance of Big Trotter or wolf, Black God or crow, Talking God, and other hunting deities and animal companions were sung as rocks glowing red hot were brought in the lodge. Round after round was sung as steam-laden air seared the men's lungs and boiled their skins. Those who were faint of heart kept their faces close to earth to breathe, but those who were intent on accruing hunting power only sang with more ferocity.

As the ceremony progressed, a change came over those whose voices reverberated in the close confines of the lodge. A strange reversal was taking place among these hunters, whose eyes gleamed in the dim preternatural light of the lodge. They were no longer men, these hunters, and their songs were no longer just songs, but wolf howls rising, wavering and dying away. The flap door of the lodge was thrown aside and these hunters loped into the carmine glow of gathering dusk.

For the next two to fifteen days they were transformed, eating as wolves eat, running as wolves run, thinking and feeling as wolves think and feel. In this way the power of wolves entered them so that they ran with tremendous speed without faltering even at night. They slept on their sides with their knees flexed so their campfire would not weaken them by entering the soles of their feet and they dreamed of killing or the chase, relating their visions to one another before they sang morning hunting songs, blessed their weapons, and sought the deer.

JAMES C. BURBANK, *Vanishing Lobo*

Through the sweat-lodge ritual, Burbank notes, Navajo hunters could break the bonds of time and "return to a pre-emergence world where all beings shared a common identity. . . ."

"Changeable Wolf Man," painting by Ha So Da/Narciso Abeyta (Navajo), 1958.

NAVAJO STALKING WAY SONG
▾▾▾▾▾▾

He goes out hunting

Big Wolf am I

With Black bow he goes out hunting

With tail feathered arrow he goes out hunting

The big male game through its shoulder that I may shoot

In death it obeys me

W. W. HILL

FOOLISH COYOTE AND WISE WOLF

Many Native American myths tell of a Keeper of the Animals, who gives people what they need as long as none is wasted. In this northern Paiute story, the Keeper is the conscientious Wolf, whose work is undone by his scatterbrained brother Coyote:

Wolf kept all the game of the country in a cave and brought out one at a time—only what could be eaten each day. Coyote, the impatient one, pestered his older brother until Wolf told him the secret of the cave and Coyote found it. Then he tried to lift the skin on the door only a crack, enough for one animal. But at the sight of all those elk, buffalo, and deer, Coyote got excited and let the opening gape as wide as his open mouth. As all the animals pounded out in a crush of hooves and dust, Coyote shot but hit nothing. Too late, he rushed about shouting at the remaining deer, trying to herd them back into the cave. One tiny deer hid behind a shrub;

Coyote triumphantly drew his bow and shot it, just as Wolf came up.

Coyote was not discouraged. He proudly served his deer to Wolf, saying, "Well, it looks like the animals have found new homes. How can we hunt them now?" Wolf, of course, had magical powers. "We put sagebrush into piles," he replied. "Soon the piles will fill with rabbits." He warned Coyote not to grow careless and let the Indians catch him as he hunted. Coyote remembered his instructions for a few minutes. He heaped sagebrush into piles; soon they were full of rabbits. But instead of taking them home to share, as Wolf would have done, Coyote ate them all on the spot.

Now that Coyote's stomach was full, he wanted to play, not work. The Indians spotted and pursued him, and Wolf had to rescue him, getting killed in the process. Poor Coyote had to spend years learning the discipline and resources to take revenge and bring home his brother's remains so that Wolf could return to life.

Adapted from *Wolf! A Modern Look*

PAWNEE WOLVES

Among the Plains tribes, the Pawnee were the most closely associated with wolves. From the word for wolf, *Skiri-ki,* came the name of one of the chief Pawnee bands, the Skidi. Like real wolves, they were also known as the most skillful scouts. The identical hand sign, using two fingers to mimic the wolf's alert ears, was used to signify "Pawnee," "wolf," and "scout."

Their neighbors and foes the Cheyenne, Wichita, and Comanche all referred to the Pawnee as wolves, because they shared the animal's endurance, could travel all day and dance all night, and survive on carcasses found along their way (or no food at all). When on the warpath, the Pawnee usually carried wolf robes to disguise themselves and thereby sneak up on their enemies' camps.

LEFT: Pawnee making the sign for "wolf" and "scout." ABOVE: "Moon When Coyotes Are Frightened," by Linda Lomahaftewa (Hopi), 1993. OPPOSITE: "Untitled" (Shaman), by Simon Tookoome (Baker Lake), 1971.

SHAPING THE EARTH

At the time of creation, man (the "hero") and wolf are twin brothers. The hero names all the plants and animals of the world, and after finishing this task, he and his wolf brother retire to live in a small dwelling at the edge of a large lake. The wolf hunts for his brother, and they are content. There are evil beings in the lake, however, and the hero warns his brother that they wish him harm, so he must never cross the water. But after a long day's hunt, the wolf forgets; he tries to swim home across the lake and is destroyed by the spirits. His brother's mourning ripples across the earth, causing the hills to form and valleys to sink. When his brother wolf comes back as a shade, the hero tells him to go and rule in the land of the dead; in time they will meet again there.

Menomini creation myth

In a famous story, a Crow medicine man named Bird Shirt uses wolf medicine on a warrior named Swan's Head, shot in the chest in a battle with other tribes. After moving the victim to a specially built brush lodge, Bird Shirt produces a stuffed wolfskin from his medicine bundle, paints himself to resemble the decorated totem, and goes to work. The storyteller reports:

Suddenly the drums changed their beating. They were softer and much faster. I heard Bird Shirt whine like a wolf mother that has young pups, and saw him trot, as a wolf trots, around the body of Swan's Head four times. Each time he shook his rattle in his right hand, and each time he dipped the nose of the wolf skin in water and sprinkled it upon Swan's Head, whining continually as a wolf mother whines to make her pups do as she wishes.

I was watching . . . when Swan's Head sat up. We then saw Bird Shirt sit down like a wolf, with his back to Swan's Head, and howl four times, just as a wolf howls four times when he is in trouble and needs help. I could see that Swan's Head's eyes were now open, so that he could see Bird Shirt stand and lift the medicine wolf skin above his own head four times . . . and each time there was, I saw, a change in Swan's Head. The fourth time Bird Shirt lifted the wolf skin, Swan's Head stood up.

American: The Life Story of a Great Indian, Plenty Coups of the Crows

The West is where we belong, the Wolves
and I, and my old friends now dead.
May we meet again on the Other Side.

BLUE HORSE, Lakota warrior,
recorded in 1906 by Natalie Curtis

OUT OF THE DARKNESS

▼▼▼▼▼

Well into this century, the business of exterminating wolves went on in the U.S.—and still does elsewhere. But in the last thirty years or so, thanks to a conjunction of scientific and social progress, the wolf has emerged from the shadows of ignorance and superstition where it lingered so long.

The first comprehensive book, Stanley P. Young's *The Wolves of North America*, appeared in 1944. It is historically interesting but biologically suspect, relying on tall tales and dubious evidence. At about the same time, Adolph Murie was writing up the results of his firsthand studies in Alaska, Rudolf Schenkel was studying the social interaction of captive wolves in Germany, and Durward Allen was soon to begin his long-term work on Isle Royale. In the 1950s Lois Crisler and her husband embarked on their arctic adventure, gleaning intimate details of wolf personality. The late 1960s brought Rutter and Pimlott's *The World of the Wolf* and 1970 David Mech's authoritative *The Wolf*.

Around these landmarks in wolf knowledge other ideas were gathering. The environmental movement, spurred by the writings of Rachel Carson, gained force as the quality of life seemed to decline. The fate of Native Americans struck our social conscience, and was clearly linked to the fate of native creatures. Wildlife films became a major source of entertainment and insight. As a result of all this, wolves have "suddenly become the symbols of a born-again wilderness," as Candace Savage notes. Farley Mowat's *Never Cry Wolf* has reached generations of enthusiastic readers and many more in its film version. Kevin Costner's *Dances With Wolves* drew on newfound sympathy for both Native Americans and wolves. New and untarnished wolf portraits abound in fiction, poetry, and children's literature.

BELOW LEFT: Road sign in Tyrell County, North Carolina. Jim Merlin/Valan Photos. ABOVE: Aerial of the Malberg Lake pack taking a sun break at Kiwishui Lake, northern Minnesota. Layne Kennedy.

Some of the new mythmaking may not serve wolves much better than their old evil reputation. Longing to reclaim and possess something of the wild, people have tried to keep or raise wolves, an endeavor almost doomed to failure despite great devotion by the keepers. Images of wolves behaving in nice but unwolflike ways do not deepen understanding or aid the wolf's cause. We have come far in clearing our minds about wolves, and the new images probably are healthier than the old, for both ourselves and wolves. But much about the wolf remains mysterious. We need to explore that mystery further, and also respect it.

THE WOLF MEN

The modern study of American wildlife may be said to have begun with Adolph Murie, who, writing about the wolves of Mount McKinley in 1944, realized there was not much point in a scientist's shooting them; so few wolves were left that this would be killing the goose laying the golden eggs. In those days even the biologists dealing with animals which weren't considered varmints mainly just boiled the flesh off their heads to examine the knobs on their skulls, or opened their stomachs to see what they ate. . . . Murie, in the field and looking at scats, could do a more thorough investigation of diet than the autopsy fellows, who, as it was, knew almost nothing else about the life of wolves.

Murie and Ian McTaggart Cowan in Canada were the best of the bedroll scientists. They could travel with dogs all winter in the snow or camp alone on a gravel bar in a valley for the summer, go about quietly on foot and record everything that they saw. No amount of bush-plane maneuvering and electronic technology can quite replace these methods, by which the totality of a wilderness community can be observed and absorbed. Young scientists such as L. David Mech, who has been the salvation of wolves in Minnesota, which is practically the only place in the lower forty-eight states where they still occur, try to combine the current reliance on radiotelemetry with some of that old bedroll faithfulness to the five senses shared by a man with the animals he is studying.

EDWARD HOAGLAND,
Red Wolves and Black Bears

David Mech eartags a wolf for tracking, northeastern Minnesota. Lynn and Donna Rogers.

WINTER SONG

On windless winter nights a quiet of dramatic purity pervades the forests of Isle Royale. In the looming presence of ancient ridges there is come-what-may stability that makes one stand and listen, and smile to himself. . . . The night comes early and we wonder about the wolves seen yesterday, less than an hour off at the mouth of the harbor. . . .

Then we hear what we might have hoped for—a low moaning call that rises, lingers, and dies away. Like the keening of a lorn soul, it resounds across the ice-bound harbor and ridges beyond. It comes again, this time with accompaniment on a higher key, a soaring note that breaks downward in rich contralto. The spirit catches them, and a medley of many voices join in, each on its own scale and tempo. . . .

Above us the forest, the harbor, and the brushy hillside. Above us the darkened sky resplendent with jewels of the galaxy. We shrink to nothingness under the inscrutable regard of Sirius, Aldebaran, and Betelgeuse. These were watching when Isle Royale's ridges were formed, before earth's highest animal life had learned to crawl across the ocean floor. They will still be watching when . . .

Nature has shown us many moods, but this is the fulfillment of it all. . . . Not entirely by chance, we and the pack were in the right place at the right time.

We listened for a voice crying in the wilderness. And we heard the jubiliation of the wolves!

DURWARD L. ALLEN, *Wolves of Minong*

SANCTUARY

In Anne Arensburg's 1980 novel Sister Wolf, *the daughter of exiled Hungarian aristocrats turns her Massachusetts estate into a wolf haven.*

[O]ne after another, in a recurring arc, like trained divers, five wolves jumped into the pool of light, moving, when they landed, to the edge of the pool, into shadow. They jumped in order of their precedence in the pack. Big Swan, the father, and Lakona, the pregnant mother. George, the lame uncle, his coat matted with a yellow salve. The two young wolves, a male and a female, born in the zoo eleven months before.

In the Dangerfield Zoo, the wolves had lived in a fine cage, in a spacious lair made out of rock, like a cave. They had climbed on stone ledges, graded in size, which descended from the cave down to a gully in front of the spectators' railing. Down the ledges ran a thin stream of water, which provided drink and kept the cage clean. In the Northwest Territories, trailing caribou and elk, the wolves used to travel fifty miles in a day. . . . In their cage in Dangerfield they huddled like immigrants in a refugee camp who may wait many years for acceptance in their new country. . . .

One day Marit had walked, on an impulse, into the office of

Harrison Feitler, the zoo's director, who had encouraged her to make her land into a wildlife refuge. . . Forthwith and outright, Feitler had given his wolves to Marit, warning her only of their hostility to the lynx.

Now, as she watched them in the beam of her flashlight, shivering and uncertain, she knew how far their wildness had been compromised. Was she a stouter guardian than the iron bars of their cage? She had rescued them from humiliation, but she could not guarantee their safety. She had put up a fence, but the fence might be too low, or the lock too easy. The zoo had a squad of keepers; she was the only warden of her preserve. In order to protect the wolves, she must harbor them in secret. . . .

Marit was used to keeping secrets. She guarded herself closely, since she did not like people well enough to give them any rope to hang her. Wolves are the most important northern predator upon the larger mammals; people are the only predators of wolves. In the zoo the wolves were prisoners; behind bars they could be mistaken for big lazy dogs. Roaming unlicensed on her estate, they would be outlaws. They already had a legendary criminal record. Every right-thinking person knew that wolves attacked homesteads, ravaged herds, relished a child as much as a calf, cheated the hunter out of his yearly kill, loomed against the moonlight with red eyes and rabid jaws. . . . In fact, they were shy and private; they mated for life and stayed in a jealous family circle. They were as frail as Marit—even frailer, for they pulled hatred the way magnets pull metal filings.

Marit loved wolves more than any other animal, because they were the most reclusive and least valued. They tallied with her image of herself, but she did not try to scale them to her size. They were creatures and she was human, and she cherished the difference more than any likeness. When she was close to the wolves, she would learn what they could teach her: loyalty, endurance, stoicism, and courage, the traits that made them symbols of survival.

ANNE ARENSBURG, *Sister Wolf*

Wolf on frozen lake, northern Minnesota. Layne Kennedy.

THE WOLF INSIDE

In a secret recess of my being a wolf had been born. She nurtured herself there in my body's den until she had grown into her fullness and vitality. She spoke to me of her wolf secrets —the power that causes her fellows to avert their gaze from her eyes.

To speak with her, I turned my eyes from her face and heard her utter words within me as if her voice was one with my own. She spoke to me of a time before time when humans and wolves talked to one another—when the world was green, numinous, unripe, and unformed.

"The Wolves (Balkan War)," painting by Franz Marc, 1913. A critic writes that "Natural laws and especially those of the animal world reinforced [Marc's] belief in the basic ethical values of spontaneity, deep inner freedom, and the unity of the individual with the entire universe."

This she-wolf told me how people long ago had discovered a way up through into the world above where time had hardened, and wolves and humans no longer understood one another, the birds and deer possessed their own tongues.

I had struggled up from below and things were ready, things were prepared, she told me. This journey had occurred a long time in the past and I remembered nothing of my travels, but she would tell me in her own way, in a way that I might hear this tale and learn her secrets.

"Now you are strong, because I have given you strength," she said. "Have courage, look into my eyes." I did as she demanded and gazed directly into her green and glowing eyes.

Reflected in each of her pupils I saw a small image of my own face lined with fear. Slowly her black lips pulled back and she sneered, revealing her long sharp teeth. Her broad forehead wrinkled and a deep growl rumbled in her chest, shaking the earth.

I saw how completely separate she was from me as if she had risen up out of me. Now she stood utterly apart and wild in her ferocity.

With a sudden leap she attacked me, tore at my clothing with her teeth, knocked me down. Her strength overwhelmed me and she stood over me, her eyes afire, her head erect, her ears forward. I looked around and I saw standing about me various other predators. The raptors looked down on me and the mountain lions and the coyotes fixed me with their gaze. They were all there, the predators.

"Get up now," commanded this she-wolf. "We are your friends. We love you." As I stood she embraced me, pulling me to her with her paws. I sensed she was part human, this wolf, and I was part wolf. Then she gave me tools to survive, weapons so that I might hunt as a predator hunts and roam as a predator roams. As she embraced me, she melted into me and disappeared inside where for awhile I heard her voice, so much like my own voice that it too faded from my awareness.

JAMES C. BURBANK, *Vanishing Lobo*

Burbank's dream of a personal "wolf guide" echoes the Tewa Pueblo emergence story where the predators initiate humans into the ways of survival.

THE THING IN ITSELF

Part of the creative genius of *Homo sapiens* is to see the things around him and convert them for his own uses. . . . The world is seen in terms of one's needs, and a new discovery, a new source of energy, or a faster or more productive machine is a mark of progress. The male ego is fed by values supporting growth, progress, and exploration and operates by controlling, manipulating and exploiting.

The tragic flaw in human perception, though, is that modern man does not really see the world as it really is. It is seen only in terms of how it can satisfy certain needs. "See me for what I am, not as you wish to use me," is the silent cry of wilderness, of wolf, whale, forest, and ocean alike.

Seeing an eagle, a puma, a wolf, or a whale as the thing in itself, no man could kill it without first questioning his own reasons for doing so. In seeing, such a man has matured at last beyond the primitive ego that feels pride and status in hunting and killing. He has matured by establishing a new connection in his brain and by breaking an old one that he inherited from his forefathers. The new connection gives him a greater awareness, which is the key to understanding life for what it is and others for what they are. The old connection tied him to the world, where the world of nature is merely an extension of himself, an egosphere, if you wish. Once broken, he becomes a free man, no longer controlled by or imposing his needs, values, and rights on others, be they wolves or other men. Other people, wolves, and indeed all living things suddenly have rights and intrinsic values in themselves. . . .

Once a man can see a tree, a wolf, or his fellow and value the other for what it, he, or she is, then his world will be very different. He will rediscover the brotherhood of humanity and reverence for all life, and foster this in others and in his children.

MICHAEL W. FOX, *The Soul of the Wolf*

LA LOBA

There is an old woman who lives in a hidden place that everyone knows but few have ever seen. As in the fairy tales of Eastern Europe, she seems to wait for lost or wandering people and seekers to come to her place.

She is circumspect, often hairy, always fat, and especially wishes to evade most company. She is both a crower and a cackler, generally having more animal sounds than human ones. . . . She is called by many names: *La Huesera*, Bone Woman; *La Trapera*, The Gatherer; and *La Loba*, Wolf Woman.

The sole work of *La Loba* is the collecting of bones. She is known to collect and preserve especially that which is in danger of being lost to the world. Her cave is filled with the bones of all manner of desert creatures: the deer, the rattlesnake, the crow. But her specialty is said to be wolves.

She creeps and crawls and sifts through the *montañas,* mountains, and *arroyos,* dry riverbeds, looking for wolf bones, and when she has assembled an entire skeleton, when the last bone is in place and the beautiful white sculpture of the creature is laid out before her, she sits by the fire and thinks about what song she will sing.

And when she is sure, she stands over the *criatura,* raises her arms over it, and sings out. That is when the rib bones and leg bones of the wolf begin to flesh out and the creature becomes furred. *La Loba* sings some more, and more of the creature comes into being; its tail curls upward, shaggy and strong.

And *La Loba* sings more and the wolf creature begins to breathe.

And still *La Loba* sings so deeply that the floor of the desert shakes, and as she sings, the wolf opens its eyes, leaps up, and runs away down the canyon.

One of the things we heard from a lot of people was "Don't use wolves." They're one of the most difficult animals to work with, and ours ran true to form—but I really didn't think we could get away with not using them.

We looked at a lot of film of half-breeds, malamutes, huskies. And though they may look like a wolf, they don't walk like a wolf. Wolves have a very distinctive way of walking on those long, thin legs, and the wolf lope is unmistakable.

There's just something about it when they look at you and the camera catches them just right—a glint in the eye—a true wildness that was worth all the frustration. To name the picture *Dances With Wolves* and not use real wolves I think would have been a travesty.

KEVIN COSTNER AND JIM WILSON,

Dances With Wolves: The Illustrated Story of the Epic Film

Somewhere in its running, whether by the speed of its running, or by splashing its way into a river, or by way of a ray of sunlight or moonlight hitting it right in the side, the wolf is suddenly transformed into a laughing woman who runs free toward the horizon.

So it is said that if you wander the desert, and it is near sundown, and you are perhaps a little bit lost, and certainly tired, that you are lucky, for *La Loba* may take a liking to you and show you something—something of the soul.

CLARISSA PINKOLA ESTÉS, *Women Who Run With the Wolves*

In Women Who Run With the Wolves, *Jungian analyst and cantadora storyteller Clarissa Estés shows how women can benefit psychologically from rediscovering a more natural, adventurous, "wild" self through archetypal tales like this one. Conversely, many men today see the wolf as a model—not of one who preys on women but of loyalty and family devotion.*

OPPOSITE: *Gray wolf in autumn landscape, Alaska. Tom and Pat Leeson.*
LEFT: *Female figure with wolf head, Tuniit culture, central Arctic.*

HOW IT STANDS FOR WOLVES

▼▼▼▼▼

Wolves have been fully protected in this country under the Endangered Species Act since 1973, but they are seriously endangered (or absent) in all but a few places. There are upwards of 10,000 in Alaska, though its government persists in trying to reopen aerial hunting of wolves despite public pressure and threatened tourism boycotts. Minnesota, thanks to effective public education, has the

next largest population (not to mention a professional basketball team called the Timberwolves). It is also home to the International Wolf Center, an educational facility that encompasses a resident wolf pack, the famous "Wolves and Humans" exhibit, and popular programs offering wolf walks and howling excursions.

Wolves are slowly recolonizing Wisconsin, Michigan, and the northwestern states, especially around Glacier National Park in Montana. Strong resistance to their return exists among ranchers, however, and official protection is sometimes ignored under the motto: "Shoot, shovel, and shut up." Especially controversial are efforts to deliberately reintroduce wolves to former habitat. The major focus currently is on the Yellowstone ecosystem, where wolves are the only important fauna missing; the Wyoming-based Wolf Fund and other wildlife groups are leading this fight.

Canada has the most wolves—perhaps 55,000—and populations are viable despite its status as fair game for trappers. Overseas the picture is pretty bleak except in remote parts of eastern Europe and Asia (see Appendix, "Where Wolves Survive"). A hopeful sidelight to the recent fall of the Soviet system is that its military-style campaign to wipe out the remaining wolves in Siberia is at least temporarily on hold.

BRINGING BACK WOLVES

Wolf reintroduction is a touchy subject; so far it has been accomplished only with the red wolf, on an isolated refuge in North Carolina and begun in Great Smoky Mountains National Park. The effort to return wolves to Yellowstone National Park and environs is spearheaded by The Wolf Fund, whose director, Renée Askins, says that Yellowstone without its chief predator "is like a watch without a mainspring."

Wolf reintroduction to Yellowstone National Park has been something of a study in dyspepsia and delay. In 1973 . . . the wolf was designated an endangered species. By law that should have prompted its reintroduction to natural habitats like Yellowstone, but it didn't. Instead, wolf opponents—mostly from the livestock industry—have been raucous in their claims that the animal is a pestilence and nimble in their efforts at blocking wolf-recovery plans. Fourteen years passed before a plan was finally approved, in 1987, and not until [1991] did Congress direct the U.S. Fish and Wildlife Service to produce an Environmental Impact Statement, the first formal step in determining whether wolves should be reintroduced.

All this, of course, could be moot if wolves return on their own, without human intervention. Already there are known to be five wolf packs in northwestern Montana, which may have made their way south from Canada, as well as confirmed wolf sightings in Idaho and Washington. Renée Askins and other conservationists say they would prefer to see wolves return to Yellowstone on their own. But they say that could take decades, so they are pushing for reintroduction.

NICHOLAS DAWIDOFF, *Aububon Magazine*

A HOWLING SUCCESS

The natural return of wolves to Michigan represents one of the great success stories of the U.S. Fish and Wildlife Service's Endangered Species Program.

Although the Endangered Species Act of 1973 did protect endangered species legally, this provision came too late for any immediate effect in wolfless Wisconsin or in Michigan where remnant animals did not constitute a viable breeding population. However, in Minnesota, where hundreds of wolves still roamed the state's extensive wilderness, the result was powerful.

To some people, of course, prohibitions against killing wolves were absurd. "Why protect the wolf? We used to bounty the varmints only 10 years ago," challenged many Minnesota locals, who knew that plenty of the big, furred predators still were left. Protest meetings and dead wolves draped on the steps of government buildings demonstrated the rage that scores of citizens felt.

Another perspective was finding its voice, however. With federal protection of wolves had come increased public interest, awareness, and sympathy—a sense that wolves like all predators have a role in nature and that people should foster biodiversity in wilderness areas such as northern Minnesota. . . . Protection in Minnesota could help restore wolves to neighboring states. . . .

[R]esearch efforts greatly increased. . . . Basic information about wolf numbers, movements, predation, mortality, survival, reproduction, and general natural history proliferated. Educational programs sprang up, fueled by the information researchers had produced. . . .

The net result was that [fewer wolves were killed in Minnesota and] wolves colonized parts of Minnesota where they had not lived for decades. As wolf numbers and range expanded, so too did wolf

OPPOSITE: *Child's drawing of a wolf, by Larry Windes, from* The Wolf Fund *newsletter, 1991.* ABOVE: *Gray wolf, Sweden. Mattias Klum.* OVERLEAF: *Two wolves backlit on a ridge. Scot Stewart.*

dispersal. By the mid-1970s, wolves had begun recolonizing nearby Wisconsin. . . . [I]t has even allowed dispersers to reach Michigan, over 100 miles away from Minnesota at most points. In 1991 a milestone was reached—the first reproduction of wolves in almost 40 years was recorded in Michigan. . . .

The recovery of the wolf in the Lake Superior region is now so well under way that there appears to be no stopping it. Minnesota wolves have reached a population of 1,550-1,750, saturating just about all available habitat. The total number of wolves in Wisconsin and Michigan is about 60 and increasing.

L. DAVID MECH, *International Wolf*

As the world's best-known wolf biologist and a tireless educator on their behalf, David Mech has had much to do with wolf recovery in the Great Lakes area.

RETURN OF THE WOLVES
▼▼▼▼▼▼

All through the valley, the people are whispering:
the wolves are returning, returning
to the narrow edge of our fields, our dreams.
They are returning the cold to us.
They are wearing the crowns of ambush,
offering the rank and beautiful snow-shapes
of dead sheep, an old man too deep in his cups,
the trapper's gnawed hands, the hunter's tongue.
They are returning the whispers of our lovers,
whose promises are less enduring than the wolves.

Their teeth are carving the sky into delicate antlers,
carving dark totems full of moose dreams: meadows
where light grows with the marshgrass and water
is a dark wolf under the hoof.
Their teeth are carving our children's names
on every trail, carving night into a different bone—
one that seems to be part of my body's long memory.

Their fur is gathering shadows, gathering
the thick-teethed white-boned howl of their tribe,
gathering the broken-deer smell of wind
into their longhouse of pine and denned earth,
gathering me also, from my farmhouse
with its golden light and empty rooms, to the cedar
(that also howls its woody name to the cave of stars),
where I am silent as a bow unstrung
and my scars are not from loving wolves.

ANITA ENDREZZE (Yaqui)

Appendix A

WHERE WOLVES SURVIVE

Because of the diversity in climate, topography, vegetation, human settlement and development, wolf populations in various parts of the original range vary from extinct to relatively pristine. The following summary, gives information by region on subspecies present, population status, approximate numbers, percent of former ranger occupied at present, main prey (where available), legal status, and cause of decline.

ALASKA: Subspecies: *ligoni, pambasileus, tundrarum, alces.* Status: fully viable, numbering approximately 6,000. Range occupied: 100%. Main prey: moose, caribou, sheep, deer, beaver, goat. Legal status: animals are hunted and trapped in limited seasons with bag limits. Some control work, enforcement active.

BRITISH COLUMBIA, YUKON: Subspecies: *crassodon, fuscus, columbianus, pambasileus, mackenzii, occidentalis, tundrarum, ligoni, irremotus.* Status: fully viable, numbering approximately 8,000. Range occupied: 80%. Main prey: game species, furbearer (BC), no closed season (Y).

Arctic wolf relaxing in a field of cottongrass, Ellesmere Island, Canada. Jim Brandenburg.

NORTHWEST TERRITORIES: Subspecies: *arctos, bernardi, columbianus, griseoalbus, hudsonicus, mackenzii, nubilus, occidentalis, pambasileus.* Status: fully viable, numbering 5,000-15,000 Range occupied: 100%. Main prey: moose, caribou, sheep, deer, beaver, goat. Legal status: furbearer.

ALBERTA: Subspecies: *occidentalis, griseoalbus, irremotus, nubilus.* Status: fully viable, numbering approximately 4,000. Range occupied: 80%. Main prey: moose, caribou, sheep, deer, beaver, goat, elk, bison. Legal status: furbearer.

SASKATCHEWAN, MANITOBA: Subspecies: *hudsonicus, griseoalbus, irremotus, nubilis.* Status: fully viable, number unknown. Range occupied: 70%. Main prey: moose, elk, deer, beaver, bison, caribou. Legal status: furbearer.

ONTARIO, QUEBEC: Subspecies: *lycaon, hudsonicus, labradorius.* Status: fully viable, number 10,000. Range occupied: 80%. Main prey: moose, deer, caribou, beaver. Legal status: furbearer.

NEWFOUNDLAND (THE ISLAND): Subspecies: *beothucus,* extinct since 1911.

LABRADOR: Subspecies: *labradorius.* Status: fully viable, number unknown. Range occupied: 95%. Main prey: moose, caribou, beaver, musk ox, hares. Legal status: furbearer.

MINNESOTA: Subspecies: *lycaon.* Status: viable, numbering approximately 1,200. Range occupied: 30%. Main prey: deer, moose, beaver. Legal status: full protection. Cause of decline; persecution, habitat destruction.

MICHIGAN AND WISCONSIN: Subspecies: *lycaon.* Status: lingering, 35 individuals. Highly endangered. Range occupied: 10%. Main prey: deer, beaver, moose. Legal status: full protection. Cause of decline: persecution, habitat destruction.

NORTHWESTERN UNITED STATES: Subspecies: *irremotus.* Status: slowly recolonizing, 30 individuals. Highly endangered. Range occupied: 5%. Main prey: deer, elk, moose, sheep, goats, beaver. Legal status: full protection. Cause of decline: persecution, habitat destruction.

MEXICO: Subspecies: *baileyi.* Status: lone wolves or pairs, <10 individuals. Highly endangered. Range occupied: 10%. Main prey: livestock. Legal status: unenforced full protection. Cause of decline: persecution, habitat destruction.

SWEDEN/NORWAY: Subspecies: *lupus.* Status: lone wolves or pairs, <10 individuals. Highly endangered. Range occupied: 10%. Main prey: moose, reindeer, livestock. Legal status: full protection. Cause of decline: persecution.

FINLAND: Subspecies: *lupus.* Status: lingering, probably only lone wolves or pairs, <100 individuals. Endangered. Range occupied: 10%. Legal status: no protection (north), game status (east), protected (south). Main prey: moose, reindeer, white-tailed deer, livestock. Cause of decline: persecution.

GREENLAND: Subspecies: *orion.* Status: lingering, 50? individuals. Threatened. Range occupied: unknown. Main prey: musk-ox, caribou. Legal status: unknown. Cause of decline: persecution.

TURKEY: Subspecies: *lupus, pallipes.* Status: viable, but in decline. Unknown number of individuals. Range occupied: unknown. Main prey: livestock, unknown. Legal status: no protection.

SYRIA: Subspecies: *lupus, pallipes.* Status: lingering, low population density, 200-500 individuals. Highly threatened. Range occupied: 10%. Main prey: livestock, carrion, small wildlife. Legal status: no protection. Cause of decline: persecution.

JORDAN: Subspecies: unknown. Status: lingering, low population density, 200? individuals. Highly threatened. Range occupied: 90%. Legal status: no protection. Main prey: unknown. Cause of decline: persecution.

ISRAEL: Subspecies: *pallipes, arabs.* Status: lingering, low population density, 100-150 individuals. Highly threatened. Range occupied: 60%. Main prey: hares, livestock, carrion. Legal status: full protection. Cause of decline: habitat destruction, persecution.

EGYPT (SINAI): Subspecies: *arabs.* Status: 30 individuals. Highly endangered.

Range occupied: 90%. Main prey: hares, livestock. Legal status: no protection. Cause of decline: persecution.

LEBANON: Subspecies: unknown. Status: lone wolves or pairs, > 10 individuals. Highly endangered. Range occupied: unknown. Main prey: garbage, carrion. Legal status: no protection. Cause of decline: persecution.

ARABIAN PENINSULA: Subspecies: *pallipes, arabs.* Status: in decline, <300 individuals. Range occupied: 90%. Main prey: garbage, carrion, livestock. Legal status: no protection. Cause of decline: persecution.

IRAN: Subspecies: *pallipes, campestris.* Status: fully viable, numbering >1000. Range occupied: 80%. Main prey: gazelle, mountain sheep, livestock, wild boar, deer, *Capra* sp. Legal status: game species. Cause of decline: persecution.

IRAQ: Subspecies: unknown. Status: unknown. Range occupied: unknown. Main prey: unknown. Legal status: unknown. Cause of decline: unknown.

AFGHANISTAN: Subspecies: *pallipes, chanco.* Status: viable, suspected decline, 1,000? individuals. Range occupied: 90%. Main prey: unknown. Legal status: unknown. Cause of decline: unknown.

PAKISTAN: Subspecies: *pallipes, campestris.* Status: unknown. Range occupied: unknown. Main prey: unknown. Legal status: unknown. Cause of decline: unknown.

BHUTAN: Subspecies: *chanco.* Status: unknown. Range occupied: unknown. Main prey: unknown. Legal status: protected. Cause of decline: unknown.

NEPAL: Subspecies: *chanco.* Status: unknown. Range occupied: unknown. Main prey: unknown. Legal status: unknown. Cause of decline: unknown.

INDIA: Subspecies: *chanco.* Status: unknown. Range occupied: unknown.

Main prey: unknown. Legal status: unknown. Cause of decline: unknown.

MONGOLIA: Subspecies: *chanco.* Status: viable, possible decline, >10,000 individuals. Range occupied: 100%. Main prey: livestock, saiga. Legal status: extermination efforts active.

CHINA: Subspecies: *chanco.* Status: extermination efforts active, population numbers unknown. Range occupied: 20%. Main prey: saiga, other ungulates, livestock. Legal status: unknown. Cause of decline: persecution, habitat destruction.

U.S.S.R. (EUROPE): Subspecies: *lupus, albus, campestris, chanco.* Status: fully viable, numbering approximately 50,000. Range occupied: 75%. Main prey: ungulates and livestock. Legal status: reduction and control even in nature reserves. Cause of decline: persecution, habitat destruction.

POLAND: Subspecies: *lupus, campestris.* Status: fully viable, numbering approximately 900. Range occupied: 90%. Main prey: (moose), roe deer, red deer, wild boar, mufflon. Legal status: partial protection. Cause of decline: persecution, habitat destruction.

CZECHOSLOVAKIA: Subspecies: *lupus.* Status: steep decline/lingering, 100? individuals. Highly threatened or endangered. Range occupied: 10%. Main prey: roe deer, red deer, wild boar, mufflon. Legal status: no protection. Cause of decline: persecution, habitat destruction.

ROMANIA: Subspecies: *lupus.* Status: decline, 2,000? individuals. Range occupied: 20%. Main prey: roe deer, red deer, wild boar, mufflon. Legal status: no protection. Cause of decline: persecution, habitat destruction.

BULGARIA: Subspecies: *lupus.* Status: lingering, low population density, 100% individuals. Highly threatened. Range occupied: unknown. Main prey: no pro-

tection. Legal status: (moose) roe deer, red deer, wild boar, mufflon. Cause of decline: persecution, habitat destruction.

GREECE: Subspecies: *lupus.* Status: viable, but in decline, >500 individuals. Range occupied: 60%. Main prey: deer, wild boar, chamois, livestock. Legal status: partial protection. Cause of decline: persecution, habitat destruction.

YUGOSLAVIA: Subspecies: *lupus.* Status: steep decline, approximately 2,000 individuals. Range occupied: 55%. Main prey: deer, wild boar, chamois, livestock. Legal status: partial protection. Cause of decline: persecution, habitat destruction.

ALBANIA: Subspecies: *lupus.* Status: unknown. Range occupied: unknown. Main prey: unknown. Legal status: unknown. Cause of decline: unknown.

HUNGARY: Subspecies: *lupus.* Status: extinct. Range occupied: nil. Main prey: unknown. Legal status: protected. Cause of decline: persecution.

ITALY: Subspecies: *lupus.* Status: lingering, low population density, 250 individuals (Boitani 1987). Highly threatened. Range occupied: 10%. Main prey: garbage, livestock. Legal status: full protection. Cause of decline: persecution, habitat destruction, prey extermination.

SPAIN: Subspecies: *signatus, (lupus).* Status: lingering, low population density, 150 individuals. Highly threatened. Range occupied: 20%. Main prey: livestock, roe deer, wild boar. Legal status: partial protection. Cause of decline: persecution, habitat destruction.

CENTRAL EUROPE: Subspecies: *(lupus).* Status: extinct. Range occupied: nil. Main prey: livestock, red deer, roe deer, chamois, wild boar. Legal status: no protection. Cause of decline: persecution, habitat destruction.

ORGANIZATIONS THAT WORK FOR WOLVES

What we have loved, others will love, and we will teach them how—

WILLIAM WORDSWORTH, *The Prelude*

Defenders of Wildlife
1244 19th Street, NW
Washington, DC 20036
202-659-9510

Strives to preserve, enhance, and protect the natural abundance and diversity of wildlife through education and reasoned advocacy of appropriate public policy.

Animal Protection Institute of America
P.O. Box 22505
6130 Freeport Boulevard
Sacramento, CA 95822
916-731-5521

Believes wildlife should be managed in a coordinated, systematic framework based on principles of population dynamics and ecosystem balance with the least intrusive management activity.

Animal Welfare Institute
P.O. Box 3650
Washington, DC 20007
202-337-2333

Founded to reduce the sum total of pain and fear inflicted on animals by humans.

Fund for Animals, Inc.
850 Sligo Avenue
Silver Spring, MD 20910
301-585-2591

Works to preserve wildlife and promote humane treatment of all animals, and to ensure that government fulfills its animal protection responsibilities. Opposes lethal intervention as a method of animal damage control.

National Wildlife Federation
1400 Sixteenth Street, NW
Washington, DC 20036-2266
202-797-6800

Northern Rockies Resource Center
240 North Higgins
Missoula, MT 59801
406-721-6705

Educates, inspires, and assists individuals and organizations to conserve wildlife and other natural resources and to protect the earth's environment. NWF works with state and federal agencies to promote wolf education and wolf recovery in the Northern Rockies.

Sierra Club
730 Polk Street
San Francisco, CA 94109

Sierra Club—Northern Plains Region
Columbus Building
23 North Scott, #27
Sheridan, WY 82801
307-672-0425

Supports a timely and biologically defensible reintroduction of wolves into the ecosystem of Yellowstone, a sound plan for their management once returned, and regional and nationwide education in support of this goal.

Wildlife Information Center, Inc.
629 Green St.
Allentown, PA 18102
215-434-1637

Wolf Haven America
3111 Offut Lake Road
Tenino, WA 98589
206-264-4695

Provides home for some forty wolves on sixty acres and sponsors statewide educational programs, provides scientific information to wildlife organizations, and supports the reintroduction of wild wolves in Washington State.

Wolf Song of Alaska
P.O. Box 110309
Anchorage, AK 91511-0309
907-274-9653

Educational organization and facility that teaches about the biodiversity of Alaska, including the predator=prey relationships of wolves.

National Parks and Conservation Association
1776 Massachusetts Avenue, NW
Washington, DC 20036
202-223-6722

Nonprofit citizens' group that works to enhance and protect the national parks system. Defends park wildlife, including wolves and other predators, and is committed to restoring wolves to parks wherever they feasibly belong.

The Alaska Wildlife Alliance
P.O. Box 190953
Anchorage, AK 99519
907-277-0897

The Humane Society of the United States
2100 L Street, NW
Washington, DC 20037
202-452-1100

The nation's largest animal protection organization. Dedicated to protecting all animals through investigation, education, and legislation.

Greater Yellowstone Coalition
P.O. Box 1874
Bozeman, MT 59771
406-586-1593

An umbrella group of individuals and organizations working to preserve and protect the Greater Yellowstone ecosystem and the unique quality of life it sustains, which includes wolves.

Idaho Conservation League
P.O. Box 2671
Ketchum, ID 83340
208-726-7485

Supports efforts to preserve habitats that would encourage wolves to naturally repopulate while they are under the continuing protection of endangered species status. Not in favor of a managed reintroduction policy.

The International Wolf Center
1396 Highway 169
Ely, MN 55731
800-359-9653

Focuses on worldwide environmental education about the wolf, its relationship with other species, and the role of the wolf within human cultures.

A Michigan pack engages in a greeting ritual. Layne Kennedy.

The Wolf Fund
The Center for the Humanities
  and the Environment
Box 471
Moose, WY 83012
307-733-0740

Purpose is to restore wolves to
Yellowstone National Park at a self-
sustaining level of population.

Montana Wilderness Association
Northwest Field Office
43 Woodland Park Drive, #9
Kalispell, MT 59901
406-755-6304

MWA's educational and advocacy
efforts on behalf of wolf recovery
in the northern Rockies are part of
a broader mission to protect the
full integrity of natural ecosystems
in Montana.

National Audubon Society
700 Broadway
New York, NY 10003
212-979-3000

Wildlife Office
National Audubon Society
666 Pennsylvania Avenue, SE
Washington, DC 20003
202-547-9009

Alaska Office
308 G St., Ste. 217
Anchorage, AK 99501
907-276-7034

**Rocky Mountain Regional
Office**
4150 Darley, Ste. 5
Boulder, CO 80303
303-499-0219

Working to expedite the recovery
of healthy reproducing wolf populations in the Rockies and other
suitable areas in the United States.
(Alaska policy may differ; contact
that office.)

**Southern Utah Wilderness
  Alliance**
1471 South 1100 East
Salt Lake City, UT 84105
801-486-3161

Advocates wilderness preservation
for qualifying federal lands in
Utah's canyon country.

The Wilderness Society,
Northern Rockies Region
105 W. Main, Ste. E
Bozeman, MT 59715
406-586-1600

The Wolf Recovery Foundation
P.O. Box 793
Boise, ID 83701-0793
208-343-2248

Works to secure the recovery of
wolves in the Northern Rockies
through public education, biological research, and effective lobbying.

Text Credits

Grateful acknowledgment is made to the following for permission to reprint material copyrighted or controlled by them. Every effort has been made to determine original sources and locate rights holders. We regret any unintentional errors of fact or omission that may have resulted from the complexity of this process and time constraints. Any errors brought to our attention will be corrected in subsequent printings; please write to Walking Stick Press, 14 Gold Street, San Francisco, California 94133.

Academic Press: *Wolf and Man: Evolution in Parallel*, by Roberta L. Hall and Henry S. Sharp. Copyright © 1978 by Academic Press, Inc.

Alfred A. Knopf: *Sister Wolf*, by Ann Arensberg. Copyright © 1980 by Ann Arensberg. Reprinted by permission. Reprinted by permission of Alfred A. Knopf, a division of Random House, Inc.

Ballantine Books: *Women Who Run With the Wolves: Myths and Stories of the Wild Woman Archetype*, by Clarissa Pinkola Estés. Copyright © 1992 by Clarissa Pinkola Estés. Reprinted by permission of Ballantine Books, a division of Random House, Inc.

Broken Moon Press: "Return of the Wolves" from *At the Helm of Twilight*. Copyright ©1992 by Anita Endrezze. Reprinted by permission of Broken Moon Press.

Roger A. Caras and Roberta Pryor, Inc.: *A Celebration of Dogs*, by Roger Caras. Copyright © 1982 by Roger Caras, published by Times Books, a division of Random House Inc. Reprinted by permission of Roger Caras and of Roberta Pryor, Inc.

Carol Publishing Group: *The Werewolf*, by Montague Summers. Copyright © 1966 by University Books, Inc. Published by arrangement with Carol Publishing Group. Reprinted by permission.

Charles Scribner's Sons, an imprint of Macmillan Publishing Company: *Wild Animal Interviews*, by William T. Hornaday. Copyright © 1928 by Charles Scribner's Sons. Copyright © renewed 1956 by Helen H. Fielding. Reprinted by permission.

Clark City Press and Rick Bass: *The Ninemile Wolves*, by Rick Bass. Copyright © 1992 by Rick Bass. Reprinted by permission.

Nicholas Dawidoff: Excerpt from "One for the Wolves," *Audubon*, 1992. Copyright © by Nicholas Dawidoff.

Doubleday & Company, Inc.: *The Complete Works of Saki*, by H. H. Munro. Copyright © 1976. Reprinted by permission.

James Greiner: *The Red Snow*, by James Greiner. Copyright © 1980 by James Greiner.

Grosset & Dunlap, Inc.: *The Jungle Book*, by Rudyard Kipling. Copyright © 1893, 1894 by Rudyard Kipling. Copyright © 1894 by Harper & Bros. Copyright © 1893, 1894 by The Century Co. Copyright © 1950 by Grosset & Dunlap, Inc. Reprinted by permission.

Richard Grossman: "Wolf," from *The Animals.*, published by Graywolf Press, 1990. Copyright © 1983 by Richard Grossman.

Harcourt Brace, Inc.: *The Complete Poems of Carl Sandburg*. Copyright © 1969, 1970 by Lilian Steichen Sandburg, Trustee. Reprinted by permission.

HarperCollins Publishers Inc.: *Arctic Wild*, by Lois Crisler. Copyright © 1958 by Lois Crisler. Copyright © 1956 by the Curtis Publishing Company. Reprinted by permission.

HarperCollins Publishers Inc.: *Captive Wild*, by Lois Crisler. Copyright © 1968 by Lois Crisler. Reprinted by permission.

HarperCollins Publishers Inc.: *Julie of the Wolves*, by Jean Craighead George. Copyright © 1972 by Jean Craighead George. Reprinted by permission.

HarperCollins Publishers Inc.: *The World of the Wolf*, by Russell J. Rutter and Douglas H. Pimlott. Copyright © 1967 by Russell J. Rutter and Douglas H. Pimlott. Reprinted by permission.

Henry Holt and Company, Inc.: *In Praise of Wolves*, by R. D. Lawrence. Copyright © 1986 by R. D. Lawrence. Reprinted by permission.

Houghton Mifflin Co.: *My Ántonia*, by Willa Cather. Copyright © 1918, renewed 1946 by Willa Sibert Cather. Reprinted by permission.

Houghton Mifflin Co.: *Wolves of Minong*, by Durward L. Allen. Copyright © 1979 by Durward L. Allen. Reprinted by permission of Houghton Mifflin Co. All rights reserved.

Johnson Books: *Vanishing Lobo: The Mexican Wolf and the Southwest*, by James C. Burbank. Copyright © 1990 by James C. Burbank. Reprinted by permission.

Little, Brown and Company: *Never Cry Wolf*, by Farley Mowat. Copyright © 1963 by Farley Mowat Ltd., renewed 1991 by Farley Mowat Ltd. By permission of Little, Brown and Company.

Lyons & Burford: *The Soul of the Wolf*, by Michael W. Fox. Copyright © 1980 by Michael W. Fox. Reprinted by permission of Lyons & Burford, New York.

Louise Murie MacLeod: *A Naturalist in Alaska*, by Adolph Murie. Copyright © 1961 by Adolph Murie. Copyright © 1990 by Louise Murie MacLeod. Reprinted by permission.

Macmillan Publishing Co.: *Last of the Loners*, by Stanley Young. Copyright © 1970 by Nydia A. Young. Reprinted by permission.

Macmillan Publishing Co.: *The Order of Wolves*, by Richard Fiennes. Copyright © 1976 by Richard Fiennes. Reprinted by permission.

McGraw-Hill Inc.: *Dance of the Wolves*, by Roger Peters. Copyright © 1986 by Roger Peters. Reprinted by permission.

McGraw-Hill Inc.: *Wild Echoes: Encounters With the Most Endangered Animals in North America*, by Charles Bergman. Copyright © 1990 by Charles Bergman. Reprinted by permission.

McIntosh and Otis, Inc. for Ed Young: *Lon Po Po*, published by Philomel Books. Copyright © 1989 by Ed Young. Reprinted by permission.

Mercury Press, Inc.: "Loups-Garous" by Avram Davidson. Copyright © 1971 by Mercury Press, Inc. Reprinted from *The Magazine of Fantasy & Science Fiction*, by permission of the Estate of Avram Davidson and its agent Richard D. Grant.

Newmarket Press: *Dances With Wolves: The Illustrated Story of the Epic Film*, by Kevin Costner, Michael Blake and Jim Wilson. Copyright ©1990 by Newmarket Press. All rights reserved. Reprinted by permission of Newmarket Press.

Duane Niatum: "Wolves" from *Drawings of the Song Animals: New and Selected Poems*, by Duane Niatum. Copyright © 1991 by Duane Niatum, Holy Cow! Press. Reprinted by permission of author.

NorthWord Press, Inc.: *White Wolf: Living With an Arctic Legend*, by Jim Brandenburg. Copyright © 1988, 1990 by Jim Brandenburg. Reprinted by permission of NorthWord Press Inc., Minocqua, Wisc.

Philomel Books: "Moon When Wolves Run Together" (Lakota Sioux) from *Thirteen Moons on Turtle's Back*, by Joseph Bruchac and Jonathan London. Text copyright © 1992 by Joseph Bruchac and Jonathan London. Reprinted by permission.

Random House, Inc.: *Red Wolves and Black Bears*, by Edward Hoagland. Copyright © 1972, 1973, 1974, 1975, 1976 by Edward Hoagland. Reprinted by permission of Random House, Inc.

Suhrkamp Verlag, Germany: *Steppenwolf*, by Hermann Hesse. Copyright © 1963 by Random House, Inc. Copyright © 1929 by Henry Holt and Company, Inc. Reprinted by permission.

Sierra Club Books: *The Kingdom: Wildlife in North America*, by Art Wolfe and Douglas Chadwick. Text copyright © 1990 by Douglas Chadwick. Reprinted by permission.

St. Martin's Press: *Turtle Island Alphabet*, by Gerald Hausman. Copyright © 1992 by Gerald Hausman. Reprinted by permission.

Sterling Lord Literistics, Inc. for Barry Lopez: *Of Wolves and Men*, by Barry Holstun Lopez, published by Charles Scribner's Sons. Copyright ©1978 by Barry Lopez. Reprinted by permission.

University of Nebraska Press: *The Custer Wolf: Biography of an American Renegade*, by Roger A. Caras. Copyright © 1966 by Roger A. Caras. Reprinted by permission of University of Nebraska Press.

University of Oklahoma Press: *The Wolves of Heaven: Cheyenne Shamanism, Ceremonies, and Prehistoric Origins*, by Karl H. Schlesier. Copyright © 1987 by the University of Oklahoma Press. Reprinted by permission.

University of Oregon Press: *The Wolf Ritual of the Northwest Coast*, by Alice Henson Ernst. Copyright © 1952 by University of Oregon. Reprinted by permission.

University Press of New England: "The Heaven of Animals" from *Drowning with Others*, by James Dickey. Copyright © 1962 by James Dickey, Wesleyan University Press. Reprinted by permission.

Viking Penguin: *Selections: Novels and Stories, The Call of the Wild*, by Jack London. Copyright ©1982 by Puffin Books. Reprinted by permission.

Viking Penguin: "The Red Wolf" from *The Complete Poems of D. H. Lawrence*, edited by V. de Sola Pinto & F. W. Roberts. Copyright © 1964, 1971 by Angelo Ravagli and C. M. Weekley, Executors of The Estate of Frieda Lawrence Ravagli. Used by permission of Viking Penguin, a division of Penguin Books USA Inc.

Viking Penguin: *The Canine Clan*, by John C. McLoughlin. Copyright © 1983 by John C. McLoughlin. Used by permission of Viking Penguin, a division of Penguin Books USA Inc.

Voyageur Press: *The Arctic Wolf: Living With the Pack*, by L. David Mech. Copyright © 1988 by L. David Mech. *The Way of the Wolf*, by L. David Mech. Copyright © 1991 by L. David Mech. Reprinted by permission of Voyageur Press, 123 North 2nd Street, Stillwater, Minn. 55082, 1-800-888-9653.

Watkins Loomis Agency, Inc: *The Bestiary: A Book of Beasts*, by T. H. White, G.P. Putnam's Sons, 1954.

Illustration Credits

Page 4. "Wolf," copper over wood sculpture by Joan Brown, 1986, 49 x 65 x 25 in. Collection of Rene and Veronica di Rosa Foundation, Napa, California. Photo courtesy Frumkin/Adams Gallery, New York.

Page 8. TOP: Illustration of Miacis, by John McLoughlin, from *The Canine Clan*, copyright © 1983 by John C. McLoughlin, published by The Viking Press. BOTTOM: Painted pottery fragment (Mimbres), c. 1050-1250. University of New Mexico–Maxwell Museum of Anthropology, Albuquerque.

Page 9. Hopi wolf kachina standing on a kiva, by Tino Youvello, 1970s. Photo © Jerry Jacka 1993.

Page 11. "U?Mata Ya," by Frances Dick (Kwakiutl), 1990. Silkscreen print. Courtesy of the artist.

Page 15. Head of Anubis. Stuccoed wood and paint. Musée du Louvre, Paris. Photo Giraudon/Art Resource, New York.

Page 18. Gundstrup cauldron, inner plate, Cernunnos holding snake and torque, surrounded by animals. Embossed silver, gilded (probably from Gaul). National Museum, Copenhagen. Photo Erich Lessing/Art Resource, New York.

Page 23. Rock painting of archer and dog, c. 6000 B.C., North Africa. Douglas Mazonowicz photo.

Page 24. "Canoe of Fate," by Roy De Forest, 1974. Polymer on canvas, 66 3/4 x 90 1/4 in. Philadelphia Museum of Art, The Adele Haas Turner and Beatrice Pastorius Turner Fund.

Page 26. "The Wolf," engraving from *Thiere*, by J. B. Meyer, Nuremberg, 1748.

Page 38. "Wolf," by William and Martha Noah, 1969. Stencil on paper, 66.1 x 50.8 cm. Gift of the Women's Society of the Edmonton Art Gallery, 1970. H. Korol photo.

Page 46. "Howl," by Luis Jimenez, 1977. Lithograph, 36 x 28 in. Courtesy of the artist.

Page 52. Illustration by John Schoenherr from *Julie of the Wolves*, © 1977. By permission of Harper Collins Publishers Inc.

Page 59. Wolf cognitive map, drawn by John Slater, from *Wolf and Man: Evolution in Parallel*, by Roberta L. Hall and Henry S. Sharp, © 1978. By permission of the authors.

Page 60. "Buffalo hunt under the wolf-skin mask," by George Catlin, 1832-33. National Museum of American Art, Washington, D.C./Art Resource, New York.

Page 63. Illustration by Prill Barrett, from *The Wolf: A Species in Danger*, by Eric Zimen, © 1981 by Souvenir Press, Ltd.

Page 64. Netsuke wolf with skull, Edo Period, 18th century, Japan. The Seattle Art Museum, Duncan McTavish Fuller Memorial Collection.

Page 66. Wolf mask, Kuskokwin River Eskimos, Alaska, c. 1935. Painted wood with separately carved ears and teeth, 8 1/2 in. h. Collection of the Newark Museum. Purchase 1938 W. R. Olsen, Bethel Collection.

Page 71. Illustration from *The Bestiary: A Book of Beasts*, by T. H. White, Capricorn Books, 1960. First published in the U.S. by G. P. Putnam's Sons, 1954.

Page 82. "Wolf," by Ken Carlson, 1988. Oil on canvas, 23 x 35 in. Courtesy of the artist and the National Wildlife Art Museum, Jackson Hole, Wyoming.

Page 95. "The Moon and the Wolf," by Susan A. Point (Coast Salish), 1991. Serigraph, 10 1/2 x 9 1/4 in. Courtesy of the artist and Coast Salish Arts, Vancouver.

Page 102. "Flight of the Shaman," by Jessie Oonark (Baker Lake, Northwest Territories), 1970. Stencil, stonecut on paper, A/P, 52.3 x 67.0 cm. William and Martha Noah, printmakers. The Swinton Collection, Winnipeg Art Gallery. Sheila Spence photo. 6-76-846.

Page 107. "Timber Run," by Tim Jessell, 1991. Courtesy of the artist and Conrad Represents.

Page 110. Old Hopi kachina dolls representing wolf and deer. The Barry Goldwater Collection at the Heard Museum, Phoenix. Photo © Jerry Jacka 1993.

Page 115. "White wolves attacking a buffalo bull," by George Catlin, 1832-33. Oil on canvas, 19 1/2 x 27 5/8 in. National Museum of American Art, Washington, D.C./Art Resource, New York.

Page 118. Illustration by Fritz Eichenberg for "Reynard and Isengrim."

Page 120. "Bear and Wolf," by Patrick Amos, 1992. Courtesy of the artist.

Page 122. "Hamatsa Raven," by Bruce Alfred (Kwakiutl), undated. Painted wood, 12 1/2 x 58 x 9 in. Courtesy of the artist. Photo by Trevor Mills.

Page 128. "The werewolf," after a tableau by Maurice Sand, 1857.

Page 130. "The big bad wolf of legend," anonymous illustration for Little Red Riding Hood, undated. Mary Evans Picture Library, London.

Page 132, TOP. Drawing by Frank LaPena (Wintu-Nompitom), 1992. Courtesy of the artist. BOTTOM: Ojibway petroglyph of wolf, northern Minnesota. Photo by Scot Stewart.

Page 134. "Two wolves tearing at a ram," Greece, 575 B.C. Terracotta figurine in the Louvre, Paris. Erich Lessing/Art Resource, New York.

Page 135, TOP. "Romulus and Remus suckling the wolf," Peter Paul Rubens. Capitoline Museum, Rome. Scala/Art Resource, New York. BOTTOM: "Lycaon turned into a wolf by Jupiter," anonymous engraving. Bibliothèque Nationale, Paris.

Page 136. "Wolves drawing the chariot of Mars," c. 1600. Illustration in Splendor Solis, manuscript. Germanisches Nationalmuseum, Münich.

Page 137. "Fenris and the ash-tree," undated. Miniature from quarto manuscript. Stofnun Árni Magnússonar á Íslandi, Reykjavík.

Page 138. "Du loup et de sa nature," by Gaston Phébus de Foix, 16th century. From Le Livre de la Chasse, French manuscript. Giraudon, Paris.

Page 139, LEFT. Illustration of wolf-charmer, 1881, Scribner's Magazine. Mary Evans Picture Library, London. RIGHT: The Beast of Gévaudan, anonymous engraving, 18th century.

Page 140, TOP. "The Wolf of Gubbio," by Luc Olivier Merson, 1877. Jardin de Musée des Beaux-Arts, Lille/Lauros-Giraudon, Paris. BOTTOM: "Shepherds putting a wolf to flight," Greek manuscript, 479 A.D. Marciana Library, Venice/ Lauros-Giraudon, Paris.

Page 142. Illustration by Warren Chappell from Peter and the Wolf, by Serge Prokofieff. Copyright ©1940, renewed 1968 by Alfred A. Knopf, Inc. Published by Alfred A. Knopf, Inc.

Page 143. "Attacked by the wolves," by Nicolas Wassilievitch Orloff, c. 1900. Gavin Graham Gallery, London/Bridgeman-Giraudon, Paris.

Page 144. Greek miniature illustrating Aesop's Fables, 15th century. Bibliothèque Nationale, Paris.

Page 145, TOP. "Wedding party attacked by wolves," lithograph from Le Petit Journal, 1894. Photo Jean-Loup Charmet, Paris. BOTTOM: "Le loup et l'agneau," by Jean-Baptiste Oudry, c. 1750. Engraving. Bibliothèque Nationale, Paris. Giraudon/Art Resource, New York.

Page 146, TOP. "Wolf and man-wolf," drawings by Charles LeBrun, 17th century. BOTTOM: "The Werewolves," 1865. Illustration from The Book of Werewolves, by the Rev. S. Baring-Gould.

Page 147. Portrait of the "hairy man," Petrus Gonsalvus, anonymous (German school), 16th century. Schloss Ambras, Innsbruck. Photo Erich Lessing/Art Resource, New York.

Page 148, TOP. Still photo from The Wild Child, a film by François Truffaut, © 1970 by United Artists. Photo Ronald V. Borst/Hollywood Movie Posters. BOTTOM: Drawing by W. Miller, © 1993, The New Yorker Magazine, Inc.

Page 149. Illustration from The Jungle Book, by André Collot, 1937.

Page 150. Hand-hooked rug depicting the fox and the crane, French-Canadian, c. 1930-1950. Wool and cotton on jute cloth. Canadian Museum of Civilization, Quebec.

Page 151. Illustration from Lon Po Po: A Red Riding Hood Story from China, by Ed Young, 1989. By permission of the artist and McIntosh and Otis, Inc.

Page 152, TOP. "The wolf become shepherd," by Jules David, c. 1850. Engraving for The Fables of La Fontaine. Bibliothèque Nationale, Paris/Lauros-Giraudon, Paris. BOTTOM: Illustration by Lane Smith from The True Story of the 3 Little Pigs, by Jon Scieszka, illustrations copyright © 1989 by Lane Smith. Published by Viking Penguin, a division of Penguin Books USA Inc.

Page 153. Illustration by Jessie Wilcox Smith for Little Red Riding Hood, 1911.

Page 156. "A wolf had not been seen in Salem for thirty years," by Howard Pyle, 1890. Oil on canvas. Delaware Art Museum, Museum Purchase, 1912.

Page 157. "Landscape with a Herd of Buffalo on the Upper Missouri," by Karl Bodmer, 1833. Watercolor on paper, 9 5/8 x 12 3/8 in. Joslyn Art Museum, Omaha, Nebraska.

Page 158. "Moonlight Wolf," by Frederic Remington, c. 1909. Oil on canvas, 20 1/16 x 26 in. Addison Gallery of American Art, Phillips Academy, Andover Massachusetts, gift of the Members of the Board of Trustees. 1956. All rights reserved.

Page 159. Drawing by Ernest Thompson Seton, c. 1895.

Page 160. Kawadelekala, by Frances Dick (Kwakiutl), 1986. Silkscreen print. Courtesy of the artist.

Page 162. Native group in ceremonial dress with carved wolf dishes, photograph by C. F. Newcombe, 1911. Royal British Columbia Museum, Victoria, B.C.

Page 163. "Changeable Wolf Man," by Ha So Da/Narciso Abeyta (Navajo), 1958. Casein on paper, 77.0 x 56.0 cm. California Academy of Sciences, San Francisco.

Page 164. "Moon When the Coyotes Are Frightened," drawing by Linda Lomahaftewa, 1993. Courtesy of the artist.

Page 165. "Untitled" (Shaman), by Simon Tookoome (Baker Lake), 1971. Colored pencil, graphite on paper, 75.2 x 57.8 cm. The Swinton Collection, The Winnipeg Art Gallery. Sheila Spence photo. G-76-855.

Page 169. "The Wolves (Balkan War)," by Franz Marc, 1913. Oil on canvas, 27 7/8 x 55 in. Albright-Knox Art Gallery, Buffalo, New York, Charles Clifton, James G. Forsyth and Charles W. Goodyear Funds, 1951.

Page 171. Female figure with wolf head, Tuniit culture, central Arctic. Canadian Museum of Civilization, Quebec.

Page 172. Drawing of wolf's head by Larry Windes, from the Wolf Fund newsletter, 1991.

Acknowledgments

We wish to convey our grateful appreciation to the many individuals and entities who helped this book into being. First and foremost, to the project staff at Walking Stick Press: especially Linda Larsen, who put in long and conscientious hours of typesetting, and Miriam Lewis, who did nearly everything, from research and clerical work to art work and paste-up, not to mention making available at a critical time the computer belonging to her and Douglas Mandell. Indispensable contributions were also made by Karen Pike, Christine Kristen, and Laurie Donaldson.

The merchandising staff of The Nature Company—Doug Orloff, Cathy Kouts, and Anni Lazarus—were unfailingly supportive and responsive; we wish especially to note Cathy Kouts's close and thoughtful involvement with every stage of the project.

Many people involved with the world of the wolf provided or checked information, notably L. David Mech, who consulted on the map and text; wildlife biologist Steven Fritts of the U.S. Fish and Wildlife Service, working on wolf recovery programs in Montana, who read and commented on the manuscript; Mary Ortiz and Rob Brown of the International Wolf Center; as well as all the representatives of organizations working on behalf of wolves who responded to our request for information.

Thanks also to freelance contributors Lindsay Kefauver, whose expertise in fine art research turned up more wolf images than we had imagined could exist, and her Paris associate Maria Vincenza Aloisi; Reineck and Reineck of San Francisco for their excellent work in cartography; our calligrapher, Verne Lindner; production assistant Nancy Barnes; the staff of Northern Lights Photo; Allen McKinney and Kevin McGehee of Graphic Impressions for creating the wolf print background pattern; and Lon Huber of Fotolithics.

The photographers and photo agencies whose images are reproduced, in particular Mattias Klum, who took time from his schedule to travel to northern Sweden and shoot new photographs for publication here, and Jim Brandenburg, who in the midst of producing a book of his own, shared his pictures and wolf lore, accommodating our urgent needs with patience and good humor.

The fine artists, museums, galleries, and archives who provided wolf images and permission to reproduce them, and the authors, publishers, and literary agents whose texts are excerpted or who helped us obtain permission to do so.

The capable and hard-working personnel at A. Mondadori, Verona and New York: Tamara Beckwith, Nancy Freeman, Sergio Brunelli, Rolando Aratri, Annalisa Gambin, Enrico Battei, Enrico Bighim, Laura Brancato and others who helped the book into its final printed and bound form.

Thanks especially to Barry Lopez for his early support and encouragement of our project.

To our nearest and dearest: Greg, Wayne, and Dana, for their patience with our long absences and short attention spans while the schedule was at white heat.

To the wolves of the Sonora Desert Museum, who obliged us by leaving their tracks on paper, to be reproduced in the background pattern that appears on some of these pages— and to all the world's wolves, who should not have to answer any human need except that fulfilled by our knowing they are living as they are meant to live, part of the substance and spirit of the wild.

Diana Landau and Linda Herman
Walking Stick Press

Wolf

SPIRIT OF THE WILD

Designed by Linda Herman and produced at Walking Stick Press, San Francisco. Composed by Linda Larsen in Minion; the part titles were hand-lettered by Verne Lindner.

Photo above by Lynn and Donna Rogers

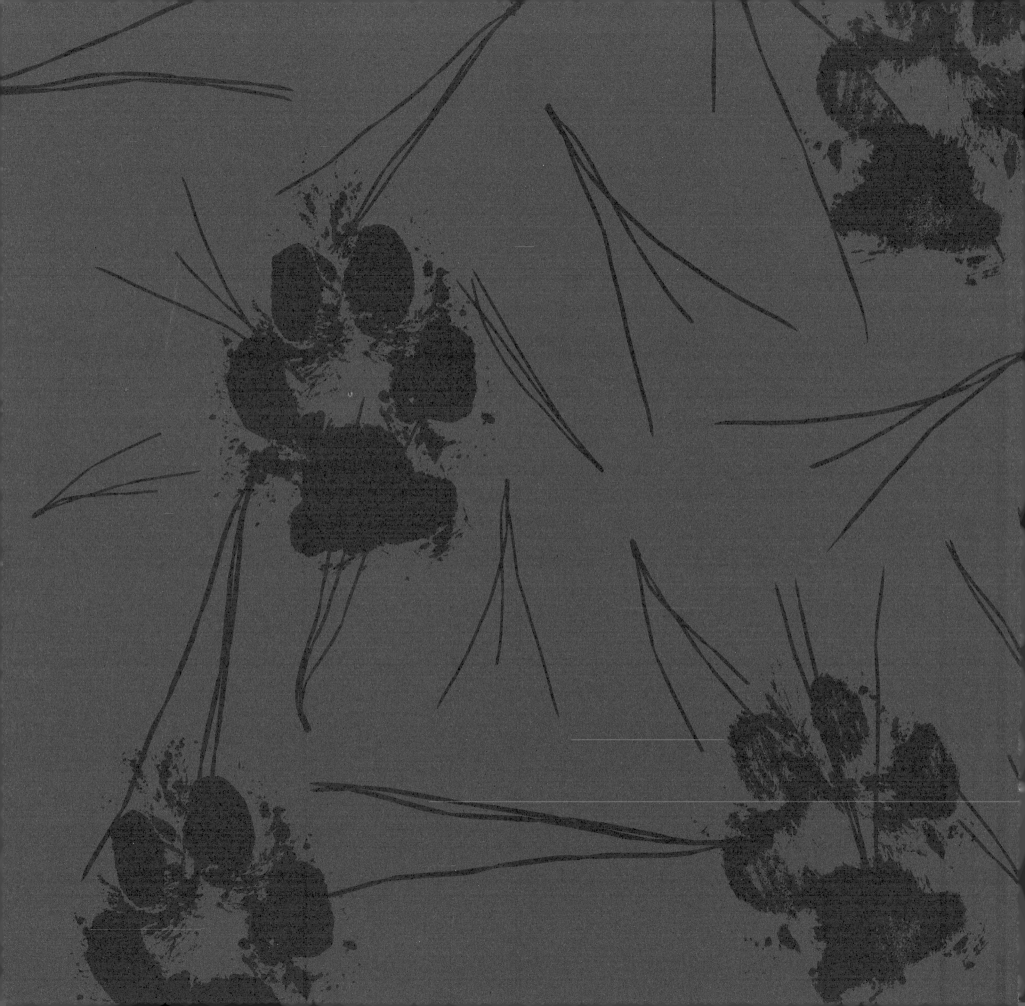